ECONOMIC ISSUES, PROBLEMS AND PERSPECTIVES

# COGNITIVE FINANCE: BEHAVIORAL STRATEGIES OF SPENDING, SAVING AND INVESTING

# ECONOMIC ISSUES, PROBLEMS AND PERSPECTIVES

Additional books in this series can be found on Nova's website at:

https://www.novapublishers.com/catalog/index.php?cPath=23_29&seriesp=Economic+Issues%2C+Problems+and+Perspectives

Additional e-books in this series can be found on Nova's website at:

https://www.novapublishers.com/catalog/index.php?cPath=23_29&seriespe=Economic+Issues%2C+Problems+and+Perspectives

ECONOMIC ISSUES, PROBLEMS AND PERSPECTIVES

# COGNITIVE FINANCE: BEHAVIORAL STRATEGIES OF SPENDING, SAVING AND INVESTING

PHILIPP ERIK OTTO

Nova Science Publishers, Inc.
*New York*

For permission to use material from this book please contact us:
Telephone 631-231-7269; Fax 631-231-8175
Web Site: http://www.novapublishers.com



**LIBRARY OF CONGRESS CATALOGING-IN-PUBLICATION DATA**

Otto, Philipp Erik.
Cognitive finance : behavioral strategies of spending, saving and investing / Philipp Erik Otto.
p. cm.
Includes bibliographical references.
ISBN 978-1-60876-279-8 (hbk.)
1. Finance--Psychological aspects. 2. Consumption (Economics)--Psychological aspects. 3. Saving and investment--Psychological aspects. I. Title.
HG101.O88 2009
332.01'9--dc22

2009036575

*Published by Nova Science Publishers, Inc. ✝ New York*

# CONTENTS


| | | |
|---|---|---|
| **Abstract** | | **vii** |
| **List of Figures** | | **ix** |
| **List of Tables** | | **xi** |
| **Chapter 1** | **Introduction** | **1** |
| | *1.1. Context Specific Strategy Usage* | *1* |
| | *1.2. Changes in Strategies* | *5* |
| | *1.3. Behavioral Finance* | *7* |
| | *1.4. Methods for Capturing Cognitive Processes* | *11* |
| **Chapter 2** | **Spending Strategies** | **17** |
| | *2.1. Behavioral Evaluation* | *17* |
| | *2.2. Usage of Behavioral Data* | *23* |
| **Chapter 3** | **Saving Strategies** | **39** |
| | *3.1. Saving Literature* | *39* |
| | *3.2. Saving Concept (Study 1)* | *43* |
| | *3.3. Saving Differences (Study 2)* | *50* |
| | *3.4. Saving Solutions* | *55* |
| **Chapter 4** | **Investment Strategies I** | **59** |
| | *4.1. Company Concept (Study 3)* | *61* |
| | *4.2. Company Evaluation (Study 4)* | *65* |
| | *4.3. Company Positioning (Study 5)* | *70* |
| | *4.4. Company Characteristics* | *74* |

**Chapter 5** **Investment Strategies II** **81**
*5.1. Performance Prediction* *81*
*5.2. Company Selection in Different Environments (Study 6)* *93*
*5.3. Company Selection with Memory Costs* *104*
*(Study 7)* *104*
*5.4. Company Selection with Information Costs (Study 8)* *111*
*5.5. Process Modeling* *119*

**Chapter 6** **General Discussion** **129**
*6.1. Characterizing Mental Processes* *129*
*6.2. Financial Personality* *131*
*6.3. Economic Evaluation* *133*

**Acknowledgements** **137**

**References** **139**

**Appendix** **163**

**Index** **179**

# ABSTRACT

Research in economics is increasingly open to empirical results. Here, advances in behavioral approaches are analyzed with respect to finance strategy. By applying cognitive methods to financial questions, behavioral approaches can provide a better perspective insight. The field of "cognitive finance" is approached by exploring decision strategies in the financial settings of spending, saving, and investing. Individual strategies in these different domains are searched which explain observed irregularities in financial decision making. Strong context-dependency and adaptive learning form the basis for this cognition-based approach to finance. Experiments, ratings, and real world data analysis are carried out in specific financial settings that combine different research methods to improve the understanding of natural financial behavior.

People have a tendency to use decision strategies within three finance domains: spending, saving, and investing. Specific spending profiles can be elaborated to obtain a better understanding of individual spending differences. Four different spending categories have been determined as *General Leisure, Regular Maintenance, Risk Orientation*, and *Future Orientation*. Saving behavior is strongly dependent on how people mentally structure their finance, and on their self-control attitude regarding *decision space restrictions, environmental cues*, and *contingency structures*. Investment strategies toward companies, where investments are placed, are evaluated by factors such as *Honesty, Prestige, Innovation*, and *Power*, but different information integration strategies can be learned in decision situations that provide direct feedback.

The mapping of cognitive processes in financial decision making is discussed and adaptive learning mechanisms are proposed for observed behavioral differences. The construal of a "financial personality" is proposed, in accordance with other dimensions of personality measures, to better acknowledge and predict variations in certain financial behavior.

This perspective enriches economic theories and provides a useful ground for improving individual financial services.

# LIST OF FIGURES

**Figure 2.1.** Debit channel usage frequency 20

**Figure 2.2.** Annual and weekly volatility of credit card spending 22

**Figure 2.3.** Age distribution of the 300,000 customer sample 23

**Figure 2.4.** Loan holdings for debit factors four and five 32

**Figure 2.5.** Response rates for standard and debit factor model 34

**Figure 3.1.** Saving labels 46

**Figure 3.2.** Saving structures 47

**Figure 3.3.** Self-control tools in saving structures 48

**Figure 3.4.** Self-control demands 51

**Figure 3.5.** Saving factors 52

**Figure 4.1.** RepGrid example solution 63

**Figure 4.2.** Model fit for the number of clusters in the Ward cluster history 68

**Figure 4.3.** Hierarchical clustering tree for the highly differentiating adjectives 69

**Figure 4.4.** Eigenvalues for the different number of factors 71

**Figure 5.1.** Decision situation 94

**Figure 5.2.** Learning curves in different environments 96

**Figure 5.3.** Predicted choices for Study 6 101-98

**Figure 5.4.** Learning curves for the different environments with memory costs **107**

**Figure 5.5.** Predicted choices for Study 7 **108**

**Figure 5.6.** Learning curve in the different environments with information costs **114**

**Figure 5.7.** Predicted choices for Study 8 **115**

# List of Tables

**Table 2.1.** K-means debit category cluster solution 24

**Table 2.1.** K-means debit category cluster solution 25

**Table 2.2** Equamax rotated factor solution 28

**Table 2.3.** Debit factor correlation 32

**Table 3.1.** Factor based groups 53

**Table 4.1.** Differentiation dimensions elicited for the generated companies 64

**Table 4.2.** Co-occurrence of named adjectives from different sources 65

**Table 4.3.** Most stable differentiating company adjectives 67

**Table 4.3.** Most stable differentiating company adjectives 68

**Table 4.4.** Equamax rotated factor solution 71-76

**Table 4.5.** Factor spearman correlation for company performance measures 73

**Table 5.1.** Optimized parameter values for Study 6 100

**Table 5.2.** Optimized parameter values for Study 7 109-114

**Table 5.3.** Optimized parameter values for Study 8 117

*Chapter 1*

# INTRODUCTION

Research in cognitive finance has a long tradition between the interaction of psychology and economics (Lewin, 1996). Economic questions can be seen as one of the reasons for the initiation of psychological research. Fechner's (1860) theory of psychophysics, for example, is based on the St. Petersburg paradox discovered by Daniel Bernoulli in 1738, describing a behavioral irregularity in gambling. Currently these two disciplines that had drifted apart are now being brought together in multiple ways. In behavioral finance, scientific research on human, social, cognitive, and emotional biases are used to better understand economic decisions. The specification of cognitive finance will focus on methods developed in psychology, and are applicable for financial questions.

A combined usage of cognitive methods for specific financial agendas is proposed. These financial agendas are derived from problems observed in behavioral finance (e.g. context dependency, self-control, and mental accounting) and are discussed for spending, saving, and investment strategies. This introduction provides a review of the research in this field, outlining central problems, current approaches, and the methods that are later applied to acquire new knowledge about decision strategies in cognitive finance.

## 1.1. CONTEXT SPECIFIC STRATEGY USAGE

Since Simon (1955, 1956), economic questions have been seen more and more under the constraint of being boundedly rational. This means that we show different behavior that does not necessarily fall under the general paradigm of rationality. Instead it stresses the characteristics of the task and a "satisficing" strategy is assumed, due to memory and general computational limitations. Decisions are satisfying but also sufficient where decisions can be seen as being ecologically rational once the specific conditions of the task are taken into account. Under the concept of ecological rationality, the guiding circumstances in which decisions take place are moving into focus, meaning the evaluation of reasons that make a decision rational.

Accordingly, external conditions and task characteristics influence what kind of behavior people choose in the end. The question of context-dependency is tackled by varying the characteristics of the tasks or by looking at decisions in different domains.

### 1.1.1. Context Dependency and Framing

A vast number of experiments now exist that examine how behavior changes according to variations of the task. Here only the more prominent are described to illustrate the potential variability in behavior. In their heuristics and biases program Daniel Kahneman and others (i.e., Tversky & Kahneman, 1974, 1983; Gilovich *et al.,* 2002; Kahneman & Tversky, 2000; Kahneman *et al.,* 1982; Tversky *et al.,* 1990) illustrated in a number of experiments how behavior depends on the format of the question. This variability is contrasting standard probability theory, where only the underlying numerical information should be taken into account.

By varying the task characteristics or the frame of a decision, systematic changes in peoples' behavior can be observed. The framing of a decision therefore can play a crucial part in the sort of answers people respond with. The conjunction fallacy nicely illustrates this dependency, where simply the general description of the task guides the answering behavior and thereby influences the resulting choice. Thus, by introducing a strong frame, decision processes are activated which contradict probability.

In the conjunction fallacy, one example that is repeatedly discussed in the heuristics and biases program, the probability of two events which occur together is rated higher than a single event that form the conjunction. The following "Linda problem" became famous (Tversky & Kahneman, 1983, p. 297):

Linda is 31 years old, single, outspoken, and very bright. She majored in philosophy. As a student, she was deeply concerned with issues of discrimination and social justice, and also participated in anti-nuclear demonstrations.

Which of the following is more likely?

1) Linda is a bank teller.
2) Linda is a bank teller and is active in the feminist movement.

Note that 85% of those asked, ranked the likelihood of option 2 higher than of option 1. However, mathematically, the probability of two events occurring in conjunction will always be less than or equal to the probability of either one occurring alone. Here the description of the person frames the answering behavior.

The Allais paradox (Allais, 1953) is another example of framing that shows when adding a common consequence to two given alternatives can reverse choices; and thus, this observed behavior contradicts the independence axiom of choice components. This especially is the case if one alternative gains certainty by the added common consequence, also called "the sure thing principle." Other framing effects that also result in preference reversals are documented by the differences in answering behavior between probability and dollar bets in gambling (e.g., Lichtenstein & Slovic, 1971). Though high probability bets are normally preferred in choice situations, high dollar bets receive higher values when the answering mode is in selling prices or certainty equivalents. Accordingly, the framing of the task or question violates procedural invariance.

Various explanations have been discussed to capture these observed irregularities. Tversky and Kahneman (1974) proposed three heuristics, namely "representativeness," "availability," and "adjustment and anchoring," to explain these observations. Later prospect theory and cumulative prospect theory were introduced (Kahneman & Tversky, 1979; Tversky & Kahneman, 1992). However, framing results mainly point out how variable behaviors within experimental designs are when making decisions under uncertainty. This general conclusion is further supported by research regarding the dependency for decisions on the underlying choice set (Roe *et al.*, 2001; Simonson & Tversky, 1992; Stewart *et al.*, 2003). Simply the variation of the existing alternatives in the choice set influences the choice itself. For two-dimensional alternatives similarity, attraction, and compromise effects have been shown, when adding a third alternative to a set of two alternatives alters the decision dependent on the individual distances between each of the alternatives. A range of alternative theories to capture framing effects have been proposed (Roe *et al.*, 2001; Stewart *et al.*, 2006; Usher & McClelland, 2004). Summing up, the stability and universality of the utility concept is questioned by these results and only process models that take the different influences of the task environment into account can explain these context dependent variations.

### 1.1.2. Context Dependency and Domain Specificity

An alternative approach to context dependency is to assume that behavior is task or domain specific. Here different sorts of behavior are directly dependent upon the characteristics of the task. Thus different strategies are picked according to the environment. Gigerenzer *et al.* (1999) proposed the metaphor of an "adaptive toolbox" where different mental tools are selected dependent on the specifics of the task. Some tools work well in certain domains but not in other domains.

Research on expert decision making isolates different types of mechanisms which were acquired to meet the specific demands of a task domain (i.e., Ericsson & Lehmann, 1996). Examples for domain specific strategy usage are the 'hot hand' strategy when using streaks of successful shots by players as allocation cues for further hits in basketball (Burns, 2004) or the 'tit-for-tat' strategy for reciprocal interaction in social settings (Axelrod & Hamilton, 1981). These heuristics can improve overall behavior, gaining more hits in the first case and achieving cooperative behavior in the second. Heuristic strategies are successful shortcuts that are used under specific conditions like time restrictions or memory constraints; and thus, are "satisficing". Such heuristic strategies could also be important for financial decisions by experts as well as non-experts.

In general, it is assumed that environmental conditions trigger the usage of one or the other strategy. Accordingly, in some environments more complex or rational strategies are used. In other environments the usage of heuristic strategies is predominant. But when are which strategies selected and how does this strategy selection process take place? This question has yet to be answered. Here, references to learning and adaptation mechanisms can be made. For now, the assumption that people use different strategies in different domains is important. When different strategies exist for specific tasks; and when these strategies are adaptive to that environment, the question arises what strategies are used in specific financial domains. This is the fundamental reason to look at the different financial areas of spending, saving, and investment separately.

## 1.2. Changes in Strategies

A long established tradition in psychology research focuses on how behavior changes. This change of behavior over time falls under the term of 'learning.' More evolutionary influenced theories see changes in behavior as adaptations shaped over the history of the human species. These two approaches are briefly introduced. They can be seen as two interacting processes, where adaptation is the result of evolutionary learning; and the lack of adaptation a necessary condition for individual learning to take place.

### 1.2.1. Learning

Many learning models have been proposed in psychology. Here we concentrate on one specific but simple learning form namely 'reinforcement learning.' It is seen as the most fundamental type of learning in repeated decisions. Thus, reinforcement learning could be relevant to different kinds of repeated economic interactions. According to reinforcement learning, successful behavior or successful strategies are supported and become more frequent. This assumption was introduced by Thorndike (1898) under the term "law of effect." If a strategy produces the desired outcome, it is used more frequently under recurring conditions.

An important criterion of reinforcement learning is the assumption of strategies that reflect the goal orientation of behavior. These strategies are linking perceived states of the environment to actions taken when in those states. The strategies are selected depending on their reward function (the immediate intrinsic desirability) and their value function (the long term desirability). An optimization of behavior is achieved by mapping strategies to environments or/and by matching the distribution of strategies in environments. Accordingly, one important part is finding the best strategies for specific environments. The other part is to adapt the strategy usage to varying environments to optimize behavior over time.

The key element of reinforcement theories, the trial-and-error learning with delayed rewards, therefore must be seen in combination with the following two other characteristics. It is a learning process that is based on a goal directed interaction with an uncertain environment, and results from the trade-off between exploration and exploitation. Reinforcement models are all derived from these fundamental principles but formalize the learning process differently. Sutton and Barto (1998) provide a detailed overview about different reinforcement models. The central assumption here is that specific reinforcement processes are also taking place in the domain of financial behavior, which form the strategies we observe in financial decision making. Financial strategies then are seen as the result of learning processes or more generally as the result of adaptation and not of optimized utility maximization.

### 1.2.2. Adaptation

Learning is a form of adapting to current environments. But adaptation can also be seen as an evolutionary process where specific strategies have been developed depending on the demands of the environment. The adaptation to ancestral environments is often seen as the reason for current misadaptation (Tooby & Cosmides, 1990a). This misalignment between behavior and current environments is only of interest here, inasmuch as ancestral mental mechanisms are developed to be used for present-day tasks. Therefore, mechanisms that were successful in the past are assumed to be applied to the demands of the modern world. Adaptation then mainly means that we have developed different strategies to cope with the demands we face in the interaction with our environment, with a differentiation mechanism that fosters some strategies in some situations. This mainly supports the assumption that behavior is domain specific and that we have to investigate the peculiarities of the task.

Some examples should provide a better intuitive understanding of this relation between adaptation and financial behavior. First, with respect to someone's saving behavior, diversification can be seen as a successful individual strategy. By spreading one's wealth into different categories the risk of a total failure is minimized and therefore the chances for survival are improved. When we say "don't put all our eggs into one basket" a similar optimization process is in place, as it was in former times. A simple 1/n-rule (Benartzi & Thaler, 2001), where funds are equally distributed over investments, might have its origin in this historically approved strategy. Second, spending behavior can be seen as a set of strategies in a population for spreading consumption over different goods. Group selection in sociobiology (Wilson, 1975; Wilson & Sober, 1994) documents that it is important for the success of a population to have different strategies in place to optimize its supply as a whole. Similar mechanisms of strategy diversity could be in place now that might have led to the existence of qualitatively different spending strategies in our population. Third, investment behavior might show similar mechanisms as ancient evaluations. The evaluation of food or people might have its parallel to the evaluation of companies. When we have specific mechanisms for the categorization of objects these might just as well apply for the categorization of companies and for respective investment strategies.

This gives an impression of how financial behavior can be reframed under the assumption of evolutionary adaptation. However, evolutionary theory is mainly seen as a possibility to generate new ideas for a theory of cognitive finance. Obviously there is a gap between modern financial decisions and the environments in which humans evolved. But adaptations may, however, set some of the cognitive background. The detection of "cheaters" (Cosmides, 1989) and the building of trust are modern examples of mechanisms which have a long tradition not only in the human race and could also form an important basis for financial coopcration.

## 1.3. Behavioral Finance

Within finance research, experimental and behavioral observations produce a growing area of interest. In contrast to standard finance theory which is mainly interested in optimal behavior; behavioral finance takes empirical observations into account, and aims to integrate them into finance theory. Linked to the areas of spending, saving, and investment the following research topics are important.

### 1.3.1. Hedonics of Spending Strategies

Within spending behavior, a purely affective component can be stressed. In contrast to standard economic theory, where preferences of choices are the basis for constructing utility functions; the focus is when emotions occur with the choice activity. This highlights the hedonic experience of a choice and how it can influence the spending behavior people show. Prelec and Loewenstein (1998) propose "double-entry" mental accounting theory that formalizes the hedonics of a spending experience. It postulates an interaction between the pleasure of consumption and thc pain of paying; and assumes a "coupling process" that refers to what degree consumption calls thoughts of payment, and vice versa. The first determinant of coupling is the degree of temporal separation. The second factor is the diversity of benefits associated with a payment, or the diversity of payments associated with a benefit, making it more or less possible to assign a particular payment to a particular benefit. Similarly, Gourville and Soman (1998) researched the behavioral implications of temporally separating the cost and benefits of consumption. The results suggest that individuals mentally track the cost and benefits of a consumer transaction in order to reconcile those expenses and its benefits on completion of the transaction. When cost precede benefits this can lead to a systematic and irrational attraction to a loss in value; 'sunk costs,' meaning an overspending if the result is not yet achieved. Consumers gradually adapt to a historic cost with the passage of time, an effect known as "payment depreciation," this devaluates costs and can lead to sunk cost processes. Soman (2001) tested the hypothesis where the payment method alters the strength of the relationship between past expenses and future spending. Expenditure reduces budgets, and hence decreases future spending. Past payments strongly reduced purchase intention when the payment mechanism requires the consumer to write down the amount paid, such as a check that requires filling in, unlike a credit card slip where one simply has to sign. Purchase intention was also reduced when the consumer's wealth is depleted immediately rather than with a delay, such as a payment made by cash or debit card. The first is attributed to a rehearsal taking place and the second considers the immediacy of the payment. It is proposed that these phenomena are due to their effect on memory and recall.

Generally, as spending is closely associated with consumption, we can assume that affective dimensions influence this behavior. Loewenstein (1996, 2000) stresses the influence of immediate emotions on behavior. In a similar strain the so called two-system or dual process models of reasoning have been proposed (i.e., Evans, 2003; Sloman, 1996). But how these systems integrate to form the overall behavior and how differences in spending behavior can be explained, is still an open question.

### 1.3.2. Mental Accounting and Self-Control in Saving Strategies

It is well documented that people organize their finances in "mental accounts" with strong influences on the resulting behavior (Heath & Soll, 1996; Thaler, 1985, 1999). Mental accounting assumes that wealth is mentally divided into different categories that are used to guide behavior. Specific wealth can be labeled and then used accordingly. This approach is transferred by Shefrin and Thaler (1988) to a life-cycle theory in one's saving behavior. Households act as if they use a system of mental accounts that violate the principle of fungibility. For example, one's mental approach toward accounts considered "wealth" less tempting than those that are considered "income." Thus the level of saving is affected by the way in which incremental wealth is framed; and income paid in the form of a lump sum bonus will be treated differently from regular salary income, even if the bonus is completely anticipated. An empirical investigation of this behavioral life-cycle savings model (Levin, 1998) supports that consumption spending is sensitive to changes in income and liquid assets which are assets that are relatively easy to transform into cash, but not to changes in the value of other types of assets, i.e. non-liquid assets such as houses and social security. This occurs despite the fact that the value of non-liquid assets is relatively large for most of the households in the sample. The findings hold when liquidity constraints of borrowing against future income are taken into account. The composition of spending is also sensitive to the composition of wealth in different income and asset types, again contrary to classical economic theory.

Closely related to mental accounting is the theory of self-control. Thaler and Shefrin (1981) proposed a model of saving that includes internal conflict, temptation, and willpower. Individuals are assumed to behave as if they have two sets of preferences: one concerned with the short run (the "doer") and one concerned with the long run (the "planner"). Since willpower represents the real psychic costs of resisting temptation, as costly; the planner also uses rules and mental accounting to restrict future choices in order to smooth consumption over time. For example, Bertaut and Haliassos (2001) assume self-control mechanisms to explain the "puzzle of debt revolvers." About two thirds of US households have a bank-type credit card, and despite high interest rates most maintain a significant credit card debt. Yet the majority of these debt revolvers have substantial liquid assets with which they could pay off this debt. The fact that they do not, violates economic arbitrage. This behavior is explained as a self-control mechanism. An "accountant self" controls the expenditures of a "shopper self" by only paying off a portion of the credit card debt, limiting the purchases that can be made before encountering the credit limit. This documents that there are some self-control mechanisms in place. However the larger range of mechanisms and how they are applied in detail is not yet researched.

### 1.3.3. Risk and Incentives in Investing Strategies

Investment behavior is closely linked to the perceived risk associated with the investment. The conventional economic approach copes with risk of outcomes by assuming a maximization of the expected utility or the subjectively expected utility (Edwards, 1954). Kahneman and Tversky (1979) later expand this model by proposing four key features in their prospect theory of choice under uncertainty:

- Reference point: outcomes are assessed relative to a reference point which often is the status quo but can be manipulated by the framing of a decision.
- Risk attitude: general risk aversion for gains and risk seeking for losses.
- Loss aversion: losses loom larger than gains.
- Non-linear decision weights: over-weighting of small probabilities relative to highly probable events and under-weighting of outcomes that are merely probable in comparison with outcomes that are certain.

These features enable the prediction of a large number of biases and deviations from economic theory that are observed in laboratory studies of decision-making.

A conceptually different approach to choice under uncertainty is to stress the incentives people have for a specific choice. The choice of an investment can be understood by the factors supporting that specific choice. Fox and Tversky (1998) for example, provide an empirical test of the implications of support theory, which states that probability judgments are weighted by a "level of support" factor. They show that judgments concerning specific events are more strongly supported than those concerning combined events, as pertinent information is more easily recalled or assessed. The sum of the judged probabilities of individual events is therefore greater than the judged probability of the same combined events. Unpacking the ways in which an investment might be profitable can increase the attractiveness of the investment. Other approaches stress the post-decisional evaluation stage, which is anticipated in the choice situation. Loomes and Sugden (1982) for example point out the importance of an anticipated regret of an investment failing.

Various choice models pointed out different factors of importance. It is clear that we have incentives for our choices. Macmillan *et al.* (1985) give an overview of different incentives venture capitalists have for investing in companies. However, Zacharakis and Meyer (1998) see a lack of insight by venture capitalists and in general by experts into their own decision processes. In particular, it is not clear how we link the perception of a company we want to invest in, to these investment incentives and how the available information is integrated into a choice.

## 1.4. METHODS FOR CAPTURING COGNITIVE PROCESSES

Various methods have been proposed to capture or describe mental processes on the individual level (i.e., think aloud technique, introspection) and diverse imaging methods are on the advance. In the following, a combination of different methods is applied, which work on an aggregated level, to capture the underlying cognitive processes in place. Here an overview is provided about the different methods. Specifics are discussed later in the respective chapters.

### 1.4.1. Experiments

A classic research vehicle in psychology, and also to a growing extent in economics, is the experiment. This formalized method allows for systematic hypothesis testing of behavioral questions. In an experiment, a specific research question is isolated that can then be investigated more systematically. Real world situations are translated into an experimental setting where key variables can be selectively manipulated to find their causal consequences. This is a huge advantage for experiments in contrast to observations where causation is often only inferred from correlation.

While in the standard experiment variables are manipulated to find causal relationships between each other, exploratory experiments can be used for the development of ideas. The latter is useful in new settings for the generation of hypotheses. A further specification is to separate between field and laboratory experiments, that enable one to vary the abstraction level of the behavior of interest.

In the cognitive sciences another distinction is made between process and outcome orientation. Generally, behavioral outcomes are the experimental focus. Alternatively, process variables can be used as a dependent variable to give insights into the procedural mechanisms involved (Covey & Lovie,

1998). This appears to be an important approach for a better understanding of the underlying cognitive mechanisms of behavior.

However experiments, as theoretical abstractions of real world situations, always bring a simplification with them. Therefore in a new setting it is often useful to also use other explorative techniques.

### 1.4.2. Ratings

An easy and straight forward method for evaluations is the use of ratings. Here the area of interest is formalized into questions that are rated on a scale. A classical example for this is test-theory where questionnaires for individual differences are developed to capture specific dimensions of personality.

The main questions regard the stability and variability of constructs and respective ratings. One common finding is that Likert scales with a neutral middle point give the best results here (Likert, 1932). Keeping also Miller's (1956) results in mind, regarding a working memory limitation of seven plus-minus two, a five point Likert scale appears to provide a useful basis for psychological rating scales.

Diverse concepts and behavioral aspects have been examined; and behavioral constructs exist for sensation seeking (Zuckerman, 1971, 1984, 1994), risk taking (Coombs, 1975; Weber *et al.*, 2002), empathy (Chlopan *et al.*, 1985), and many other personal characteristics. But besides capturing personal characteristics, ratings have been developed for much more diverse areas and even situations or objects are the included in this method (Osgood *et al.*, 1957).

### 1.4.3. Real World Data

An additional category of methods that have yet to be developed in cognitive sciences, and thus will be a growing importance is real world data analysis. This is a systematic analysis of existing behavioral data, with the advantage of directly describing the behavioral facets in a real world environment. Examples of this come from practitioners, where data storage systems have been employed. Large customer warehouses do exist but often, for a behavioral analysis, the academic know-how or incentives are lacking. Yet these databases often allow a systematic tracking of behavior in diverse areas.

Some research areas traditionally work with real world data. Market data for example is extensively analyzed. But mainly aggregated behavior is the focus. In marketing a frequent approach is to break this market down into segments, often working with demographic differences. Thus a direct analysis of behavioral differences is rare. An exception is the current customer relation management practice where individual behavior is tracked over time. However customer relation management research in academia remains nascent (Kamakura *et al.*, 2005).

This documents the need for behavioral methods in specific financial agendas. Many approaches of behavioral analysis exist but not in linkage to the specifics of financial domains. A domain specific analysis could help to clarify the importance and universality of behavioral effects and would help to better understand the behavior in financial settings. The research question is threefold: First, what strategies do people use in different financial domains? Second, how different are the financial strategies people use within a domain? Third, is the selection of different strategies adaptive and can be explained by learning processes?

Chapter 2 describes an example of behavioral tracking of natural spending strategies in. This examines individual differences in spending behavior and differentiates between different spending styles based on the debit transactions recorded by a financial service institution. Chapters 3 through 5, utilize ratings and experimental methods respectively for saving and investment strategies. In Chapter 3, individual saving concepts and saving structures, as well as differences in self-control demands and self-control features are researched. Chapter 4 introduces a method of how companies are evaluated based on semantic differences. Then in Chapter 5 different inference strategies for integrating company information into a choice are compared, followed by a final discussion and outlook in Chapter 6.

*Chapter 2*

# SPENDING STRATEGIES

In this chapter we look at peoples' spendings to better understand their behavior, and to investigate the differences people show in this domain. The analysis is made on real financial data and introduces a method for identifying psychological differences in financial behavior based on real world data.

When companies introduce customer segmentation, a common strategy is to use individual differences as a predictor of future behavior. Recent advances in data management used by large financial institutions give an unprecedented and potentially powerful source of data for identifying such differences. It is shown that spending data can substantially help to target the direct marketing of a savings product. Behavior-based segmentation does not simply align with classic demographic information. In particular, a systematic combination of this independent source and more traditional measures can enhance the predictive power of marketing research and improve the relationship with customers. Customer data is a direct source for a better understanding of individuals and can easily be applied for deriving and testing psychological assumptions about financial behavior.

## 2.1. BEHAVIORAL EVALUATION

Spending in general, but especially shopping, can be seen as one of the most direct expressions of the underlying demand structure. When fulfilling needs or generally pursuing happiness, we display various purchase behaviors differing in sort, frequency, and variability. These recorded differences in spending activity can be used to characterize different sorts of behavior. In the following, a method is provided for using these tracks of spending behavior to capture individual behavioral differences.

### 2.1.1. Spending Literature

Economic literature on spending behavior traditionally focuses on consumer intentions and consumer attitudes, as well as purchase incidents (i.e., Dreze & Modigliani, 1972; Goodhardt *et al.*, 1984; Juster, 1966; Tobin 1959). Optimal consumption strategies are derived based on different utility functions (Hakansson, 1970; Mirman 1971), but also the elasticity of demand is discussed as price dependent changes in purchase quantity (Oliveira-Castro *et al.*, 2006). Another focus lies on the temporal distribution of spending over time. The life-cycle permanent income hypothesis (Friedman, 1957; Modigliani, 1966, 1986; Modigliani & Brumberg, 1954) is central here, which proposes that anticipated earnings are taken into account by current spending behavior to optimize and respectively equalize spending over one's lifetime. Alternatively, smoothing spending behavior over time can be the result of buffer stock as a precautionary saving motive (Campbell & Mankiw, 1990; Carroll, 1997).

Also, emotions have been stressed as important in spending behavior (Hirschman, 1984; Hirschman & Holbrook, 1982; Holbrook & Hirschman, 1982) where experiential and hedonic aspects are highlighted. Closely related are impulsive buying or compulsive spending (i.e., Rook & Fisher, 1995; Weinberg & Gottwald, 1982), which are specific manifestations of emotional spending behavior. Other features of spending behavior can be ecological aspects such as sustainability and social responsibility. Reisch and Røpke (2004) provide an overview about ecological economic consumption.

A further characterization of spending behavior is the usage of different transaction channels. Generally the best channel structure for a company to optimize profits is searched for (i.e., Coughlan, 1985; Jeuland & Shugan, 1983; Schoenblacher & Gordon, 2002; Trivedi, 1998). In addition, the usage of specific channels like the internet (Dewan *et al.*, 2000) or credit card usage (Plummer, 1971) has been researched.

## 2.1.2. Individual Spending Differences

The improved storage and processing of transactional data by large financial institutions makes it possible to analyze these differences in detail. Existing research in this field mainly concentrates on purchasing frequency, retention, or customer loyalty (i.e., Eriksson & Vaghult, 2000; Stern & Hammond, 2004; for a critical comment see Reinartz & Kumar, 2002). In this chapter, a psychometric approach is adopted that examines the underlying consumption styles as differences in financial behavior. Based on a rich set of automatically processed and readily available data in personal financial services, a new differentiation method is introduced that extracts financial traits directly corresponding to the observed behavioral data.

Customer segmentation is widely used in marketing, where different predictive characteristics like "attitudes," "lifestyles," "psychographics," or "purchasing involvement" have been adopted (Gould, 1997; Hustad & Pessemier, 1974; Lockshin *et al.*, 1997; Pernica, 1974; Plummer, 1974; Slama & Tashchrian, 1985). Lesser & Hughes (1986) provide a generalizability test for psychographic market segments. For an early critic of segmentation compare, for example, Wells (1975). Our focus is on the understanding of the individual customer and different dimensions are described that can be used as a multiple purpose tool for improving customer relations. The method proposed in this chapter differentiates between customers by using directly observed behavior. A promising psychological concept in this context is that of personality factors to account for differences in financial behavior. The records of manifested behavior are analyzed to extract the underlying personal financial characteristics, which represent the main individual differences. The advantage of this direct behaviorally based differentiation is that it is independent of additionally gathered data; and thus, can supplement information on attitude, interests, or demographic data.

First, the underlying data source and the employed data sample are described. Then follows an outline of the method of behavioral differentiation that includes data aggregation, as well as, data interpretation, and the advantages of the derived method in relation to a direct mailing example are reported.

### 2.1.3. Behavioral Analysis

Behavioral data can easily be used in a variety of data-rich areas. Nowadays large quantities of behavioral data are mostly gathered automatically by large corporations and government, and prove easily accessible. But often this data is not exploited effectively by organizations. For example, in designing coupon programs, Rossi *et al.* (1996) have shown that the largely neglected purchase history can be highly valuable for improving the profitability of direct marketing. The importance of categorized purchases is further supported on the household level by Ainslie and Rossi (1998), as well as, Bucklin and Gupta (1992). The lack of direct data evaluation is mostly due to the absence of corresponding resources in this fast-developing domain. Thus customer information is often not processed systematically by practitioners or academics, and hence its full potential is not exploited. Easily accessible behavioral data is the primary data for the advantages of being robust against manipulation, errors, and over-interpretation.

For our purpose, the data of a financial services retail institution is used with highly sophisticated records of customers' regular spending behavior. This pre-recorded information was aggregated and made usable through standard statistical procedures. The data processing is mainly automatic and can be applied for a variety of purposes. The proposed procedure involves low running costs and can serve marketing purposes, as well as, support and structure the financial service itself.

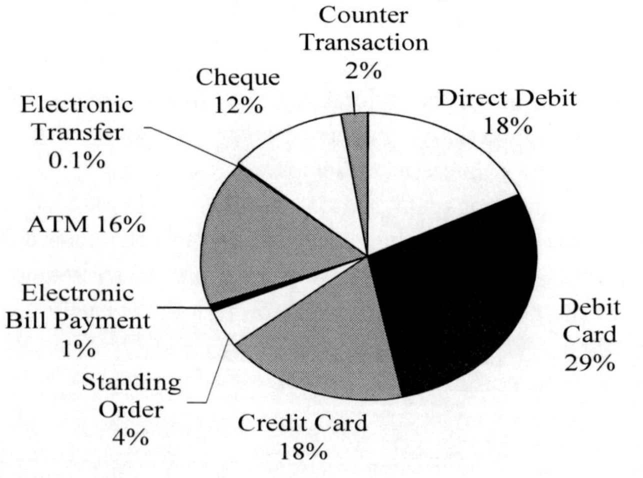


Figure 2.1. Debit channel usage frequency

***Data Description***

The processed source data consisted of debit transactions made within the different payment mechanisms shown in Figure 2.1. This data is available at an individual level in the customer information warehouse alongside other personal information such as, demographics, credit scores, lifestyle variables, etc. All recorded transactions are evaluated on the basis of the British merchant Standard Industry Classification (SIC). This information allows a separation of different types of spending behaviors. The transactions are separated into 370 different debit categories, describing specific groups of goods sold by these industries. This data classification is completely automated and thus reliable within the constraints of the formalized classification procedure. The predefined categories allow an evaluation of individual spending behavior, and provide behaviorally meaningful data by enabling a characterization of individuals according to what they spend their money on, how much they spend, and how spending in the different areas is distributed over time. Though in this analysis, the focus is on the spending frequency and the amount of money spent in the different debit categories over one year.

It is important to consider however, and inevitably stress the partial nature of this available data, since it is analyzed from a single company. Hence possible transactions by other providers are not captured. When working with the data of only one provider a common problem is to miss out on possibly relevant parts of the behavioral style. I addressed this problem by evaluating only customers who predominantly bank with onc institution, lcaving out about half of the customers. This guarantees a sample that provides the most transactions are captured, but it potentially neglects behavioral variations of people who are more flexible in the use of financial providers. A more adequate consideration of this bias is only possible when customer information is shared by different institutions (Lin *et al.*, 2003). But the chosen method of data analysis proves to be robust against missing data (Kamakura & Wedel, 2000). The considered information is further restricted to informative transactions only. Within the recorded transactions the cash retrievals (ATM) and some of the other transactions which do not classify as specific purpose transactions are not followed up. The categorized transactions constitute 74% of the total number of transactions.

***Sample Description***

For computational ease in the analysis, the total customer base of 20 million individuals was reduced. Initially only “active customers” were selected, where "active" is defined as those customers who have both a credit card and a debit card with the financial institution; and, who show at least one transaction on each within the last three months. From the resulting 10 million active customers, a sample of 300,000 was randomly selected. Even though, in the analysis I used the aggregated annual transactions, an examination of the daily data shown in Figure 2.2 illustrates that there are also significant weekly (with the highest spending on Fridays and the lowest on Sundays) and seasonal patterns (mainly showing spikes related to different holidays) that are not further considered here.

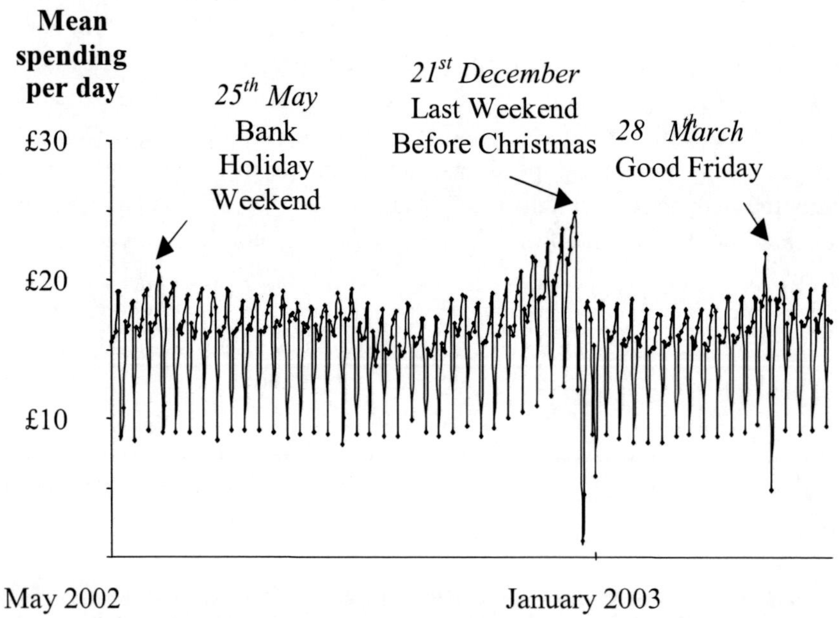


Figure 2.2. Annual and weekly volatility of credit card spending

The sample includes only the age groups between the ages of 18 and 99 years. The age distribution with their amounts spent is shown in Figure 2.3. In addition, the definition of active customers influences the representation of this sampling. Generally the sample is representative for adults of the UK. However, as only credit card holders with a regular spending pattern with one provider were included, parts of the total population have been left aside. Therefore, the following observations of spending behavior are restricted to these customers only and are to be interpreted within these limitations. The average annual income for example is £38,000, slightly above the average income of the total UK population of £34,000. The selected data provide a substantial record of differences in purchasing behavior for a specific sample of 300,000 customers.

Figure 2.3. Age distribution of the 300,000 customer sample

## 2.2. Usage of Behavioral Data

Using the data of financial services institutions allows individual differentiation on multiple purchasing events which leaves aside specific shopping characteristics such as brand switching, and focuses on more general drivers guiding the variation in overall behavior. The aim was to reduce the mass of behavioral data into a limited number of useful and manageable factors that can then be employed to provide a better understanding of individual customers, and be used in specific marketing campaigns as a direct business application; thereby promoting individualized services in the private financial sector.

### 2.2.1. Data Aggregation

The first step in our analysis consisted of finding a suitable level of aggregation for the expense data. The expenditure categories needed to be sufficiently aggregated in order to enable useful comparisons across individuals. The goal was to prevent the analysis from being swamped by noise from very small expense categories, and to make the analysis tractable. Notably to have a sufficient number of expense categories to ensure that spending behavior could be differentiated across individuals.

Therefore, the initial 370 categories were grouped into larger categories. This was done by a cluster analysis of the 370 debit categories into 32 new spending classes. Thus, similar debit categories are grouped together forming more or less homogeneous groups of spending incidents depending on the data. For the purpose of achieving a specified number of homogenous clusters, the k-means method (MacQueen, 1967) was applied to generate different solutions based on the number of clusters specified. The analysis is based on the correlation of the number of transactions within the different categories and searches for the lowest sum of deviations from the clusters' means. The number of transactions was taken here to reflect every single action but not to rely on the spending category dependent pound values.

**Table 2.1. K-means debit category cluster solution**

| | **Spending Cluster** (in order of avg. member distance from centroid) | **Number of Members** | **Debits in £ Million** | **Root Mean square** | **Max. Distance from Centroid** | **Nearest Cluster** | **Distance to near. Cluster** |
|---|---|---|---|---|---|---|---|
| 1 | **Catalogue Shopping** | 1 | 0.18 | . | 0 | 28 | 1.17 |
| 2 | **Loan Repayments** | 2 | 100 | 6.2% | 0.62 | 31 | 1.03 |
| 3 | **Subscriptions** | 2 | 20 | 6.3% | 0.63 | 28 | 0.94 |
| 4 | **Home Maintenance** | 3 | 14 | 5.9% | 0.70 | 29 | 0.98 |
| 5 | **Household Bills** | 6 | 308 | 5.3% | 0.85 | 9 | 0.84 |
| 6 | **Petrol & DIY** | 3 | 385 | 6.0% | 0.84 | 20 | 1.12 |
| 7 | **Children & Graduates** | 3 | 6.7 | 6.3% | 0.73 | 29 | 0.92 |
| 8 | **Specialist Holidays** | 3 | 16 | 6.4% | 0.75 | 29 | 0.96 |
| 9 | **Mortgage & Assurance** | 4 | 906 | 6.4% | 0.97 | 5 | 0.84 |
| 10 | **Education** | 5 | 17 | 6.2% | 0.80 | 29 | 0.88 |
| 11 | **Pensions & Insurance** | 5 | 44 | 6.2% | 0.80 | 29 | 0.89 |
| 12 | **Leisure – Luxury** | 4 | 229 | 6.6% | 0.99 | 22 | 0.82 |
| 13 | **Charity** | 8 | 5.6 | 6.1% | 0.84 | 29 | 0.93 |
| 14 | **Television** | 4 | 46 | 6.6% | 0.87 | 29 | 0.89 |
| 15 | **Retail – Other** | 6 | 17 | 6.3% | 0.83 | 28 | 0.98 |
| 16 | **Health** | 6 | 47 | 6.3% | 0.84 | 29 | 0.90 |
| 17 | **Services – Financial** | 7 | 276 | 6.2% | 0.85 | 31 | 0.85 |
| 18 | **Retail - Food & Drink** | 6 | 38 | 6.4% | 0.85 | 29 | 0.92 |

**Table 2.2. K-means debit category cluster solution**

| | **Spending Cluster** (in order of avg. member distance from centroid) | **Number of Members** | **Debits in £ Million** | **Root Mean square** | **Max. Distance from Centroid** | **Nearest Cluster** | **Distance to near. Cluster** |
|---|---|---|---|---|---|---|---|
| **19** | **Services - Commercial** | 6 | 13 | 6.4% | 0.89 | 29 | 0.88 |
| **20** | **Retail – General** | 11 | 247 | 6.2% | 0.98 | 24 | 0.87 |
| **21** | **Services – Other** | 9 | 26 | 6.2% | 0.85 | 29 | 0.89 |
| **22** | **Leisure – Creative** | 14 | 116 | 6.1% | 0.89 | 26 | 0.75 |
| **23** | **International Travel** | 4 | 167 | 6.8% | 0.89 | 30 | 0.89 |
| **24** | **Retail - Clothing & Home** | 13 | 926 | 6.3% | 1.01 | 20 | 0.87 |
| **25** | **Car Purchase & Running** | 8 | 99 | 6.4% | 0.90 | 29 | 0.91 |
| **26** | **Leisure - Intellectual** | 12 | 2 | 6.3% | 0.92 | 22 | 0.75 |
| **27** | **Leisure – Sports** | 10 | 27 | 6.3% | 0.98 | 29 | 0.92 |
| **28** | **Services - Professional** | 5 | 80 | 6.8% | 0.94 | 31 | 0.87 |
| **29** | **Investment & Self Employed** | 4 | 93 | 7.0% | 0.90 | 31 | 0.82 |
| **30** | **Travel & Cash** | 8 | 112 | 6.8% | 1.02 | 31 | 0.85 |
| **31** | **Payment Cards** | 8 | 519 | 6.8% | 0.98 | 29 | 0.82 |
| **32** | **Career Specific** | 10 | 64 | 6.7% | 1.05 | 29 | 0.86 |

One advantage of k-means clustering is that distance information for the items to the cluster's mean and for between the clusters becomes readily available. Table 2.1 shows the 32 spending clusters derived from the 370 debit categories. It simplifies the understanding and interpretation of the cluster results. Outliers and central categories can be easily determined and explanations for discrepancies sought. In cases where the reason for the behavioral similarity is not immediately obvious, further investigation into the categories could prove useful in understanding the dependencies between the categories. For example the grouping of 'Stockbrokers', 'Investment', 'Department of Social Security' (DSS) and 'Rent' initially seemed counter-intuitive. However, once it is understood that the data underlying 'Rent' relate more to 'commercial rent' than to 'private rent,' and that DSS largely consists of National Insurance payments on the part of small businesses, then the grouping makes much more sense, and can be taken to reflect the spending behavior of small businesses or individual entrepreneurs.

Besides the clusters' interpretability, the heterogeneity or stability is of empirical importance. The distance of each item from its centroid (cluster mean) and the distances between the centroids themselves are good indicators of the clusters' stability. The clusters vary greatly and have strong overlaps with each other, often with single outliers distorting the cluster solution. The

32 spending clusters provide broader classes of spending behavior that can be applied to further analysis.

### 2.2.2. Data Interpretation

But what does the data tell us regarding individual differences in spending behavior, and cognitive or psychological spending characteristics? For a deeper understanding of the personal differences in financial behavior an abstraction method to find the underlying differences in the purchasing characteristics is needed. Exploratory factor analysis is a common statistical technique in psychometric tests to determine the fundamental dimensions of differences within observed data. This method is used to compress variables into a limited number of factors and account for these differences. The derived factors are orthogonal, where scores on each factor are uncorrelated and hence independent from each other. Each factor thus reflects a different behavioral aspect. The underlying aim thereby is to evaluate spending behaviors and to find the dimensions to differentiate between customers. Personal diagnostic factors are differentially dependent on specific behaviors and, therefore, describe different aspects of the overall behavior. They are seen as the underlying dimensions of behavioral variation, presumed to reflect an underlying trait and thereby a propensity for a specific behavior (Cattell, 1965; Eysenck & Eysenck, 1985; Fishbein & Ajzen, 1975). The results of the 32 derived spending clusters provided the starting point for a factor analysis; considering the individual amount spent in each cluster.

It is desirable to use the smallest number of factors while explaining as much variance as possible. To determine the optimal number of factors, all 32 possible factors are generated along with the variance they explain. Starting with the strongest factor the explained variance decreases over the factors. A measure for selecting a useful number of factors is the eigenvalue of the factors, which measures the importance of a factor, by giving an estimation of the variance explained by that factor in a given data set. A common heuristic is to keep all factors with an eigenvalue of at least one, thus all these factors explain more variance than the underlying variable. In our final solution seven factors where the eigenvalue is clearly above one were selected. This limit was chosen because only strong, clearly interpretable factors are useful, and factors eight to ten, though slightly above one, were not directly interpretable. In the next step the factors were rotated and made more distinct. The initial factor solution takes the variance between the input variables into account and not the differences between the factors themselves. In order to derive comparable factors, which explain a higher proportion of variance, a factor rotation method has to be used. With more than one explanatory factor needed, where the factors themselves are highly distinct according to the input variables, an equamax rotation has to be applied (Landahl, 1938). This is a standard optimization method of orthogonally rotating the factors according to the data fit. Through this process the factors' differences in explained variance is decreased, and high factor loadings for only a few variables on each factor are obtained; rendering the factors more distinct from each other and making them directly interpretable. The higher the factor loading of the spending cluster the more important is that specific variable for that factor. The loadings of the spending clusters determine the factor and are used for the factor interpretation. The shaded loadings in Table 2.2 show the categories that were most important for the factor interpretation. The first factor, for example, is highly dependent on the spending clusters 'Leisure-Luxury,' 'Travel&Cash,' 'International Travel,' and 'Payment Cards' and is, therefore, called 'Leisure & Travel'. All the factors received labels as they appear to capture specific characteristics, though these labels are subjective interpretations. Together the factors describe a substantial amount of the variance in the underlying data with the first two as the main dividers (see Table 2.2). The seven derived debit factors are shown with their assigned naming and the variance explained, measured by their eigenvalue. For each factor the loading of the spending classes are listed as the standardized factor loadings, representing the weight of this variable for the respective factor.

The factor analysis was used to find regularities in the personal differences, to reveal the underlying dimensions of buying behavior. The seven generated factors systematically represent the different characteristics in spending behavior; and, therefore, reflect seven dimensions of financial personality. As the factors describe different parts of the individual personality, they can be used to differentiate customers on these dimensions. Every customer can be assigned a specific score on each factor by multiplying their percentage of the amount spent in each of the derived spending clusters by the loading on the factor. These loadings are summed up to create the respective factor score. The factor score stands for the degree of a specific behavioral trait (described by that factor) and can be attributed to that individual or group of individuals. For example, the behavioral trait of the 'Leisure & Travel' factor is determined by weighting the proportion of spending in each of the clusters by the appropriate loadings. Thus, People who

## Table 2.3 Equamax rotated factor solution

| **Factor 1 LEISURE & TRAVEL** | | **Factor 2 GENERAL** | | **Factor 3 MAINTENANCE** | | **Factor 4 REGULAR PAYMENTS** | | **Factor 5 RISK & SOCIAL** | | **Factor 6 SERVICE ORIENTATION** | | **Factor 7 FUTURE ORIENTATION** | |
|---|---|---|---|---|---|---|---|---|---|---|---|---|---|
| ***Eigenvalue*** | *2.08* | | *2.07* | | *1.6* | | *1.5* | | *1.35* | | *1.17* | | *1.12* |
| **Leisure - Luxury** | 0.68 | Services - Professional | 0.93 | Home Maintenance | 0.68 | Television | 0.62 | Pensions & Insurance | 0.69 | Services - Commercial | 0.72 | Children & Graduates | 0.75 |
| **Travel & Cash** | 0.65 | Subscriptions | 0.93 | Petrol & DIY | 0.59 | Loan Repayments | 0.60 | Household Bills | 0.46 | Retail - Other | 0.53 | Education | 0.43 |
| **International Travel** | 0.51 | Retail – General | 0.38 | Retail - Clothing & Home | 0.44 | Household Bills | 0.44 | Charity | 0.45 | Financial Services | 0.39 | Mortgage & Assurance | 0.22 |
| **Payment Cards** | 0.41 | Leisure - Creative | 0.21 | Retail - General | 0.37 | Mortgage & Assurance | 0.41 | Health | 0.37 | Services - Other | 0.24 | Payment Cards | 0.16 |
| **Retail - Clothing & Home** | 0.40 | Retail - Clothing & Home | 0.19 | Leisure - Creative | 0.34 | Car Purchase & Run. Costs | 0.27 | Education | 0.19 | Payment Cards | 0.19 | Career Specific | 0.15 |
| **Leisure Creative** | -0.39 | Payment Cards | 0.17 | Services - Other | 0.32 | Payment Cards | 0.24 | Retail - Clothing & Home | 0.18 | Travel & Cash | 0.13 | Household Bills | 0.13 |
| **Leisure - Sports** | 0.35 | Leisure - Luxury | 0.16 | Mortgage & Assurance | 0.18 | Catalogue Shopping | 0.022 | Leisure - Luxury | 0.17 | Leisure - Luxury | 0.12 | Retail - Clothing & Home | 0.12 |
| **Retail – General** | 0.31 | Petrol & DIY | 0.09 | Leisure - Luxury | 0.18 | Retail - Clothing & Home | 0.21 | Mortgage & Assurance | 0.17 | Leisure - Creative | 0.12 | Leisure - Luxury | 0.11 |
| **Car Purchase & Run. Costs** | 0.23 | Health | 0.09 | Household Bills | 0.17 | Petrol & DIY | 0.19 | Payment Cards | 0.16 | Loan Repayments | 0.10 | Financial Services | 0.11 |
| **Health** | 0.22 | Travel & Cash | 0.09 | Retail - Food & Drink | 0.17 | Financial Services | 0.19 | Leisure - Creative | 0.16 | Charity | 0.10 | Travel & Cash | 0.09 |
| **Retail - Food & Drink** | 0.21 | International Travel | 0.08 | Car Purchase & Run. Costs | 0.16 | Retail - General | 0.15 | International Travel | 0.13 | Catalogue Shopping | 0.09 | Charity | 0.08 |
| **Mortgage & Assurance** | 0.09 | Leisure – Sports | 0.08 | Health | 0.15 | Retail - Food & Drink | 0.10 | Investment & Self Employed | 0.11 | Education | 0.07 | Leisure - Creative | 0.07 |
| **Petrol & DIY** | 0.09 | Television | 0.08 | Payment Cards | 0.13 | Leisure - Sports | 0.10 | Retail - Food & Drink | 0.11 | Retail - Food & Drink | 0.06 | Petrol & DIY | 0.07 |

## Table 2.3 (Continued)

| Factor 1 LEISURE & TRAVEL | | Factor 2 GENERAL | | Factor 3 MAINTENANCE | | Factor 4 REGULAR PAYMENTS | | Factor 5 RISK & SOCIAL | | Factor 6 SERVICE ORIENTATION | | Factor 7 FUTURE ORIENTATION | |
|---|---|---|---|---|---|---|---|---|---|---|---|---|---|
| **Leisure Intellectual** | –0.09 | Retail - Food & Drink | 0.07 | Retail - Other | 0.11 | Pensions & Insurance | 0.08 | Services - Other | 0.06 | Retail - General | 0.06 | Services - Commercial | 0.05 |
| **Retail – Other** | 0.08 | Services - Commercial | 0.05 | Leisure - Sports | 0.09 | International Travel | 0.08 | Financial Services | 0.06 | Specialist Holidays | 0.06 | Health | 0.05 |
| **Catalogue Shopping** | 0.06 | Household Bills | 0.05 | Investment & Self Employed | 0.07 | Leisure - Creative | 0.08 | Television | 0.06 | Subscriptions | 0.06 | Retail - General | 0.05 |
| **Investment & Self Employed** | 0.04 | Retail – Other | 0.05 | International Travel | 0.07 | Leisure - Luxury | 0.07 | Specialist Holidays | 0.05 | Services - Professional | 0.05 | Car Purchase & Run. Costs | 0.05 |
| **Television** | 0.02 | Car Purchase & Run. Costs | 0.04 | Education | 0.05 | Education | 0.06 | Subscriptions | 0.05 | Retail - Clothing & Home | 0.05 | International Travel | 0.04 |
| **Education** | 0.02 | Mortgage & Assurance | 0.04 | Career Specific | 0.03 | Leisure - Intellectual | 0.04 | Petrol & DIY | 0.04 | Home Maintenance | 0.03 | Leisure - Sports | 0.03 |
| **Household Bills** | 0.01 | Charity | 0.04 | Specialist Holidays | 0.01 | Retail - Other | 0.02 | Travel & Cash | 0.04 | Petrol & DIY | 0.02 | Retail - Food & Drink | 0.02 |
| **Charity** | 0.01 | Leisure - Intellectual | 0.03 | Subscriptions | 0.00 | Specialist Holidays | 0.01 | Services - Commercial | 0.03 | Leisure - Sports | 0.02 | Subscriptions | 0.01 |
| **Services Commercial** | –0.00 | Services - Other | 0.03 | Services - Professional | 0.00 | Subscriptions | 0.01 | Services - Professional | 0.03 | Leisure - Intellectual | 0.01 | Services - Professional | 0.01 |
| **Specialist Holidays** | -0.01 | Loan Repayments | 0.02 | Leisure - Intellectual | -0.01 | Services - Professional | 0.01 | Leisure - Sports | 0.01 | International Travel | 0.01 | Loan Repayments | 0.00 |
| **Children & Graduates** | -0.02 | Pensions & Insurance | 0.02 | Charity | -0.01 | Children & Graduates | 0.01 | Retail - General | 0.01 | Mortgage & Assurance | 0.01 | Television | -0.01 |
| **Services – Other** | -0.02 | Investment & Self Employed | 0.01 | Television | -0.01 | Health | 0.00 | Retail - Other | 0.00 | Health | 0.00 | Home Maintenance | -0.01 |
| **Services Professional** | –0.03 | Children & Graduates | 0.01 | Financial Services | -0.02 | Services - Other | -0.02 | Home Maintenance | -0.04 | Career Specific | 0.00 | Services - Other | -0.01 |

## Table 2.3 (Continued)

| Factor 1<br>**LEISURE & TRAVEL** | Factor 2<br>**GENERAL** | Factor 3<br>**MAINTENANCE** | Factor 4<br>**REGULAR PAYMENTS** | Factor 5<br>**RISK & SOCIAL** | Factor 6<br>**SERVICE ORIENTATION** | Factor 7<br>**FUTURE ORIENTATION** |
|---|---|---|---|---|---|---|
| **Subscriptions** - 0.04 | Education 0.00 | Travel & Cash - 0.04 | Travel & Cash - 0.04 | Car Purchase & - Run. Costs 0.04 | Household Bills 0.00 | Leisure - - Intellectual 0.05 |
| **Financial Services**- 0.04 | Catalogue 0.00 Shopping | Loan - Repayments 0.04 | Services -- Commercial 0.05 | Career Specific - 0.04 | Television - 0.01 | Retail - Other - 0.06 |
| **Pensions** &- **Insurance** 0.06 | Home 0.00 Maintenance | Services -- Commercial 0.06 | Investment &- Self Employed 0.07 | Catalogue - Shopping 0.07 | Pensions &- Insurance 0.02 | Investment &- Self Employed 0.06 |
| **Career Specific** - 0.07 | Specialist 0.00 Holidays | Pensions &- Insurance 0.08 | Home - Maintenance 0.10 | Leisure -- Intellectual 0.10 | Children &- Graduates 0.03 | Specialist - Holidays 0.08 |
| **Loan** - **Repayments** 0.10 | Financial 0.00 Services | Children &- Graduates 0.09 | Career Specific - 0.11 | Children &- Graduates 0.15 | Car Purchase &- Run. Costs 0.06 | Pensions &- Insurance 0.09 |
| **Home** - **Maintenance** 0.18 | Career Specific - 0.01 | Catalogue - Shopping 0.09 | Charity - 0.12 | Loan - Repayments 0.20 | Investment &- Self Employed 0.19 | Catalogue - Shopping 0.39 |

spend a lot of their money on leisure goods and travel receives a high score. People who instead spend their money on loan repayments and home maintenance are described by a low or negative score on this factor.

It appears that people have a complex "spending personality" and can be described by seven defined factors. This is a rather new approach for understanding differences in spending and captures one aspect of a "financial personality." It nicely describes observable differences and enables a differentiation of customers on a psychological or cognitive basis. The seven spending dimensions can be applied in a multitude of ways. One possibility is to segment the customer base according to the likelihood of a specific purchase. To validate the results, an example for predicting new data is given for loan products, as shown in the next section. But these methods could in principle serve any business strategy where individual spending differences are of importance and correlate with the behavior of interest.

### 2.2.3. Customer Understanding

The main question then is what the dimensions of spending behavior tell us besides the already known and frequently used personal characteristics like demographic information or "lifestyle variables." What additional explanatory value do they provide and, perhaps more importantly, how can these insights be used in customer relation management or marketing in general?

In the first step it has to be shown that these seven spending dimensions do not simply align with demographic information that is usually applied in the domain of targeting or individualized services. Table 2.3 shows that this is not the case, and that the Pearson Correlation with standard demographic measures like sex, age, and income is in general relatively low, although substantial correlations exist for some product usages. Therefore, we can conclude that additional information is provided by this type of spending analysis allowing us to better differentiate between customers. Although the relation between the different personal variables needs further investigation, one obvious advantage of the factorial approach is that it is not purpose-bound and provides a continuous variable that can be applied in different areas – possibly in addition to existing measures. For the cases of 'Loan,' 'Pension,' 'Saving Online,' 'Saving General,' 'Funds,' and 'Mortgage' in Table 2.3, the usage of the products is captured by the number of entries representing the holding of the product. 'Credit Card,' 'Debit Card,' 'Direct Debit,' and 'Overdraft' usages are described in terms of amounts. The gender is coded 0 for female and 1 for male. 'Spending' is the total amount spent in the last year, and 'Debits' is the total number of outgoing transactions in the last year.

**Table 2.4. Debit factor correlation**

| | | Factor 1 | Factor 2 | Factor 3 | Factor 4 | Factor 5 | Factor 6 | Factor 7 |
|---|---|---|---|---|---|---|---|---|
| | **Variable** | Leisure & Travel | General | Main-tenance | Regulars | Risk & Social | Service Orien-tation | Future Orien-tation |
| **General Charac-teristics** | Age | -.07 | .01 | .08 | .04 | .37 | -.18 | -.14 |
| | Sex | -.11 | -.12 | -.12 | .05 | -.08 | .03 | .02 |
| | Spending | .01 | -.12 | -.18 | -.04 | -.09 | .15 | .17 |
| | Debits | .06 | -.07 | .06 | -.02 | -.05 | .07 | .15 |
| **Product Usage** | Credit Card | .22 | .09 | .04 | -.20 | -.06 | .07 | .00 |
| | Debit Card | .09 | -.02 | -.01 | -.10 | -.12 | .09 | .01 |
| | Direct Debit | -.11 | -.19 | -.24 | .09 | -.04 | .12 | .22 |
| | Overdraft | .06 | -.01 | .02 | -.02 | .03 | -.01 | .05 |
| | Loan | -.11 | -.06 | -.11 | .15 | -.17 | .05 | -.07 |
| | Pension | -.04 | -.04 | -.02 | .03 | -.04 | .00 | .04 |
| | Saving Online | .02 | .00 | -.05 | -.03 | -.03 | .05 | .02 |
| | Saving General | .01 | .00 | -.03 | -.06 | .00 | .00 | .01 |
| | Funds | .00 | .00 | .00 | -.03 | .05 | -.04 | -.02 |
| | Mortgage | -.07 | -.09 | -.06 | .12 | -.01 | -.01 | .15 |

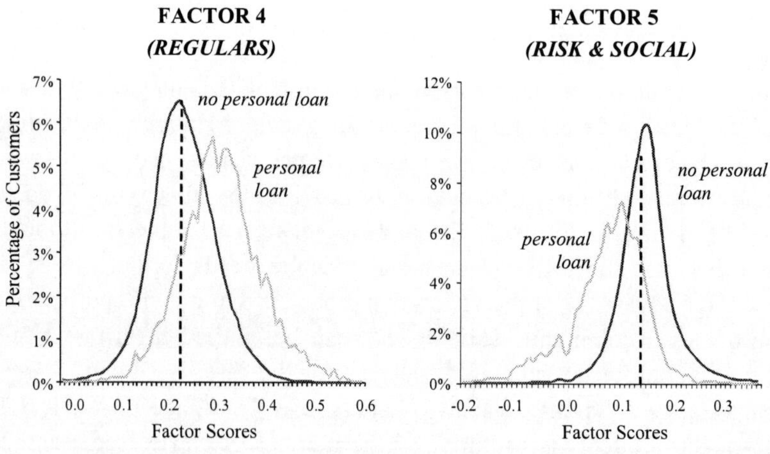


Figure 2.4. Loan holdings for debit factors four and five

To illustrate how to apply the debit factors an example is provided. The factors can be used to optimize the targeting method for products with a high factor correlation, serving as a predictor for purchasing likelihood. This application can be seen as an experiment to test the robustness of the underlying factors in predicting behavioral differences. Therefore, the model's relevance for applications is used to document its theoretical significance for describing differences in financial behavior. A simplistic method to improve the likelihood of a specific behavior is to use the expenditure database for cut-off based segmentation. Those debit factors that best distinguish customers concerning the criteria of interest were used to limit the customer base. In the case of loan holdings, factors four and five are the most predictive. Figure 2.4 shows the distribution of loan holdings for the factor values of these two factors for the 300,000 sample. If a specific sample size is desired, the cut-off can be set accordingly. The differentiation value of the two factors is visualized by the cut-off example. Initially, half of the customers who score highly ($F4 \geq .22$) on the fourth factor were selected. Subsequently, this number of customers was further decreased according to their score on the fifth factor ($F5 \leq .13$). The two factors were selected according to their high correlation with the targeted behavior. The restriction of the customer base with regard to these two factor scores can significantly increase the identification of those customers likely to hold loans from 1% to 9%. The first selection criterion leaves 166,000 customers with 3% holding a loan. The final selection results in 45,000 customers of which 9% are holding a loan.

This straightforward hierarchical selection method has been used with an implementation of the debit factors in direct mailing to improve the mailshot selection, as well as, to optimize the mailshot size. The likelihood of holding a loan was used to predict purchase probability. In a sample independent test the additional usage of the debit factors nearly doubled the response rate compared to only demographic and lifestyle based data from 0.196% to 0.341% (Figure 2.5). In addition to the existing predictors, the alternative direct mail selection method took the debit factors into account where the spending was averaged over the past year. This information was used for the following month's direct mailing. All customers approached were new customers not holding a loan with the provider. The response rate is the percentage of people who purchase a loan within two months after the mailshot. Although no response data was available for a large part of the debit factor mail sample, this substantial uplift in the response rate is assumed to be valid for the whole debit factor mail sample. Alternatively the debit factors can be used to optimize the size of the standard mail sample.

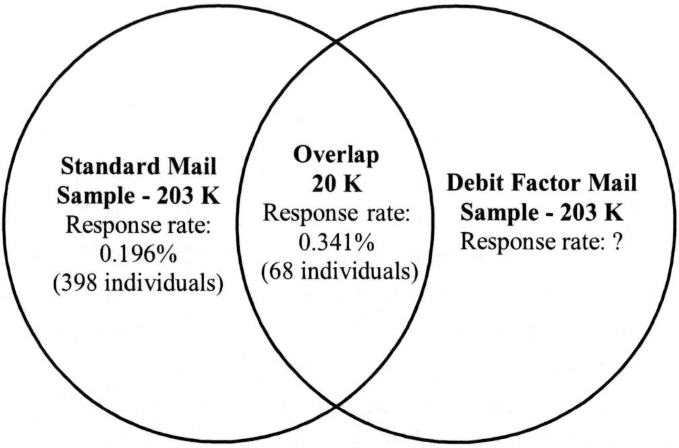


Figure 2.5. Response rates for standard and debit factor model

In both cases all available customer information was taken to select the most responsive mailing sample in a logistic regression. This is the standard procedure for model building in financial services. Both selection models have in common financial behavior, product holdings, risk scores, and household information. They are derived in the same way and trained on past mailings. All data preceding the mailing are regarded, but only the alternative model includes the debit factors. The uplift in the response rate by this additional information is substantial, as achieving the same number of responses with the standard model would mean doubling the mailing size and would add a cost of approximately £100,000 (assuming £0.50 per mail). Thus, on economic grounds alone the debit factors achieve a fundamental gain, in addition to the reduction in "annoyance of the customer" by additional mail.

This illustrates how the debit factors can be used to substantially improve the effectiveness of a direct marketing campaign. The outlined method supports the idea of one reason decision making (Gigerenzer & Goldstein, 1999), yet leaves room for improvements and only exemplifies how the debit factors can be used. To be conclusive, the temporal as well as interregional stability of the debit factors would need further investigation. Also, other methodological issues and the different advances in the field of segmentation have not been investigated in full detail (for a summary see Wedel & Kamakura, 2000; Wind, 1978). Therefore, the real value of debit factor based differentiations and the space for applications has yet to be further explored. The main result is a two step approach, where the first step is a systematic understanding of customer behavior, that can substantially change and improve the efficacy of customer relation management in service industries;

although long-term effects, resulting from a better understanding of the customers' needs could be more prominent.

Generally, this application experiment stresses the close link of the factors to concrete behavioral differences in natural everyday behavior. Therefore, this psychologically grounded theory of individual differences in consumer spending has strong implications for practical applications, as well as, for economic theory as it illustrates systematic variations in spending behavior.

### 2.2.4. Conclusion

Data gathering and data evaluation play a growing role in the digitalization of transactions. In order to add value to this growing amount of reliable data, it is important to develop an explanatory theory. The focus on the individual enriches the data evaluation and allows for individualized services. This sort of direct data evaluation improves service orientation. It can be seen as a crucial economic factor in the further development of customer services.

Also important is to incorporate the customer perspective into this progress. On the one hand data protection and information control have been raised as issues for public policies and legislation matters (Goodwin, 1991; Milne, 2000; Phelps *et al.*, 2000). On the other hand, the role and potential of personal data in customer relation management has been stressed (Godin, 1999; Milne & Boza, 1998). Only when using behavioral data in a way that supports all concerned, then real improvement of data-based customer services can be achieved.

As demonstrated, transactional data cannot only be easily transformed into useful information for marketing purposes, it can also help to build psychological models to provide a better understanding of the customers in general. This can be seen as a method of systematically putting an understanding of the customer first, using data drawn from their own behavior; thus emphasizing the key moment for building and maintaining useful customer warehouses. Preferably by the use of dimensions rather than segments, I want to promote the development toward individual specific relations that would enable services to relate directly to individuals and their demands.

The new technological possibilities demand a new way of thinking and definitely new ways of marketing that go hand in hand with the improvement of analytical and statistical methods. Only by fundamental understanding in the accessible data; and with the adequate methods at hand, can we provide reliable resources for coping with the changing demands in personal services and finally reach the land beyond targeting alone – enabling the delivery of products and information that is personalized for each customer.

This new way introduces a study that applies previously hidden aspects of human behavior to understand individual personal differences. It enlarges the concept of personality to behavioral differences in a concrete setting and describes a method of using financial direct data to enrich psychological theory in regard to individual differences in spending behavior.

*Chapter 3*

# Saving Strategies

At least since Keynes (1936), it is part of economic theory that we have a variety of different motives for saving, including the need to secure means for the future. To bridge the gap between motives and observed behavior, it is necessary to understand how people actually try to achieve their saving goals. A new visualization method for existing saving concepts is introduced here, and shows that individuals apply a range of saving strategies to organize their finances. Based on a financial personality survey it is shown how external, as well as, internal control for saving can be improved systematically.

## 3.1. Saving Literature

When thinking about the use of specific sums of money, such as a Christmas bonus, we often decide to spread consumption and thus keep some portion for a later point in time. However, once the day approaches and this fund is available we tend to spend it all. This can be seen as a momentary failure and a lack of providing means for the future. This chapter investigates the different aspects of saving and how self guiding tools can be used to improve individual commitment.

Saving behavior is a universal activity to ensure that demands are met in the future. Humans apply different strategies to achieve this goal of uncertainty reduction. Most prominent is the delay of gratification, namely the issue of self-control in favor of future consumption. The classic example, for coping with the lures of the moment, is Ulysses who binds himself to the mast of his ship (Homer, 900-600 B.C, Book 12). More generally, environmental structures can help to achieve self-control. These self-control mechanisms and structures are focused for the domain of saving behavior. Elster (1979) and Mele (1995) provide a detailed discussion of the different aspects of pre-commitment and the relation to freedom of will and autonomy. In the economic literature the problem of inter-temporal inconsistency first appears with Strotz (1955) as "spendthriftiness" followed by a more general overview provided by Ainslie (1975) under the label of "impulse control."

### 3.1.1. Economic Model

Starting with Strotz (1955) the standard economic model of wealth distribution over the lifecycle as an overall utility maximization (Ando & Modigliani, 1963; Friedman, 1957; Modigliani & Brumberg, 1954; Modigliani, 1966, 1986) has been challenged repeatedly (i.e., Bernheim *et al.*, 2001; Cordes, 1990; Loewenstein, 1987; Loewenstein & Prelec, 1992; Thaler, 1980, 1985). The two main observations contradicting the integration into one category of total discounted wealth are the additional utility of direct or anticipated consumption (self-control) and the segregation into financial categories (mental accounting). The behavioral life cycle model proposed by Shefrin and Thaler (1988, 1992) generates these two effects by assuming non-fungible components in wealth based on mentally divided accounts. Also other models capturing these behavioral characteristics have been proposed. Laibson (1997; Angeletos *et al.*, 2001; Harris & Laibson, 2001) incorporates hyperbolic discounting functions to model dynamically inconsistent preferences and asset specific spending. In contrast to the standard lifecycle model it predicts that spending tracks income. Others explain the immediacy effect by incorporating a "reference point" in the utility function (Loewenstein, 1988), by "dynamic self-control" preferences (Gul & Pesendorfer, 2001, 2004), or by "temporal construals" where the richness of mental representations of event features depends on the distance in time (Trope & Liberman, 2003).

Equally inherent in the models are two distinct intrapersonal mechanisms. This separation goes back to Descartes and has entered modern sciences via Freud (1911) who distinguished between primary processes ("pleasure principle") and secondary processes ("reality principle"). Later, saving behavior was described as a conflict between multiple selves (i.e., Thaler & Shefrin, 1981). All models have in common the assumption of a conflict between different selves or the now and the future, reflecting a struggle between a “myopic doer” versus a “farsighted planner”. Implicitly this follows a deficit orientation that can be seen as individual self-regulation failure (for an overview see Baumeister & Heatherton, 1996; Metcalfe & Mischel, 1999). I postulate a different conceptualization of self-control that stresses its potential of integrating the construct of the self via action (compare Kivetz & Simonson, 2002; Rachlin, 1995). Self-control as an activity, therefore, can serve to foster long term saving (utilitarian goals), as well as impulsive spending (hedonistic goals). This defines self-control as a mechanism for integrating the different motivational drives without favoring one or the other.

### 3.1.2. Behavioral Aspects

Various patterns of self-control have been described in the literature of financial behavior. In line with Schelling (1984) and Ainslie (1975) these can be categorized into three different types.

First, there is the physical or mental restriction of the decision space. Direct acts of pre-commitment or personal rules like budgeting describe this category. One sort of self restriction is the a priori elimination of behavioral alternatives. The “virginity principle” (e.g., “I do not borrow”) is an example for a universal self-control mechanism where specific behaviors are debarred from the decision space. A weaker restriction is the reduction in liquidity. It describes active limitations of possible future behavior (Bertaut & Haliassos, 2001; Gross & Souleles, 2002) or mental structuring of event categories (Benartzi & Thaler, 2001; Heath & Soll, 1996; Moon *et al.*, 1999).

A second way of controlling future behavior is the manipulation of the environmental structure. Here the likelihood of the demanded activity is increased by adding situational components that support this activity or vice versa removing deviation-evoking stimuli. Various changes concerning the perception of the consequences of an event like costs and benefits have been discussed. These concern the elaboration of events (Gourville, 1998), the grouping of events (Soman & Gourville, 2001), and temporal factors influencing the event evaluation (Gourville & Soman, 1998; Prelec & Loewenstein, 1998; Soman, 2001).

The third and most common solution is to change the contingency structure between the behavior and its outcome. This can be done by side bets that include behavior contingent penalties or rewards. A saving behavior example is a saving account that has a penalty for early withdrawals or a saving account that has a reward of a higher interest rate if the money is not accessed for a specific time period. But when altering the effect of an event, the specification of exceptions from the rule becomes important. The structure must be as restrictive as possible while being flexible enough to capture the respective behavior. Ainslie (1975, p. 481) stresses that to make the rule effective exceptions must be rare and uncontrollable. Controllable events can only be part of the concept if they are combined with a high level of effort. Softer self-control mechanisms in this case are self manipulations that change the interpretation or the psychological meaning of an event. An individual standard can evaluate the behavior itself, or the inclination to apply effort can serve as a self-control tool to create costs which bolster against less desired activities (Soman, 1998; Trope & Fishbach, 2000).

### 3.1.4. Applied Cognition

Many behavioral patterns use different mechanisms in combination to guide saving. The earlier categorization illustrates the variety of possible alternatives that can be applied. External control goes hand in hand with internal preparedness, and they are, therefore, difficult to distinguish from each other. In general internal and external mechanisms go together for exerting self-control. Next, we evaluate whether people actually use self-control strategies to guide saving behavior. A lack of sufficient saving for retirement could be due to missing self-control devices. By contrast, it could simply be a result of limited control, reflecting human imperfection or akrasia. To evaluate these opposing concepts of saving behavior deficits, needs a closer look at the demands in the domain of future savings and the ways in which people try to achieve them. The level of sophistication and differentiation in self-control demand and self-control strategy use will serve as a willingness indicator for saving. Goal specification is often left aside in behavioral research, and commonly the general aim of value maximization is assumed, but a more specific goal can be essential for the selection of the self-control strategy.

To explore the definition and incentives people have for saving, we need to first analyze the dimensions of saving and the different saving structures people employ. Only then, a systematic analysis of individual differences in saving behavior can be provided. This can be seen as a bottom-up approach to improve the understanding of the self-control problem. As participants' payments were not dependent on the performance in the following saving experiments and only reported behavior was taken into account, more direct evaluations can be asked for to support the derived conclusions. Only this would cancel out a possible misalignment between reported and actual behavior, or the danger that specific behavioral parts are left aside.

## 3.2. Saving Concept (Study 1)

To understand peoples' saving behavior, we need to examine their actual savings. Rather than asking hypothetical questions, an in-depth analysis is provided of what people actually do, to stress the ecological validity of the saving concept.

In order to evaluate the different approaches to saving, it is necessary to know how people understand this problem and what their saving goal is. It has been shown that often diverse motives for saving exist (Horioka & Watanabe, 1997; Keynes, 1936; Lindqvist, 1981). Thus, we have to understand saving behavior as a motivational configuration that can serve different goals. Also the individual definition of the saving task can be seen as crucial for decision processes. This includes the internal construction, as well as, the external structuring of saving. Construal or mental representation is important for the various self-control initiatives, and for understanding the mental representation of saving it is useful to know how people structure their finances. The assumption of concepts stresses the importance of cognition. Mental events are understood as the structuring causes of behavior (i.e., Dretske, 1993). This can equally be assumed for saving behavior and preliminary analyzes of the individual structure of the saving concept have been proposed (Groenland *et al.*, 1996).

This explorative experiment examines the understanding people have of saving by asking them to describe their definition of saving and by visualizing their saving structures in place. This reveals people's dimensions for saving and illustrates what different self-control mechanisms people use. The research question is twofold, covering saving construals and demands on the one hand, and existing saving features and structures on the other.

### 3.2.1. Method

The used one-to-one interview included a drawing board task. All participants held a saving product with one leading British financial institution that provided access to their customer database. The corresponding saving product allows for several separate accounts called "saving pots" and includes the possibility for different sorts of automatic transfers. In total 13 adults took part in the study: four male, nine female, with an average age of 50 years, and of which eight were full-time employed (one part time, three retired, and one unemployed). The interview, to derive the individual's understanding of saving, took approximately 20 minutes, and the drawing board procedure, to determine the individual saving structures, took approximately 40 minutes. The whole session was video taped. Compensation for the participation was £20.

The first part consisted of questions regarding the subjective understanding of saving (i.e., "What is saving?"), the saving motive (i.e., "Why are you saving?"), and the aim of saving (i.e., "What are you saving for?") in a semi-structured fashion. The duration was situation dependent and varied according to the verbal fluency of the interviewee, but at least one answer per question had to be given. The interview was transcribed and the answers categorized.

In the second part the participants visualized their existing saving structure on a drawing board. We started with explaining the task by describing different features they can use (i.e., automatic transfers, account limits, alerts, etc.). Then, the participants were provided with a large drawing board, different pens, and as many cards they need, representing different "saving pots". After possible questions were resolved, they were left alone to complete the task. They had to come up with a final structure describing their saving situation by capturing the transfers between the different "saving pots" and possible other features they use. When finished, they were confronted with different scenarios to test their saving structure and, if necessary, missing elements were added. The scenarios consisted of general "what if" questions clarifying the understanding and the functioning of the derived saving structures (i.e., "If you urgently need the extra £200 cash and your current account is empty, where do you take it from?"). The final structures were photographed and analyzed according to structure differences and featured details.

### 3.2.2. Results

The sophistication of the understanding and structuring of the individual concept for saving varies considerably between participants. This variation demands a more systematic analysis of differences in saving concepts and is focused next. These individually driven descriptions here provide the saving problem definition and isolate the first mechanisms used for self-control.

***Saving Dimensions***

All participants show a clear understanding of what saving behavior means to them and they come up with definitions capturing everything from security aspects (i.e., "Want to make sure that I do not run out of money.") to purpose specific savings (i.e., "Save that I can afford something special in the future.") and saving for growth (i.e., "Saving to generate wealth."). This demonstrates that some sort of common understanding exists of what behaviors saving covers, as at least two of these were mentioned by most individuals (purpose = 100%; security = 58%; growth = 50%). However the definition of saving behavior and the motives for saving go together in the individual understanding of saving. During the interviews it was often stressed that the definition of saving behavior concerned a general expectation about what people ought to do, and motives and behaviors were frequently mixed up. Thus, the individual saving construals seem to be driven by motives rather than actual behavior, which underline the prospective character of saving.

When asked for the aims of saving, participants come up with an average of 3.0 aims. These describe specific aims like saving for child education, a new car, retirement, etc. or general purposes like "providing a buffer" or "increase choices." They can be specific in timing and prominence or rather diffuse. Further support for the variation in saving aims can be found when considering all 350,000 customers of the provided database who hold a saving product where the different accounts ("saving pots") can receive individual names. The actual naming of the accounts can be seen as a labeling of this particular part of savings. The average number of accounts per person is 2.8. This number of accounts might just be an indicator for a high number of different saving aims as only one provider is considered and possible saving accounts with other providers are not captured. However, it also does not necessarily represent the number of accounts in use due to a large number of dormant accounts. Figure 3.1 defines the 10 most frequently used saving labels. It shows the saving names frequency for the different accounts of one financial provider where the saving product allows the savings to be divided into a maximum of twelve parts. The percentages for different saving categories in a total of one million account labels are shown. Only the 5.2% informative names that describe specific or general purposes are included in the graph. The individual naming of saving accounts is a relatively new possibility at the researched financial service institution. As a result a majority leaves the names at their defaults. Also the labels 'Instant' and 'Addition' could be less meaningful as they reflect the former products offered by this financial provider.

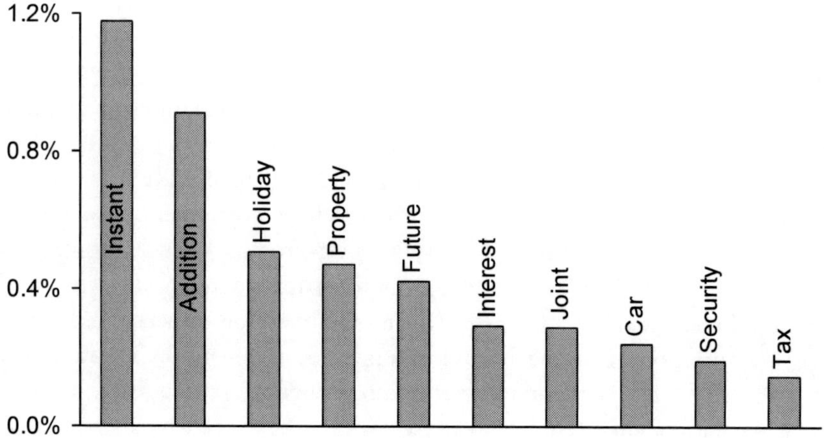


Figure 3.1. Saving labels

The correlation between categories is not analyzed and thus the simultaneity of different saving categories is not illustrated, but these labels document the variety in existing saving aims. The saving categories are representations of the three general saving motives but illustrate primary interest in specific purpose savings. The formulation of several motives and the saving descriptions together support the diversity of the saving construal. Nevertheless, it provides no information about how these goals are achieved.

***Saving Structures***

All participants have some sort of financial structure in place to facilitate saving. Yet, the general understanding of this structure is poor and is only revealed through the task. The derived saving structures, reflecting the different individual saving concepts are given in Appendix A.

The results divide into two categories: "tiered structures" and "radial structures" (Figure 3.2). These tiered and radial structures for organizing financial flows, as two different types for separating savings, are derived from the photographed individual solutions. The tiered structures (46% of the cases) serve as a sort of buffer with a different number of levels. In the radial structures (54%) the current account is in the center, and income is distributed between different saving accounts.

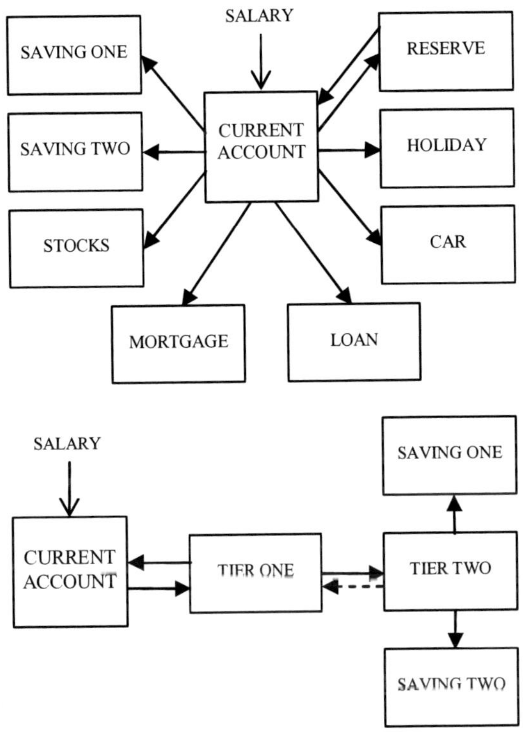


Figure 3.2. Saving structures

In all cases, a number of accounts are linked in specific ways by tools which control or guide the transfers. The corresponding self-control mechanisms and other applied self-control features are listed in Figure 3.3.

The number of participants out of all 13 who applied each of the self-control tools in their saving structure is shown. 'Automatic transfers' describes any automatic sweeps between accounts. 'Elimination of alternatives' covers limited access, as well as liquidity restriction. Under 'budgeting' falls only the explicit separation into several specific budgets. 'Supporting cues' mean automatic information given by the structure to guide saving. 'Increase distance' stands for receiving less information for parts of the structure. 'Rewards and costs' describe mechanisms that impose respective consequences for specific activities.

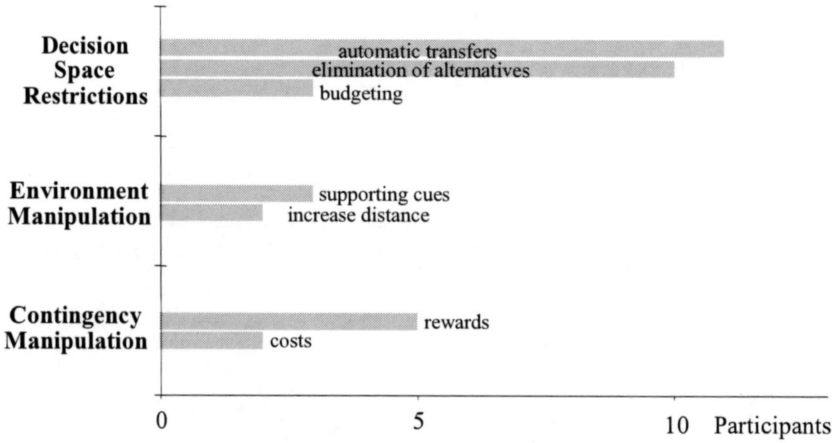


Figure 3.3. Self-control tools in saving structures

A large proportion use automatic transfers to ensure the desired monetary liquidity and saving levels. Features are 'penalties,' as well as 'bonuses,' 'information suppression,' and 'lock away periods.' These illustrate examples for all three self-control categories. Thus, methods of restricting the number of decision alternatives, changing the environmental structure, and manipulating the contingency structure itself are used. They serve different levels of self restriction, and often the maintenance of direct final control over the system is stressed. Also, the explanation process in the guidance of the task might have supported the inclusion of these features. Yet, in general the structures show typical everyday saving examples like building up a "rainy day" reserve, keeping surplus separate, or imposing commitment by the act of manually storing money. Although participants show quite sophisticated saving structures, it is not clear if these are demand driven or rather a result of product availability. On the one hand, the low initial understanding of their own saving situation supports the assumption that they are just the result of the individual historical process of taking up products. On the other hand, the actual market situation; with its homogeneity and limited flexibility of savings products, restricts the complexity of the saving structures in place. Thus, the influence of individual demands and environmental conditions are not separated.

### 3.2.3. Discussion

The different construals for saving behavior and the elicitation of the individual saving structures illustrates that multiple saving motives exist and that self-control tools are used to achieve these goals. The definition of saving is mainly determined by the motives for this behavior and actual activities seem to be less influential. The saving motives (namely security, growth, and purpose) correspond with the three main motives mentioned in the literature on saving behavior. For example "precaution," "calculation," and "foresight" as the corresponding first three individual saving motives were listed by Keynes (1936, p. 108). This formulation of different saving motives as well as the existence of simultaneous saving aims and the high number of accounts in their saving structures clearly support the existence of different mental accounts and stresses the importance of self-control in mental accounting. All three self-control categories found representations in the derived saving structures, although with a different degree of retained control. The reluctance against relinquishing control to the saving system appears more prominent. What variables do support the relinquishing of control, in favor of enabling self-control is not clear. The impression is that issues of trust and reliance have to be addressed to enforce self-control mechanism.

Of course, the derived saving structures are partly determined by the banking environment itself. But a natural view on people's savings is to regard the saving behavior in the environment people are used to; and, in which they learned to develop specific behavior. Any more abstract exploration of how people view saving is likely to ignore the important constraints that determine the actual behavior. Therefore, it is crucial to embed the decision problem in the world in which it really arises. While the relation between the derived structures and the saving motives is not established, the individual solutions indicate a possible concordance between the two. Where tiered structures are used to promote security issues as the distance to the savings is increased, and radial structures are more likely to serve specific purposes as the savings are separated into different categories. However, to support the assumption of the deliberate usage of self-control tools, the relation between demands and saving structures has to be examined more systematically. Although different self-control tools are in place, their origin and purpose seem not to be assured. Also, the strong inter-individual variation demands a further examination of the different factors that influence self-control and eventually the level of saving.

## 3.3. Saving Differences (Study 2)

The different variables influencing the application of self-control tools need to be invested in more detail. Individual characteristics are important on the one hand; the individual financial situation, demographics, and saving motives influence the way of saving. Also, the sort of personal saving strategy forms the saving behavior (Veldhoven & Groenland, 1993; Wahlund & Gunnarsson, 1996). On the other hand, environmental factors like economic conditions and financial management influence the observable behavior. The availability of self-control tools to guide saving and support in setting up and maintaining self guiding structures seem equally important. This implies a clear distinction between personal demands and environmental structures.

A specifically developed questionnaire tackles these different dimensions and evaluates their relations. This enables the measurement of the demand level and the need for self-control tools independent of the actual realization. Equally, self-control prospects and existing behavioral patterns are evaluated based on a larger body of data, linking individual differences to self-control demands and types. The questionnaire was designed in several incremental steps of constructing and evaluating suitable items. Starting with the questions from the earlier interview; and this generated additional questions regarding 'personal motives,' 'self-control tool interests,' and 'individual self-control demands.'

### 3.3.1. Method

The self-control survey was partly distributed in shopping areas and was partly an online questionnaire linked to the BBC webpage. In total 173 people took part in the survey, of which 89 answered the questionnaire online. The online data broadened the area of the study, due to the mixture of retrieval methods leading to a higher representativeness of the sample (compare Birnbaum, 2000). The participation was rewarded by inclusion in a prize draw for £400. Fifty-four percent of the overall sample was female, the average age was 36.4 years, and the average yearly household income was £32,000.

The self-control survey includes 24 items on demographics and current financial situation. Eighty-three items concern the "saving personality" on a five point Likert scale, with 15 items on personal motives (e.g., "I save to feel secure about the future."), 12 items on self-control tool interest (e.g., "I would like to be continually informed about my level of debt."), and 56 items on individual self-control (e.g., "I want to be less involved with my finances."). Appendix B shows all the "saving personality" questions used. The answers were analyzed according to self-control usage, personal differences, and group characteristics.

### 3.3.2. Results

Participants expressed high demand for general self-control and specific self-control tools. Items on overall need for self-control were rated with averages above three (total average 3.29). The results on the self-control tool interest questions also showed a number of high specific demands. Average interest for specific self-control tools on a scale from one to five (total average 3.07) are shown in Figure 3.4

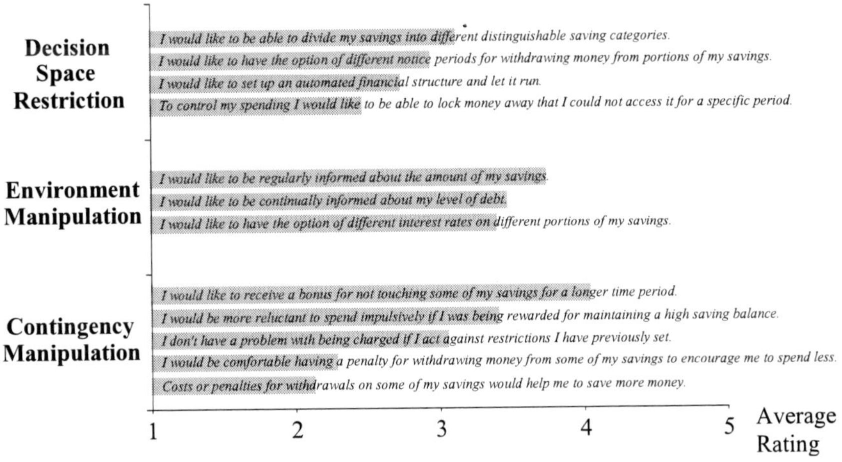


Figure 3.4. Self-control demands

In particular, the manipulation of contingencies via bonuses appeared to be in high demand. Also, guidance by environmental cues were desired, but little interest in direct restrictions was shown. Answers on the personal saving motive questions were in line with the previous results with examples for the three main saving motives receiving the highest averages: "I save to ensure my income meets my needs in the future" (security) 3.81, "I save for a number of different goals" (purpose) 3.64, and "I would like to save an increasing amount over time" (growth) 3.72.

A exploratory factor analysis conducted on the 56 self-control demand questions results in 10 dimensions for the inter-individual variation. The 10 factors account for 51.78% of the observed variance and represent approximations for the captured differences in personal characteristics. The scree plot for the initially derived factors and the given labels for the 10 factors with an eigenvalue above 1.5 after a varimax rotation are shown in Figure 3.5.

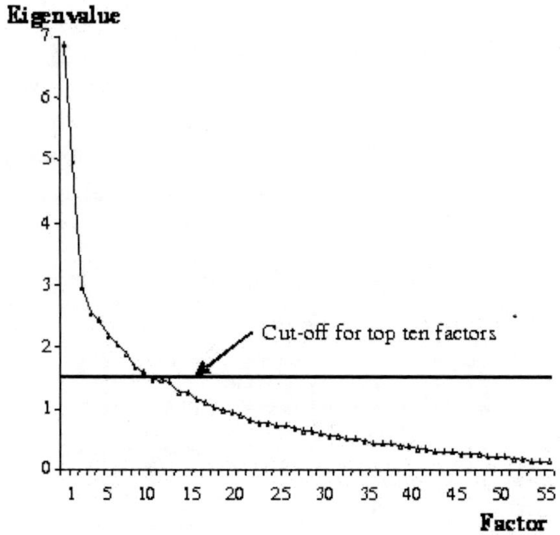


**Factor Names**

*1. Self-Control*
*2. Hands On Involvement*
*3. Need for Advice*
*4. Regular Savings*
*5. Automation*
*6. Low Effort*
*7. Integration*
*8. Security Worries*
*9. Planned Budget*
*10. Distributed Savings*

Figure 3.5. Saving factors

The first two dimensions describe general control issues, followed by more specific descriptors of saving behavior differences. Appendix B provides the loadings for all factors. To illustrate the factors' meanings and to see how they link to everyday behavioral patterns, descriptive customer samples were formed. Grouping the highest and lowest scorers on the first two factors resulted in four different groups. In Table 3.1 these exemplary self-control groups with their corresponding financial characteristics are shown. The 45% of the people with the highest respective lowest factor scores were grouped together ('concerned' = 31 people; 'assisted' = 39 people; 'controlling' = 34 people; 'unconcerned' = 35 people). Our intuitive understanding of the personality factors is reflected in the group differences. The 'concerned' group is the youngest with the lowest income with clear need for self-control. Many people in the 'assisted' group already use penalties and bonuses in their saving accounts. The 'controlling' people, as the oldest group with the highest income, need the most time for their finances. 'Unconcerned' people are likely to simplify and integrate their finances, although keeping a number of saving accounts. Marked values describe significant group differences.

A participants' high demand for self-control lead to various sorts of behavior that require different self-control tools. People are likely to impose specific self-control strategies, but the willingness for self restrictions or for relinquishing control strongly depends on the individual and corresponding environmental relations. Some people (i.e., 'assisted' group) might directly buy into self-control tools, for others (i.e., 'controlling' group) it is only possible via a process of trust building. The realization of self-control strongly depends on demographics, lifecycle, and individual variables. The way and level of self-control varies according to financial status, life stage, and personal preferences. They are interconnected and together influence the application of self-control tools, and therefore differences in self-control cannot be explained by demographics alone.

**Table 3.1. Factor based groups**

| | *concerned* | *assisted* | *controlling* | *unconcerned* | |
|---|---|---|---|---|---|
| **Self-Control** | high | high | low | low | **Total** |
| **Hands On** | high | low | high | low | **Avg.** |
| Sex (male) | 48% | 38%* | 41% | 62%* | 46% |
| Average Age | 28.4* | 31.6 | 44.7* | 39.2 | 36.3 |
| Average Number of Children | 0.19* | 0.64 | 0.91 | 0.91 | 0.71 |
| Average Household Income (£'000) | 23.1* | 32.3 | 34.1 | 32.3 | 31.7 |
| Average Number of Savings Accounts | 1.71* | 1.81 | 3.12* | 2.86 | 2.38 |
| Saving with Bonuses | 20%* | 22%* | 6%* | 11%* | 16% |
| Saving with Penalties | 14% | 19%* | 12%* | 13% | 15% |
| Integrate Current Account into a Financial Structure | 69%* | 82% | 77% | 94%* | 80% |
| Minutes Spent on Finances (monthly averages) | 51.4 | 32.2* | 77.4* | 55.0 | 56.3 |

*significant on the p<0.01 level

### 3.3.3. Discussion

The questionnaire reveals differences in self-control demands and shows correlations with the financial situation and product demands. Self-control as the guiding factor for saving behavior is supported. However, the relation between self-control demand and the actual application of self-control tools needs further support. The research design here cannot prove that people in the end are actually more controlled when provided with their specific self-control tools, which is crucial for understanding and bridging the discrepancy between planning and behavior. The existence of a high need for self-control is in line with the postulation of a "saving gap," a claim made at the individual level by Bernheim (1995) or Farkas and Johnson (1997), which stresses the importance of saving product designs to support self-control mechanisms. This lets one assume that specific features like lock away periods or channel restrictions, but also the general service including individual planning, involvement, support, and flexibility, increase self-control, and enable saving.

One distinction introduced here, for a better understanding of saving behavior and its relation with self-control, is the differentiation between types of financial personality. The proposal of individually different concepts for saving might help to understand the self-control mechanism in place and could prove useful for saving increasing policies. People tend to approach the task of saving differently, varying on important dimensions like willingness to relinquish control, demand for involvement, and level of advice accepted. Only when understanding these individual differences, one can fully embrace the concept of self-control and factor in its conditional importance. The assumption of a financial personality helps to systematically analyze attitudinal differences in relation to variations in saving behavior. Further proof is needed for establishing this claim and areas like self-awareness (O'Donoghue & Rabin, 2003) or the propensity to plan (Ameriks *et al.*, 2003) have to be addressed. Also, the relation to social theories and personality research could be important. Existing clinical measures of self-control (Rosenbaum, 1980) and the connection to other behavioral constructs like sensation seeking (Zuckerman, 1994), self-efficiency (Bandura, 1977), and locus of control (Rotter, 1966) have to be accounted for. However, the construction of a general psychometric self-control scale might be useful for various fields, including personalized financial services. This survey discovered first correlations between individual self-control, product characteristics, and saving behavior. The dependence between differences in self-control and actual saving rate has also been documented by Romal and

Kaplan (1995) to demand stronger self-control strategy encouragement. A further specification of the self-control construct in combination with the evaluation of direct behavior and its changes over time, according to lifecycle changes appears necessary.

## 3.4. Saving Solutions

The ecological reality of saving behavior shows that the intra- and inter-individual variability in relation to motives, strategies, and lifecycle issues have not been acknowledged accordingly. Multiple saving motives, differences in goal orientation and capacities, individual foci and changing needs all demand an individually centered, situation specific, expansion of the understanding of saving behavior. The different saving strategies in relation to each other could possibly better explain overall observed patterns of saving than behavioral deficit models.

### 3.4.1. Product Demands

Besides strategy similarities with a conflict between multiple selves (Schelling, 1980), a positive perspective on individual saving tools as means for self-control is provided. This assumption itself is grounded in the variations of the observed behaviors, yet is also supported by cognitive models and neurological underpinnings.

Neural processing and the interaction of multiple cognitive systems represent an integration that can be seen as an internal communication and a problem solving process rather than a conflict. Different mental functions being complementary in inter-temporal choice (i.e., Manuck *et al.*, 2003; McClure *et al.*, 2004), is in line with consistent plans over time (Becker & Murphy, 1988; Loewenstein & Prelec, 1993). For achieving commitment over time, the actual planning of future behavior is of importance. The influence of goal formation on behavior has been repeatedly documented (i.e., Bandura & Schunk, 1981; Gollwitzer, 1999). Also, the rare reversion or redistribution in saving behavior (Skinner, 1992; Venti & Wise, 1987) supports this claim. What part cognitive strategies play here and to what degree saving is influenced by mental causation (i.e., automation, sequential learning) or social mechanisms (i.e., social control, conformity) is open to future investigations. Saving behavior probably more strongly depends upon cognitive and social functioning than on economic calculus.

### 3.4.2. Prototype Generation and Selection

The underlying mental mechanisms are mainly neglected in models of saving behavior. I argue that the different areas of self-control have direct implications for public policy issues. For the incentive structure Laibson (1996) and Thaler (1994; Thaler & Benartzi, 2004) demonstrate that variations in delay, penalties, and rewards guide the saving behavior in saving schemes. The flexibility in individual saving, depending on the perceived decision space, is generally stressed in pension plans (Choi *et al.*, 2002; Madrian & Shea, 2001; Papke, 2003; Poterba *et al.*, 1996). Following that the total amount allocated to retirement savings can easily be manipulated by the introduced pension plans, there might just not be the demand matching products available on the market to enable self-control techniques which secure saving levels. A common practice to directly restrict the decision space by using credit cards and credit limits to manipulate liquidity (Haliassos & Reiter, 2006; Soman & Cheema, 2002) illustrates that self-control mechanisms are in place. Together with a supporting information structure and based on the persistence of decisions, it can be assumed that the provision for retirement can be improved substantially, and thus the lack of individual consistency can be diminished. The current observation of a "saving gap" (Bernheim, 1995; Farkas & Johnson, 1997), meaning a lack of providing means for the retirement particularly in the UK and US, might then only be a mismatch between available products and individual needs.

The individual differences in self-control strongly demand tailored solutions and stress design components to support the understanding, the involvement, the evolution, and the flexibility of financial products. Naturally the individual commitment to save also depends on the inclination for buying and related avoidance strategies (i.e., Baumeister, 2002; Benhabib & Bisin, 2005; Bernheim & Rangel, 2004; Carrillo & Mariotti, 2000; Hoch & Loewenstein, 1991; Loewenstein, 1996; O'Guinn & Faber, 1989; Wertenbroch, 1998). In contrast to this deficit orientation, I focused on the side of general empowerment to increase choice. To enforce saving behavior here, tools for all three self-control strategy categories have to be provided on an individual level: decision space restrictions, environmental cues, and contingency structures. These categories can be seen as the fundamental areas for providing people with the means for managing their behavior and as strategic tools to be used in accordance with individual demands. They stand for the differences in self-control strategies and reflect the psychological spectrum for behavioral variation, and thus the diversity of peoples' strategies.

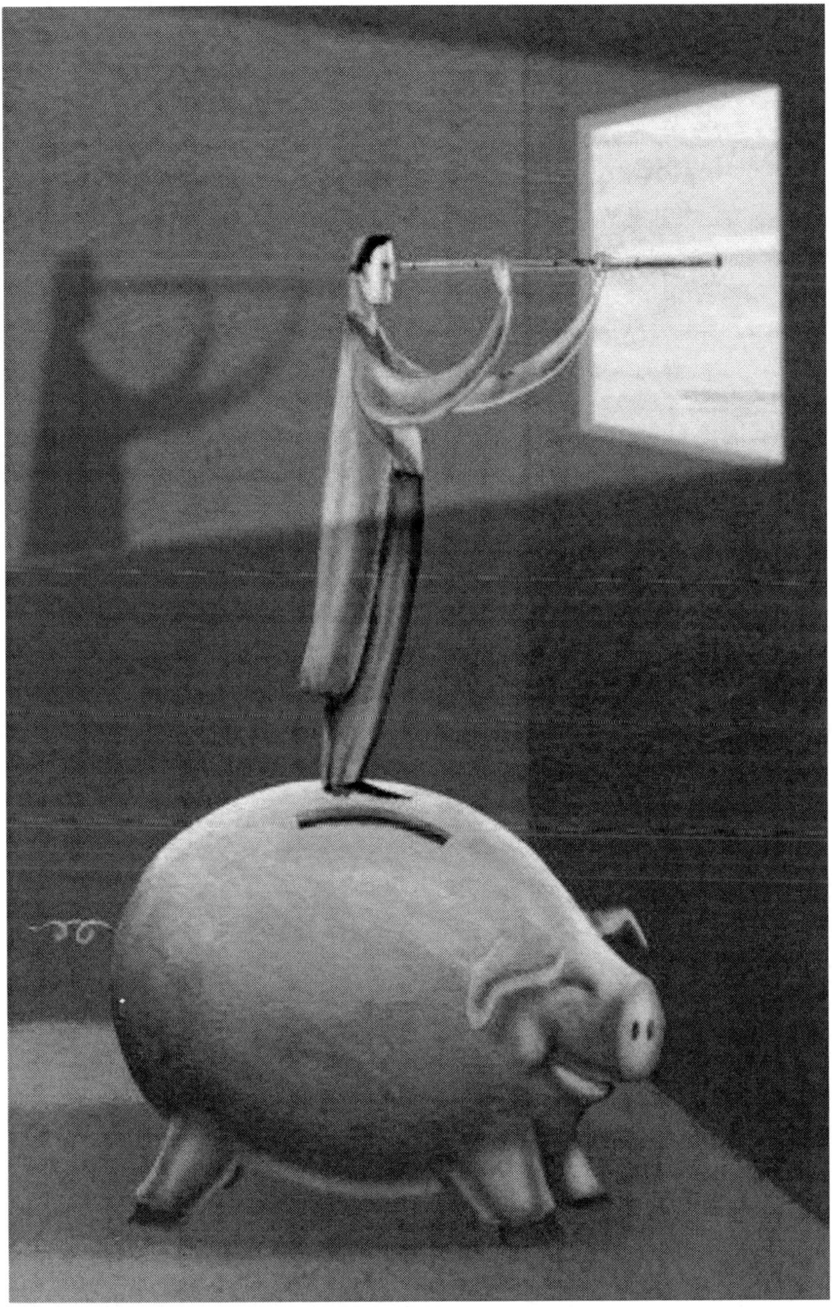

*Chapter 4*

# INVESTMENT STRATEGIES I

In previous chapters, we have seen various motives exist for saving strategies. Also, for investment strategies different motives can be present. According to portfolio theory (Friedman & Savage, 1948; Shefrin & Statman, 2000) investors have a desire for security and also an aspiration for riches; meaning their ideal portfolios resembles a combination of a bond and a lottery ticket. Leaving these investment characteristics aside, the broader question to address is the dimensions people use to generally evaluate companies. How different company characteristics can be integrated in a choice situation is the focus in Chapter 5.

Prospect theory has looked at how options or companies are evaluated, but how companies are perceived and represented is not yet researched. This appears to be an important part for company evaluations and can form the ground for company comparisons. As with any other object, people perceive companies along a number of dimensions. But what are the key psychological dimensions that best describe companies, organizations, or brands? To look at how people represent "corporate personality," research methods are applied here which were initially developed for studying attitudes, including attitudes to other people. First, repeated evaluations of a small number of companies are used to distill the most useful dimensions for company comparisons. In a second step, a broader range of companies is positioned on these derived dimensions. The major dimensions that psychologically differentiate companies can be labeled as honesty, prestige, innovation, and power. Scales of this type may have substantial commercial value in helping companies understand and track their public perception.

In the continuous interaction with our environment we need not only to be able to quickly perceive new information, we also have to rely on existing information as a benchmark. For example when eating breakfast, greeting a person, or running a business, we always have to understand the differences within the various tasks and need concepts to guide our behavior. Thus, behavior always takes place under a specific frame and is embedded in context, and evaluations are in relation to similar objects of the respective class of objects. But is there a general mechanism to describe this formation of differences between perceived objects? Does the evaluation of e.g. food, faces, and fortunes have something in common? Do we apply comparable processes in different domains? Kelly (1955) proposed the theory of personal constructs for personality evaluations, using methods that appear more generally applicable. Osgood (1962) promoted methods for finding "semantic dimensions" for objects of all kinds. More recently computational corpus analysis has been applied for "dimensionalizing" semantic materials in a uniform way (Landauer & Dumais, 1997; Griffiths & Steyvers, 2004). Moreover, in the literature on categorization, it is typically assumed that uniform principles guide the representation of diverse categories, although certain fundamental distinctions (e.g., the distinction between the natural versus artifact concepts) are sometimes viewed as representationally significant (Gelman, 1988; Murphy, 2002; Sloman & Malt, 2003).

The focus is to test how well existing research methods develop initially for uncovering psychological dimensions, and how this can be transferred to understanding how people represent companies. Public perception is a substantial factor in determining consumer purchasing decisions; and also may potentially influence investor decision making. Thus, it would be of considerable practical interest to have a workable model of the dimensions of "corporate personality." To tackle this question an evaluation process for understanding company perception is derived from the existing literature.

Research investigating how people represent complex objects goes back to Osgood and colleagues postulating general dimensions for evaluating objects (Osgood, 1962; Osgood *et al.*, 1957). In this "semantic differential" approach, lists of adjectives were searched for that best capture meaningful differences between items. The claim was made that a restricted number of descriptive properties can be sufficient to differentiate items within a wide range of categories of objects, reaching from colors and shapes to stories and people. More recent approaches have applied the semantic differential to a range of specific domains, including product categories (Hsu *et al.*, 2000; Katz *et al.*,

2002; Mondragon *et al.*, 2005), perceptual categories (Ohnishi *et al.*, 1996; Oyama *et al.*, 1998; Tessarolo, 1981), and names (Hartmann, 1985).

Another evaluation approach for complex objects is the psychometric method. Here scales are developed for capturing differences. Underlying factors are extracted that link directly or indirectly to featural differences, yet either way explain variations in observed behavior. This perspective is common in personality research where different "personality dimensions" are used to explain individual differences (compare Eysenck & Eysenck, 1985; Cattell, 1965). Prior research in brand perception has documented interesting parallels between the perception of people and the perception of brands (i.e., Epstein, 1977). A similar claim is made by Lievens and Highhouse (2003) for the evaluation of organizational attractiveness. When describing an organization, similar descriptors are used as when describing categories like 'friends' or 'strangers' - thus, it appears that people may represent organizations as having a "corporate personality," analogous to human personality. However, Aaker (1997) formalized the specific dimensions for "brand personality" and Slaughter *et al.* (2004) did the same for "organization personality" to observe differences between human and company personality.

We begin examining these issues using an exploratory study, to establish some of the natural dimensions along which people differentiate companies, using a relatively open-ended method. In the light of Study 3, Study 4 allows us to systematically evaluate these and other company dimensions, provided by the literature, to get an understanding of the relative importance of the company descriptors. Study 5 uses a subset of descriptors to position diverse companies on these dimensions and to highlight the relations to different economic characteristics.

## 4.1. COMPANY CONCEPT (STUDY 3)

The main aim here is to explore, in an open-ended way, the natural dimensions that best describe the concept "company." Later, we have people rate companies on different adjectives. However, first a method was needed to generate a list of candidate adjectives that could usefully discriminate between companies. For this an experimental technique is used, namely Repetory Grid (RepGrid) that was introduced by Kelly (1955). RepGrid was first generated by Kelly for the evaluation of individual personality differences. To make sure the concept is derived by the participant and not induced by the procedure, he introduced an iterative method to be content neutral. This keeps the guidance by the actual questions asked at a minimum; and only builds on formerly given answers without providing any specific material and only providing a content free frame. This general method is especially suitable for the generation of dimensions people naturally use to evaluate objects and can directly be applied for the analysis of any concept. The only difference in the case here is that the objects of analysis were companies instead of people. The derived concepts form the starting point for the later analysis.

### 4.1.1. Method

Six postgraduate students or university staff (three male; three female; average age 27) took part in the study and were paid £6 each. The individual RepGrid session lasted approximately 60 minutes and took place as a one-to-one interview. The material consisted of a card for each elicited company (element) and an initially blank table into which the adjectives would be written. The same table was later used for the rating of the companies. First, each participant had to generate the names of nine different well known companies, which were written on cards. This was followed by the second step, that Kelley (1955) called triadic elicitation, where triples of companies were selected by the experimenter. Repeatedly two companies were contrasted with a third one and the participant's task was to produce bipolar pairs of adjectives that differentiated the third company from the other two. In these comparisons each company was selected once as the "single" company, resulting in nine descriptions. These descriptions were always depicted in bipolar dimensions describing the two companies on the one hand and the single company on the other, presenting opposing adjectives like international versus national, large versus small, friendly versus unfriendly, and so on. In a last step all nine companies were rated on a scale from one to five on these derived bipolar adjectives, all in line with Kelly's (1955) standard RepGrid method. The results were analyzed according to concept homogeneity and inter-individual variability.

### 4.1.2. Results

All participants found it easy to generate bipolar adjectives to separate their selected companies. Also the similarity between the companies based on the rating for their elicited adjectives was supported by the participants, as the grouping of the clustering results was ad hoc confirmed by the participants. An example of a derived solution is given in Figure 4.1.

The named companies, the generated dimensions, and the ratings on these dimensions (with 1 as the extreme on the left side and 5 as the extreme on the right side of the elicited bipolar adjectives in Figure 4.1) are shown for this participant. As in the case of other participants the dimensions nicely group into higher level dimensions, shown by the hierarchical clustering results based on the individual rating. For this participant three groups of adjectives for describing company differences can be seen: qualitative aspects, personal relation, and level of luxury. For all different RepGrid solutions see Appendix C. The selected companies mainly represent large retailers or famous brands. They cover supermarkets and banks, as well as current or potential employers and favorite product producers. Participants are similar in what companies they select, with four out of the six participants picking the same company. The frequency with which the selected companies co-occur within the sample is 'Tesco' four times, 'Sainsbury' and 'Costcutters' three times, and 'H&M', 'BT', and 'Barclays' twice.

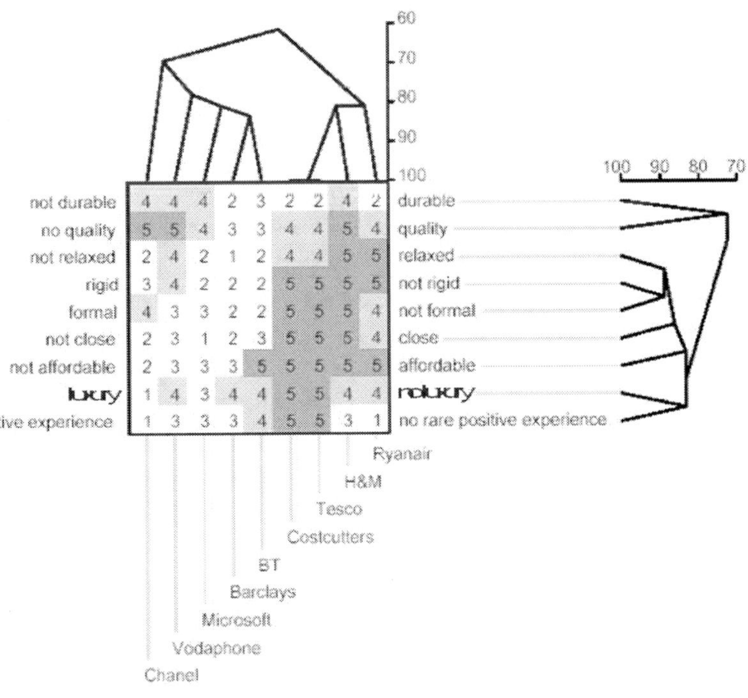


Figure 4.1. RepGrid example solution

For comparing these different companies people use similar adjectives, as is apparent from inspection of Table 4.1. Here only one adjective describing the bipolar dimension is shown. The other pole is its opposite (i.e., big-small) or simply its negation (i.e., common-uncommon). The qualitative similarities in choice of adjectives used to distinguish between generated companies broadly support the assumption of a naturally agreed concept of company differences. Common themes are quality, price, general appearance, and contact experiences. Adjectives selected more than once by different participants are highlighted accordingly.

**Table 4.1. Differentiation dimensions elicited for the generated companies**

| Person 1 | Person 2 | Person 3 | Person 4 | Person 5 | Person 6 |
|---|---|---|---|---|---|
| common | affordable | dominant | attractive | abstract | adversarial |
| enjoyable | close | freedom of action | cheap* | cheap* | big |
| essential | durable | identity | competitive | educated | competent |
| hidden importance | formal | inter-national* | distant | helpful* | concerned |
| needed | luxurious | powerful | feminine | influential | exploitative |
| nice | quality** | quality** | helpful* | physical | inter-national* |
| prestigious | rare pos. experience | spacious | modern | profes-sional | quality** |
| secondary | relaxed* | high status | regular | trustworthy | socially responsible |
| specific | rigid | Typical | relaxed* | useful | well priced |

*picked twice **picked three times

### 4.1.3. Discussion

The elicited dimensions for company evaluations have overlaps within the sample but also with other descriptors developed from previous studies (Table 4.2).

First they show similarities with the concept of brand personality (Aaker, 1997) and organization personality (Slaughter *et al.*, 2004); second with Osgood's semantic differentials (Heise, 1970; Osgood, 1962; Osgood *et al.*, 1957). In the former, a large spectrum is used to find the most useful dimensions for companies. The latter assumes more general dimensions apply for different sorts of objects and have been labeled as Evaluation, Potency, and Activity. By letting people derive the dimensions for describing differences between companies here, a more open-ended yet direct way is chosen to generate the important dimensions for differentiating between companies. The RepGrid method can be seen as a more direct approach for finding useful adjectives on which to evaluate differences between companies.

The elicited dimensions might prove useful for future evaluations of companies. They are complementary to adjectives generated in the existing literature, thus potentially adding formerly neglected areas of systematic company differences. However, only a larger dataset will allow for reliable interpretation. Therefore, Study 3 only prepares for the following Studies 4 and 5. All results derived here are used to produce a more systematic study. To further evaluate the dimensions differentiating between companies, we compare the derived company concepts with existing company descriptors in Study 4. Thereby the number of potentially useful adjectives is pruned to facilitate later evaluations.

**Table 4.2. Co-occurrence of named adjectives from different sources**

| | **RepGrid** | **Brand** | **Personality** | **Organization** | **Semantic Differential** |
|---|---|---|---|---|---|
| Total number of adjectives in the study | 19 | 12 | | 23 | 23 |
| Brand | 2 | - | | 9 | 1 |
| Organization | 2 | 9 | | - | 0 |
| Semantic Differential | 3 | 1 | | 0 | - |

## 4.2. COMPANY EVALUATION (STUDY 4)

A simple rating method is used to evaluate the different proposed descriptive adjectives. This is done to compare systematically the different sources of company descriptors. Existing company personality adjectives, the semantic differentials, and all RepGrid company adjectives generated from Study 3 are used to measure a restricted number of companies to figure out their descriptive values. Besides finding the most useful dimensions, redundancies are captured and the adjectives are put into relation. It also enables us to determine a set of adjectives that best describes company differences. This will allow a reduction in the number of adjectives required, and enable us to scale-up the resulting methods in Study 5.

### 4.2.1. Method

For the study, participants rated a list of adjectives in relation to a set of companies. As illustrated in the Study 3, the different sources show overlaps in the adjectives used. This includes all previously proposed descriptors (Aaker, 1997; Slaughter *et al.*, 2004; Heise, 1970) and our newly derived dimensions. Only redundant adjectives which describe the same dimensions were left out.

Twenty students (10 male; 10 female; average age 26) took part in the study and were paid £12 each. The computer based rating lasted approximately 120 minutes and took place in separate rooms for each individual. Participants had to rate 20 companies on all the 118 adjectives discussed in Study 3. A Likert scale from one to five was used for each adjective always taking both ends of the dimension as a single evaluation, so that ‘good’ and ‘bad’ were rated separately. The 20 companies were taken from Study 3 in the following way. All the six companies which were named more than once were included. In addition, 14 companies represented all listed industries to cover the most different companies. The companies were displayed together for each adjective, but the company order was varied within each set and the adjective order was randomized over participants.

### 4.2.2. Results

The company ratings were analyzed according to the relation of inter-company variability to inter-individual variability. For this, I introduce a measure of how far a specific adjective differentiates between companies. This measure relates the adjective’s descriptive power of differentiating between companies to their inter-individual variation. The more stable the adjective is over participants and the better it distinguishes between companies, the higher is its value. The most stable and strongest between-company differentiating adjectives are shown in Table 4.3.

The sources are as follows: RepGrid for the newly derived dimensions; SD for Semantic Differential; BP for Brand Personality; OP for Organization Personality. For the shown 31 adjectives the proportion of variance explained by company mean differences is higher than the proportion of variance over participants within a company, meaning that at least half of the total variance (total STD) is explained by the differences between company mean values (STD means). Adjectives below this cut-off of 50% were left aside due to their relative high inter-individual variability. With this criterion of stable company differentiability, RepGrid adjectives were included the most, with 14 out of 31 representing our newly elicited dimensions. For the other sources there are ten, six, and five cases in the highly differentiating group for the Brand Personality, Semantic Differential, and Organization Personality adjectives respectively. The number of 31 dimensions is in line with the hierarchical clustering results, where a strong decrease in the fit of the model, measured by R square (RSq), is observed somewhere around this number

The clustering results for the 31 most differentiating adjectives are shown in Figure 4.3. These clustering results are based on the average company values over participants. The different clustering steps describe different aggregation levels for company evaluation. The adjectives group together, forming different more abstract aspects of company characteristics. They nicely separate into four to six clusters that describe company characteristics on a higher level. Representative classes in higher order clusters are 'quality/prestige,' 'power,' and 'price,' with the adjectives 'technical' and 'quiet' as outliers. These classes form specific groups of adjectives for the evaluation of companies.

**Table 4.3. Most stable differentiating company adjectives**

| Adjective | Total STD | STD means (over companies) | STD means divided by total STD | Source |
|---|---|---|---|---|
| technical | 1.18 | 0.92 | 0.78 | BP |
| luxurious | 1.22 | 0.90 | 0.74 | RepGrid |
| international | 1.38 | 0.98 | 0.71 | RepGrid |
| upper class | 1.20 | 0.82 | 0.68 | BP |
| cool | 1.20 | 0.78 | 0.65 | BP |
| quiet | 1.07 | 0.68 | 0.63 | SD |
| formal | 1.26 | 0.79 | 0.63 | RepGrid |
| exploitative | 0.97 | 0.59 | 0.61 | RepGrid |
| leader | 1.19 | 0.72 | 0.60 | BP |
| original | 1.15 | 0.67 | 0.58 | OP & BP |
| popular | 1.07 | 0.62 | 0.58 | OP |
| noisy | 1.22 | 0.70 | 0.57 | SD |
| status | 1.13 | 0.65 | 0.57 | RepGrid |
| cheap | 1.22 | 0.69 | 0.57 | RepGrid |
| low class | 1.22 | 0.69 | 0.57 | OP |

**Table 4.4. Most stable differentiating company adjectives**

| Adjective | Total STD | STD means (over companies) | STD means divided by total STD | Source |
|---|---|---|---|---|
| young | 1.07 | 0.60 | 0.56 | BP & SD |
| quality | 1.20 | 0.67 | 0.56 | RepGrid |
| old | 1.19 | 0.65 | 0.55 | SD |
| good looking | 1.21 | 0.66 | 0.54 | BP |
| well priced | 1.06 | 0.57 | 0.54 | RepGrid |
| glamorous | 1.30 | 0.70 | 0.54 | BP |
| creative | 1.09 | 0.59 | 0.54 | OP |
| competitive | 1.01 | 0.54 | 0.54 | RepGrid |
| powerful | 1.20 | 0.64 | 0.54 | RepGrid & SD |
| educated | 1.15 | 0.61 | 0.53 | RepGrid |
| intelligent | 1.08 | 0.57 | 0.53 | BP |
| busy | 1.03 | 0.54 | 0.52 | OP |
| big | 1.06 | 0.55 | 0.52 | RepGrid & SD. |
| secure | 1.12 | 0.58 | 0.51 | BP |
| prestigious | 1.14 | 0.58 | 0.50 | RepGrid |
| secondary | 1.10 | 0.55 | 0.50 | RepGrid |

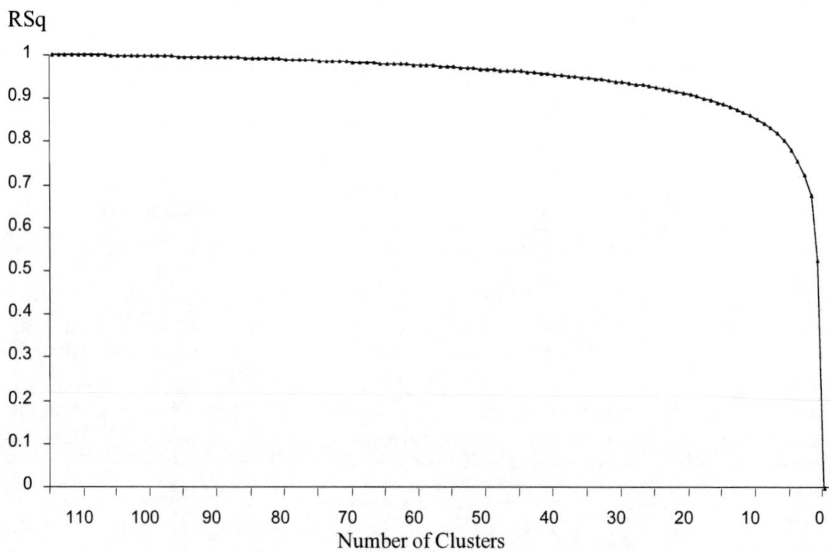


Figure 4.2. Model fit for the number of clusters in the Ward cluster history

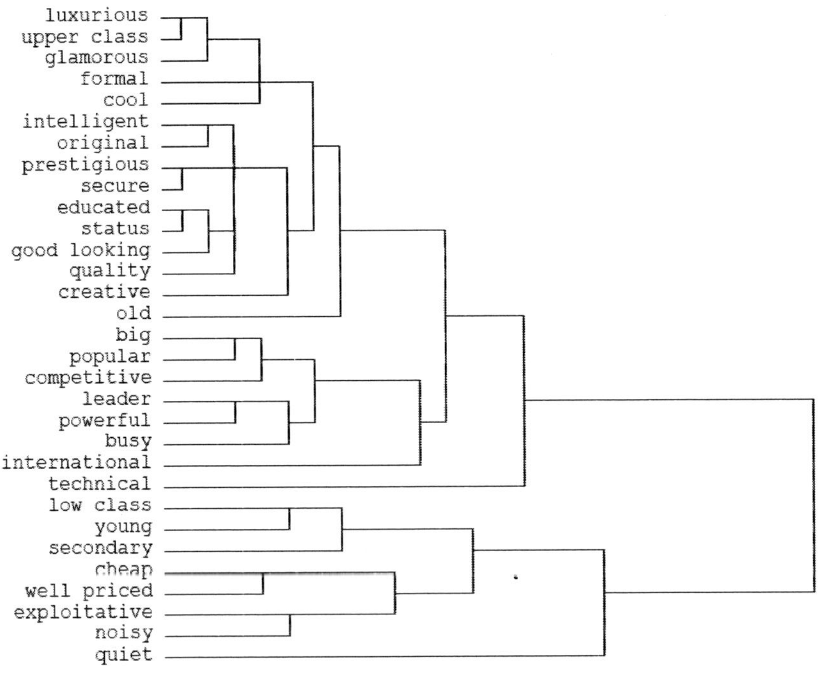


Figure 4.3. Hierarchical clustering tree for the highly differentiating adjectives

### 4.2.3. Discussion

When evaluating a larger number of adjectives from different sources, which all describe companies' characteristics, the newly elicited adjectives prove highly useful. This illustrates the possible improvements we can achieve for the evaluation of companies. By comparing the adjectives on their stability of company differentiability, the more important adjectives are isolated. These can be seen as more general descriptors for companies.

It is interesting that not only single adjectives describe companies, but that these also aggregate into factors. A first step into this direction is done in this part by grouping the adjectives into clusters. Note that these adjectives are broadly in line with Osgood's three general Semantic Differentials: Evaluation (prestige/quality), Potency (power), and Activity (price). However, a larger body of companies is needed for generating the fundamental factorial dimensions that guide company evaluations independent of the restriction to companies taken from Study 3. Thus, our next study applies a smaller number of adjectives to a much wider range of companies.

## 4.3. Company Positioning (Study 5)

To estimate the relative importance of the different company dimensions and to learn more about their similarities, a further study distills the most important factors for the evaluation of companies. Study 5 uses the adjective evaluation results of Study 4 and expands the analysis to a larger number of companies. This enables a derivation of the common company features to be related to other company characteristics.

### 4.3.1. Method

Sixty-four well known UK companies and globally operating international companies (UK: 51 companies; international: 13 companies) were evaluated on 41 adjectives in an online survey. These 41 adjectives represent the dimensions captured with the 31 adjectives from Study 4 and keeping social adjectives, like friendly and helpful, and trust related adjectives, like pleasant and personal, available in more detail in the pool to not miss out on these dimensions. In total 1282 people took part in the study (40% female, 38.5 average age). Participants were recruited and paid via Ipoints web-service. Ipoints is a platform for running experiments where people gain points dependent on the length of the task which then can be redeemed for specific products on offer. The evaluation lasted approximately 10 minutes. Every participant evaluated all 64 companies on four randomly allocated adjectives. The companies were displayed together, yet the order was randomized for each adjective. Each adjective was rated by at least 100 participants on a five point Likert scale, as in Study 4. Factor analysis is then used to describe the underlying dimensions of company evaluations.

### 4.3.2. Results

The usage of the adjectives on a broader range of companies enables a grouping of the adjectives, forming general dimensions of perceived company differences. These groups or factors illustrate the underlying categorical differences and nicely link to economic measures for company performance.

In the factor analysis, the eigenvalues of the principal factors flatten out after the fourth factor (Figure 4.4). Factor five is with an eigenvalue of 1.08 slightly above one, but due to the observed jump between factors five and four, only a four factor solution is considered in the further analysis (compare Cattell, 1966).

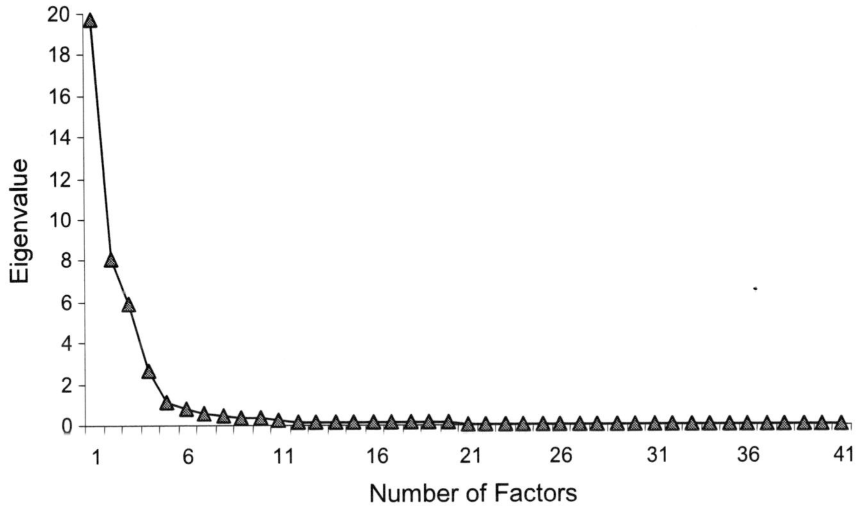


Figure 4.4. Eigenvalues for the different number of factors

The equamax rotated factor solution is shown in Table 4.4. The rotated solution nicely separates into the factors that can be labeled 'Honesty,' 'Prestige,' 'Innovation,' and 'Power.' The first factor labeled 'Honesty' captures fairness and trustworthiness of a company. 'Prestige' is a dimension of how valued a company is. 'Innovation' describes the vividness and flexibility of a company. 'Power' as the fourth factor captures the importance or dominance of a company.

**Table 4.5. Equamax rotated factor solution**

| **Factor 1**<br>*Honesty*<br>*Eigenvalue* | *14.2* | **Factor 2**<br>*Prestige* | *9.2* | **Factor 3**<br>*Innovation* | *8.4* | **Factor 4**<br>*Power* | *4.3* |
|---|---|---|---|---|---|---|---|
| fair | 0.92 | prestigious | 0.96 | fresh | 0.90 | dominant | 0.90 |
| helpful | 0.89 | luxurious | 0.96 | energetic | 0.89 | powerful | 0.81 |

**Table 4.6. (Continued)**

| **Factor 1** *Honesty* | | **Factor 2** *Prestige* | | **Factor 3** *Innovation* | | **Factor 4** *Power* | |
|---|---|---|---|---|---|---|---|
| *Eigenvalue* | *14.2* | | *9.2* | | *8.4* | | *4.3* |
| supportive | 0.88 | high status | 0.92 | fashionable | 0.85 | established | 0.81 |
| cooperative | 0.88 | formal | 0.87 | innovative | 0.84 | popular | 0.71 |
| honest | 0.87 | good quality | 0.74 | creative | 0.82 | active | 0.59 |
| caring | 0.87 | intelligent | 0.71 | original | 0.82 | essential | 0.43 |
| attentive to people | 0.87 | reliable | 0.60 | active | 0.70 | family-oriented | 0.41 |
| friendly | 0.87 | safe | 0.58 | competitive | 0.68 | exploitative | 0.36 |
| good value | 0.83 | attractive | 0.58 | popular | 0.57 | energetic | 0.32 |
| soc. responsible | 0.82 | trustworthy | 0.51 | attractive | 0.45 | high status | 0.29 |
| trustworthy | 0.82 | global | 0.48 | global | 0.43 | safe | 0.28 |
| essential | 0.81 | pleasant | 0.40 | personal | 0.40 | reliable | 0.25 |
| pleasant | 0.80 | honest | 0.39 | friendly | 0.39 | competitive | 0.25 |
| personal | 0.78 | powerful | 0.37 | dominant | 0.37 | attractive | 0.24 |
| safe | 0.68 | soc. responsible | 0.36 | attentive to people | 0.30 | global | 0.20 |
| reliable | 0.68 | caring | 0.34 | good value | 0.29 | good quality | 0.19 |
| family-oriented | 0.65 | established | 0.34 | pleasant | 0.29 | pleasant | 0.19 |
| attractive | 0.55 | fashionable | 0.32 | intelligent | 0.24 | personal | 0.19 |
| good quality | 0.54 | supportive | 0.27 | good quality | 0.24 | supportive | 0.19 |
| intelligent | 0.54 | attentive to people | 0.24 | helpful | 0.21 | creative | 0.18 |
| cheap | 0.45 | cooperative | 0.23 | reliable | 0.21 | helpful | 0.18 |
| original | 0.40 | helpful | 0.22 | fair | 0.21 | prestigious | 0.15 |
| fresh | 0.37 | innovative | 0.21 | powerful | 0.19 | original | 0.14 |
| creative | 0.33 | personal | 0.19 | cooperative | 0.19 | cooperative | 0.14 |
| innovative | 0.30 | creative | 0.16 | family-oriented | 0.19 | innovative | 0.11 |
| high status | 0.19 | fair | 0.15 | supportive | 0.19 | attentive to people | 0.10 |
| established | 0.15 | original | 0.12 | honest | 0.17 | friendly | 0.10 |
| prestigious | 0.11 | sleepy | 0.12 | caring | 0.15 | trustworthy | 0.10 |
| formal | 0.11 | fresh | 0.08 | trustworthy | 0.12 | fashionable | 0.07 |
| competitive | 0.08 | dominant | 0.01 | cheap | 0.09 | soc. responsible | 0.06 |
| sleepy | 0.06 | essential | -0.03 | essential | 0.09 | intelligent | 0.06 |
| popular | 0.04 | friendly | -0.08 | luxurious | 0.08 | tacky | 0.04 |
| active | 0.03 | family-oriented | -0.11 | high status | 0.06 | fair | 0.04 |
| luxurious | 0.03 | active | -0.14 | exploitative | 0.05 | good value | 0.04 |
| energetic | -0.01 | energetic | -0.17 | prestigious | 0.02 | luxurious | 0.03 |
| dominant | -0.05 | exploitative | -0.18 | safe | 0.00 | fresh | 0.01 |
| fashionable | -0.12 | popular | -0.22 | tacky | -0.02 | caring | -0.01 |
| powerful | -0.12 | good value | -0.33 | soc. responsible | -0.13 | formal | -0.01 |
| global | -0.24 | competitive | -0.48 | established | -0.30 | honest | -0.03 |
| tacky | -0.46 | cheap | -0.81 | formal | -0.37 | cheap | -0.04 |
| exploitative | -0.84 | tacky | -0.84 | sleepy | -0.93 | sleepy | -0.23 |

These factors are then put in relation to economic company descriptors taken from Datastream, a database which continuously provides available company information. Here the factor values for the British companies were correlated with economic measures of 'size,' 'evaluation,' 'growth,' and 'profit.' Table 4.5 shows the spearman correlation for the four factors based on the 25 companies listed on the London Stock Exchange. Company measures, as taken from Datastream, are 'size' for total assets employed, 'evaluation' for market to book value, 'growth' for three year growth in sales, 'profit' for pre-tax profit. Strongly significant correlations are marked in the table.

**Table 4.7. Factor spearman correlation for company performance measures**

| | **Factor 1** *Honesty* | **Factor 2** *Prestige* | **Factor 3** *Innovation* | **Factor 4** *Power* |
|---|---|---|---|---|
| **Size** | -0.02 | 0.56* | -0.23 | 0.06 |
| **Evaluation** | 0.13 | 0.24 | -0.27 | 0.33 |
| **Growth** | -0.14 | -0.32 | 0.52* | -0.14 |
| **Profit** | -0.14 | 0.75* | -0.31 | 0.27 |

*significant on the p<0.01 level

The derived factors show direct relations to objective company characteristics. The Prestige factor strongly correlates with the measure for company size and company profit, the Innovation factor correlates with the measure for company growth. The honesty and the power factor do not show any significant correlations with the selected economic company descriptors, but might proof useful for company developments over a longer time horizon.

### 4.3.3. Discussion

The derived factors can be of potential use for understanding company perception and for the development of evaluation criteria for companies. The factor correlation also indicates possible relations with economic measures which might prove useful as performance predictors. Evaluations over time and on a larger body of companies are necessary, though, to confirm the strength and the directionality of these relations.

Also interesting relations can be drawn from the derived factors to Osgood's concept of Semantic Differentials (Osgood *et al.*, 1957). The Innovation factor fits with their Activity dimension, Prestige goes together with their Evaluation dimension, and Power with their Potency dimension. Only Honesty comes in as an additional factor for the evaluation of companies which seems not to be part of Osgood's original schema. The broader implication of these results is discussed in more detail next.

## 4.4. Company Characteristics

The derived factors can potentially be applied in diverse areas. This potential depends greatly on the factors' universality and how stable they link to other company characteristics of interest. These two questions guide this discussion.

### 4.4.1. Universality of Corporate Personality Dimensions

Are the corporate personality dimensions universal? A first, very positive, observation in relation to the likely generalization of corporate personality factors is that they connect well with Osgood *et al* (1957) classic attempt to find universal semantic differentials. This suggests that there are general principles guiding the evaluations of objects that are structuring how people judge companies. No doubt, of course, the evaluation of companies has its idiosyncrasies and possibly other objects might have their own peculiarities too. Osgood's proposed general dimensions are Activity, Evaluation, and Potency. It is interesting to consider how these original dimensions have a clear sense when applied to, for example, living things, translate into the related factors concerning companies. The translation of the Activity dimensions, in the case of companies, into an Innovation factor appears straight forward as innovation can be seen as resulting from concerted activity within groups. Activity is somehow equal to the rate of change at which an entity updates itself. Our Prestige factor stands in close relation to Osgood's Evaluation dimension. The prestige of a company is described by evaluative qualitative criteria. Potency is a measure of strength and freedom of action, or the ability to influence and create one's environment. The power of a company directly reflects this ability. The additionally derived factor Honesty could somewhat be understood as part of the Evaluation dimension. But the results here show that a company's honesty is somehow distinct from the more general quality evaluations and should be treated as a separate dimension. In passing, it is worth noting that Honesty relates directly to questions of trust, thus the public perception of honesty is presently a central concern in many areas of commerce.

These conclusions are further supported by the work of Slaughter *et al.* (2004) that also report a honesty dimension for Organization Personality. Their first factor (Boy Scout) is described by adjectives like "friendly," "family-oriented," "pleasant," "personal," "attentive to people," "helpful," "honest," and "cooperative," and quite similar to our Honesty factor. Factor two (Innovativeness) and factor three (Dominance) are directly in line with our results. Their factors four (Thrift) and five (Style) are comparable to our Prestige factor or Osgood's general Evaluation dimension. Also Aaker's (1997) first factor, named Sincerity, describes an honesty dimension as the most important dimension for their Brand Personality with the loading adjectives "down-to earth," "honest," "wholesome," and "cheerful." Although receiving somewhat differing labels, also the Prestige factor (Competence and Sophistication) and the Power factor (Ruggedness) find their representations. An interesting question for future work is how far this viewpoint holds for future evaluations of the company concept; currently, it seems that some clearly common themes arise from different methods for evaluating how people perceive companies. So far, research appears to be showing a relatively consistent picture to represent the natural way of evaluating companies.

The Semantic Differential has been used for attitudinal research and the evaluation of diverse objects. Besides the person aspect, it has not been applied to many living objects. Yet when researching the affective characterization of cities, Ward and Russell (1981) derive similar results reporting as the main first two factors an evaluation ("angenehm") and an activity ("erregend") dimension. In light of their work, and our own results on company perception, it is natural to ask how far Osgood's dimensions apply to other types of objects, e.g., animals or celebrities. Can we find similar regularities in these domains? If so, there really might be cognitive simplification processes involved that are similar across evaluations of complex entities. If different classes of objects are mapped according to similar dimensions we might be able to derive valuable information for the understanding of basic cognitive processes. An important general question arises, such as whether the underlying dimensions are separable or integral. If these dimensions are separable, and hence can directly be judged independently by participants; or if they are integral, in which case reconstruction of the dimensions will necessarily be indirect, using methods such as that described here. In both cases the corporate factors link to behavioral variation, although separable dimensions would establish a more direct relation between the different factors and specific behaviors. Therefore, to test causal behavioral dependencies, would first require a direct evaluation of the dimensions. Only when the dimensions are separable, we can assume cognitive representations directly structure the behavior.

### 4.4.2. Stability and Usefulness of Corporate Personality Dimensions

How stable and useful are dimensions of corporate personality? The introduction of personality factors for companies can be seen as a new way to describe companies. This mainly aims as an alternative description for companies that directly reflect the public understanding of them. However we have seen that the proposed corporate factors also show links to economic variables and might in general be useful as performance indicators. Thus, tracking measures of corporate personality might add important dimensions to economic measures of company performance and could be used both in shaping marketing and brand strategy, and potentially also in evaluating and predicting company success.

One important point for the application of the factors is their variability. One can assume that the values on the factors are not stable over time and that changes can be expected over longer time horizons. This only stresses the potential of the corporate factors as indicators to track changes over time. The performance of a company over time on these dimensions could be used, for example, to evaluate the impact of a high-profile advertising campaign. Also sources of variations; due to, for example, regional differences can not be ruled out, but prior work on the inter-cultural stability of factors supports the assumption of stable dimensions for company evaluations. Geeroms *et al.* (2005) generated preferred Brand Personality factors across 11 countries. The four corporate factors find representations in their eight factor solution (i.e., Belonging, Recognition, Vitality, and Power). Although perhaps more interesting is the link they built between these factors and consumer motives, which stresses the interactive component of the evaluation process and illustrates that motives or goals can play a key role here.

There may too be a relationship of motives or goals with the factors of corporate personality. If so, there is a link to issues like consumer demands; attractiveness as an employer and employment confidentiality, differences in short term and long term performances, as well as general social acceptability of a company. Thus, improved measures of corporate personality provide the cornerstone for a wide range of practical applications, and they generally enrich economic theory. The dimensions of company personality help economists to better understand judgments about products and also about company investments that appear not to be purely based on a rational evaluation of company information. A company perception bias reflected in these dimensions can play a crucial part in these decisions. But even if we know what the considered company information is, we can assume different ways of integrating this information into a choice. The next chapter focuses on different integration strategies and provides a learning explanation of how information about companies is considered.

*Chapter 5*

# INVESTMENT STRATEGIES II

Traditionally subjective utility maximization postulates an integration of the different anticipated outcomes in a choice. If different company details are available these can be taken as predictors for the outcomes and are integrated accordingly. Here a strategy conceptualization is proposed that assumes a choice between different available strategies which are applied to predict company performance. This exemplifies how company measures can be used and describes a cognitive modeling approach of inferences under uncertainty.

## 5.1. PERFORMANCE PREDICTION

Herbert Simon (1956) promoted the idea that human cognition should be understood as an adaptation of the environment. Consequently, different environments should lead to different inference strategies, so that people develop repertoires of strategies to deal with the problems they face. The claim that human cognition can be understood by assuming that people possess a repertoire of cognitive strategies has been asserted for various domains, including probabilistic inferences (Gigerenzer *et al.*, 1999); preferential choices (Einhorn, 1970, 1971; Payne, 1976; Payne *et al.*, 1988, 1993; Rapoport & Wallsten, 1972; Svenson, 1979); probability judgments (Ginossar & Trope, 1987); estimations (Brown, 1995; Brown *et al.*, 2002); categorization (Patalano *et al.*, 2001, Schunn & Reder, 1998); resource allocations (Ball *et al.*, 1998); memory (Coyle *et al.*, 1998); cognitive development of mathematical skills (Lemaire & Siegler, 1995; Siegler, 1999); word recognition (Eisenberg & Becker, 1982); and social interactions (Erev & Roth, 2001; Fiske, 1992).

If one adopts the view that people are equipped with a strategy repertoire, the pressing question is how individuals select their strategies. This is called the strategy selection problem. As a solution to this problem, several authors have followed a cost-benefit approach to strategy selection (see Beach & Mitchell, 1978; Christensen-Szalanski, 1978; Payne *et al.*, 1988, 1993; Smith & Walker, 1993). According to this theoretical approach, individuals trade a strategy's costs against its benefits in making their selections. The costs of a strategy are related to the cognitive effort required for processing it and the benefits are related to the strategy's accuracy. People anticipate the "benefits and costs of the different strategies that are available and choose the strategy that is best for the problem" (Payne *et al.*, 1993, p. 91). The trade-off of costs and benefits is influenced by the characteristics of the task, the person, and the social context. According to Payne *et al.* (1993), the selection process could be a conscious process of applying a meta-strategy, or an unconscious decision triggered by experience. Busemeyer (1993) has made the criticism that the trade-off process has not been examined (or explicated) sufficiently. Then, it is necessary to advance the theoretical approach by providing a computational model that describes the strategy selection process. The assumption of a meta-strategy could run into the problem of an infinite regress, as the meta-strategy also needs to be selected. In addition, a meta-strategy, conceptualized as constrained optimization could make the selection process of a simple strategy. This is a rather complex cognitive process. An alternative explanation is that people do not consciously select a strategy based upon a trade-off process of the anticipated effort and accuracy of strategies, but rather they learn to select appropriate strategies. From this learning perspective, three crucial questions remain to be answered: First, do people select different inference strategies in different environments? Second, do people learn to select the strategy that performs best in a particular environment? Third, how to describe the learning process of selecting strategies?

### 5.1.1. Strategy Repertoire

Do people select different strategies for inferences? Consider this problem: Of two companies, you must choose the more creditworthy. For this inference, one could use the information garnered from different cues; for instance, the company's financial flexibility. Thus how many cues should be considered, and how should the information from the cues be used to make an inference? The focus is on this probabilistic inference problem, which differs from the preferential choices that Payne *et al.* (1988) have examined. Gigerenzer and Goldstein (1996) showed that a simple lexicographic heuristic, called Take The Best (TTB), can perform surprisingly well: Assume each cue has either a positive or a negative cue value and that the cues can be ranked according to their validities. The cue validity is defined as the conditional probability of making a correct inference on the condition that the cue discriminates; in this example, that one company has a positive and the other a negative cue value. TTB searches for the cue with the highest validity and selects the company with the positive cue value. If the cue does not discriminate, then the second most valid cue is considered, and so on. If no cue discriminates, TTB selects randomly. This inference strategy is "noncompensatory," because a cue cannot be outweighed by any combination of less valid cues, in contrast to "compensatory strategies," that integrate cue values. Gigerenzer and Goldstein (1996) showed that TTB matches or outperforms many alternative strategies in inferential speed and accuracy, including a linear weighted additive strategy (WADD). For each alternative, the WADD strategy (sometimes also called "weighted linear model"), computes the sum of all cue values multiplied by the validity of the cue, and then finally selects the alternative with the largest sum. The simplicity and accuracy of TTB makes it psychologically plausible that people select it for inference problems. However, it has been suggested that the empirical support for this heuristic is weak and that direct tests are needed (e.g., Bröder, 2000; Chater, 2000; Lipshitz, 2000). Under which conditions do people actually apply noncompensatory strategies?

Recent studies have examined how different strategies can predict inferences (Bröder, 2000, 2003; Bröder & Schiffer, 2003; Newell & Shanks, 2003; Newell *et al.*, 2003). Rieskamp and Hoffrage (1999, 2003) showed that under greater time pressure, a lexicographic heuristic achieved the best fit with experimental data and, under lesser time pressure; compensatory strategies (in particular WADD) were best in predicting participants' inferences. In a similar vein, Bröder (2000, Experiment 3) showed that TTB predicted participants' inferences best when relatively high explicit information acquisition costs existed, whereas under low information costs, compensatory strategies reached a greater fit. TTB also predicted individuals' inferences well when the cue information had to be retrieved from memory; whereas a compensatory strategy (most frequently WADD) had a better fit in predicting inferences when the information was provided via a computer screen (Bröder & Schiffer,

2003). The selection of different strategies also depends on the overall payoffs they produce, such that TTB is selected more frequently when it produces the highest payoff compared to other strategies (Bröder, 2003). Newell and Shanks (2003) and Newell *et al.* (2003) showed that the way people search for cues follows the predicted search by TTB under high information acquisition costs, whereas the search is consistent with compensatory strategies under low information costs. However, search behavior appears to be only loosely connected with the predicted information search by a particular strategy, even if the strategy predicts the choices better than alternative strategies. Often people, for instance, search for unnecessary information or look up information twice (Newell *et al.*, 2003; Rieskamp & Hoffrage, 1999). Therefore, we assume that when people apply a strategy, they will search for the information required by the strategy, but they might also search for additional information, for instance, to consolidate their preliminary decision (Svenson, 1992). Besides this recent work on inferential choice, there is a large body of research examining strategy selection for preferential choice, such as the important contribution by Payne *et al.* (1988, 1993), and by Creyer *et al.* (1990) studying learning effects. Abelson and Levi (1985) or Ford *et al.* (1989) provide an overview here.

In summary, the reported results provide evidence that noncompensatory heuristics predict favorable inferences when the costs for applying compensatory strategies are high. In contrast, when the information search is not costly or when the use of more information leads to a better performance, people rely on compensatory strategies such as WADD. Thus, people's behavior is adaptive: strategies that perform well are also appropriate for describing behavior.

### 5.1.2. Strategy Learning

Do people learn to select strategies for inferences? Most of the reported experiments gave feedback about the correct decisions; adaptive strategy selection could be the result of learning. Only Newell *et al.* (2003, Experiment 1) reported that their participants seemed to change their strategies in later trials due to learning. Unfortunately, this learning effect was not analyzed in detail. Bröder (2003) also examined learning with a preliminary learning phase, however did not observe a learning effect. The experimental design was not really suitable for testing learning effects, since it led to "a significant amount of noise" in the measurement, as Bröder admitted (2003, p. 616).

Thus, it appears necessary to examine whether adaptive strategy selection can be explained by learning.

In general, past research has presented a mixed picture of whether people are able to learn inference strategies adaptively. Learning has been studied extensively with the "multiple cue probability learning" (MCPL) paradigm initiated by Hammond (1955) and Smedslund (1955; for reviews see Balzer *et al.*, 1989; Cooksey, 1996; Klayman, 1988). A prototypical MCPL task of repeatedly estimating an object's criterion value based on several cues differs from the inference task of choosing between two objects or companies. Nevertheless, many MCPL experiments document substantial learning effects (e.g., Hammond & Summers, 1972), although the optimal response is often not reached.

Categorizations are also inferences. For instance, in a frequently used medical diagnosis task (e.g., Estes *et al.*, 1989; Gluck & Bower, 1988; Koehler, 2000; Nosofsky *et al.*, 1992; Shanks, 1991), a patient's disease (the category) must be inferred based on a set of symptoms (cues). Categorizations differ from inferential choices—only one object (patient) instead of two objects is considered, and the criterion is membership in a category instead of a continuous criterion value that defines the correct choice. Modifying the diagnosis task as an inferential choice would imply asking the participant which of two patients is more likely to suffer from a disease; although one, none, or both patient(s) might be afflicted. Despite these differences, categorization studies demonstrate that people are often very successful at learning categories of a limited number of objects. However, in general, many authors are rather sceptical about people's ability to learn to make inferences "optimally" (Busemeyer & Myung, 1992; Connolly & Gilani, 1982; Connolly & Wholey, 1988; Wallsten, 1968), whereas other authors stress how well people learn to adapt to different inference problems (Anderson, 1991; Ashby & Maddox, 1992; Massaro & Friedman, 1990).

### 5.1.3. Models for Strategy Selection

Computational learning models have a long tradition in psychology, starting with the seminal work of Estes (1950), Bush and Mosteller (1955), and Luce (1959). More recent learning theories differ from traditional ones by proposing specific learning mechanisms (e.g., Börgers & Sarin, 1997; Busemeyer & Myung, 1992; Camerer & Ho, 1999a, b; Erev, 1998; Erev & Roth, 1998; Harley, 1981; Rieskamp *et al.*, 2003; Stahl, 1996, 2000; Sutton &

Barto, 1998). These theories assume that people often do not solve a specific decision problem from scratch; they may not perform very well at the beginning; but, through learning they can improve their decisions substantially; and, potentially, find the optimal solution. We can propose learning as an answer to how people select strategies for an inference problem. Accordingly, people learn to select cognitive strategies that allow them to generalize from experience in particular situations to new situations. The following learning theory defines a strategy selection learning process.

***Strategy Selection Learning Theory (SSL)***

According to SSL, people possess a repertoire of cognitive strategies to solve the judgment and decision problems they face. Through feedback, the unobservable cognitive strategies, instead of stimulus response associations are reinforced. From their strategy repertoire, people are most likely to select the strategy they most, subjectively, expect to solve the problem. These strategies' "expectancies" change through learning depending on the strategies' past performance in solving the task. For simplicity's sake, we focus on a prototypical compensatory strategy (WADD) and a prototypical noncompensatory strategy (TTB) that are suitable to predict inferences under varying conditions as reported. .

According to SSL, individuals have a set $S$ of $N$ cognitive strategies. For the following studies let us assume that the strategy set of SSL consists of only two strategies, hence $N = 2$ and $S = \{\text{WADD, TTB}\}$. The individual's preference for a particular cognitive strategy is expressed by positive expectancies $q_i$, with $i$ as an index for the cognitive strategies. Following Luce (1959, p. 25, cf. Thurstone, 1930) the probability that strategy $i$ is selected at trial $t$ is defined by

$$p_t(i) = \frac{q_t(\mathrm{i})}{\sum_{j=1}^{N} q_t(j)}. \tag{1}$$

The strategies' expectancies in the first period of the task can differ, and are defined by

$$q_1(i) = EV_r \cdot w \cdot \beta_i, \tag{2}$$

where $EV_r$ is the random choice payoff, $w$ is the initial association parameter, and $\beta$ is the initial preference parameter. The random choice payoff is the payoff that can be expected from applying a random choice strategy for the task, letting the expectancy depend on the random choice payoff facilitates comparisons between different tasks (when $EV_r$ is zero, as in the following studies, it is set to one to avoid expectancies of zero, thus, the positive expectancies only conceptually relate to the random choice payoff of the task). The initial association parameter $w$ is restricted to $w > 0$ and expresses an individual's initial attachment to the available strategies relative to later reinforcement. SSL assumes that individuals have initial preferences for selecting particular strategies at the beginning of a task. The initial preference parameter $\beta_i$ for each strategy $i$ is restricted to $0 < \beta < 1$ and $\sum_{i=1}^{N} \beta_i = 1$. The number of initial preference parameters equals the number of strategies minus one; in the case of two strategies this implies one free parameter. Thus, we do not assume an initial expectancy parameter as a free parameter for each strategy, equivalent to the proposed model. We follow this conceptualization for two reasons. First, both parameters should present two distinct psychological mechanisms: The initial preference parameters show how participants evaluate strategies differently at the beginning of the task, whereas the initial association defines how strong new reinforcement has to be and how often it has to be provided to develop or change a strategy preference. Second, it simplifies generalizations to other tasks: When considering tasks where it is reasonable to assume several cognitive strategies; one can keep the initial association parameter, but may either increase the number of free initial preference parameters or group strategies according to their similarity and use only one preference parameter for each group. After a decision is made, the expectancies of the cognitive strategies are updated for the next trial t by

$$q_t(i) = q_{t\text{-}1}(i) + I_{t\text{-}1}(i)\, r_{t\text{-}1}(i), \quad (3)$$

where $I_{t\text{-}1}(i)$ is an indicator function and $r_{t\text{-}1}(i)$ is the reinforcement. The reinforcement of a cognitive strategy is defined as the payoff $r_{t\text{-}1}(i)$ that the strategy produced. The indicator function $I_{t\text{-}1}(i)$ equals one if strategy $i$ was selected and equals zero if the strategy was not selected. It is assumed that a strategy was selected if the necessary information for applying the strategy was acquired and the choice coincides with the strategy's prediction. This definition becomes a problem if strategies make identical predictions, when it could be incorrectly inferred that both strategies were selected. Therefore, when two or more strategies make the same prediction that coincides with the individual's choice (and the necessary information for these strategies has been acquired), it is assumed that $I_{t-1}(i)$ equals the probability with which the model predicts the selection of these strategies. In this case, the strategies' expectancies increase, but the ratio of the strategies' expectancies does not change. By definition, if $q_t(i)$ due to negative payoffs falls below a minimum value $\rho$, $q_t(i)$ is set to $\rho$; for the following studies $\rho = 0.0001$ was used. The strategies' reinforcements are explicitly defined in terms of the monetary gains and losses a strategy produces. However, in principle, reinforcements naturally also include a non-monetary aspect, such as the cognitive effort required to process a strategy (see Payne *et al.*, 1993).

Finally, SSL assumes that people make minor errors when applying a strategy, so that, by mistake, they deviate from the strategy's prediction. Without any application error, the conditional probability $p(a|i)$ of choosing alternative $a$ out of the set $\{a, b\}$ when strategy $i$ is selected is either $p(a|i) = 1$ or $p(a|i) = 0$ for deterministic strategies like TTB and WADD (in cases when the cues do not allow a discrimination between the alternatives $p(a|i) = 0.5$). Incorporating an application error $\varepsilon$ into strategy application leads to the predicted probability of

$$p_t(a|i,\varepsilon) = (1-\varepsilon)\cdot p_t(a|i) + \frac{\varepsilon}{k-1}\cdot p_t(\overline{a}|i)\,, \tag{4}$$

where $p_t(\overline{a}|i)$ denotes the probability of choosing any other alternative than $a$ out of $k$ available alternatives (i.e., alternative $b$ in the case of two alternatives), given strategy $i$ was selected. For the sake of economy, the application error is assumed to be the same across strategies. In summary, the probability of choosing alternative $a$ depends on the probabilities of selecting the strategies and the corresponding choice probabilities of the strategies, so that

$$p_t(a) = \sum\nolimits_{i=1}^{N} p_t(i)\cdot p_t(a|i,\varepsilon)\,. \tag{5}$$

Besides the psychological plausibility of human errors, the application error parameter allows an evaluation of whether a reasonable set of strategies was assumed. If people apply a cognitive strategy that differ substantially from this assumed strategy set (i.e., strategies that make different predictions), then the result will be a relatively high application error.

SSL proposes a solution to the strategy selection problem: when assuming that people possess a repertoire of cognitive strategies for the inference problems they face, SSL provides a computational description of how strategies could be selected. SSL is a simple learning model with three free parameters, implementing mechanisms that have been proposed in previous learning theories: the choice rule (e.g., Erev, 1998), expectancies for the objects (e.g., Camerer & Ho, 1999a; Erev & Roth, 1998), and conceptualizing strategies as the objects of reinforcement (e.g., Busemeyer & Myung, 1992; Erev & Roth, 2001; Stahl, 1996). SSL's prediction depends on its parameter values. Generally, however, when no extreme initial preference for one strategy exists, the initial attachment to the strategies is not too strong, and the application error rate is small, SSL predicts that the strategy that performs best in a particular environment will be selected after sufficient learning opportunity. SSL is tested against four alternative models: three of them represent more general learning models and the last represents exemplar models.

### *Alternative Reinforcement Learning Theories*

The three general learning models were constructed by extending SSL, each incorporating one additional psychological mechanism.

SSL assumes that strategies are selected according to a linear selection rule (1). This implies that even when the decision maker, due to exhaustive learning, detects the performance superiority of one strategy over another, the best-performing strategy will not necessarily be selected exclusively. Therefore, many recent learning theories apply exponential selection rules (e.g., Ashby & Maddox, 1993; Busemeyer & Stout, 2002; Camerer & Ho, 1999a, b). Consistently, SSL can be extended by a *exponential sensitivity parameter* that allows the model to predict relatively large selection probabilities, even for low-expectancy differences across strategies, in the case of a high value for the sensitivity parameter. However, in the case of low values for the sensitivity parameter (i.e., lower than one), the model can also predict that a superior strategy is not learned, since it is selected too rarely.

Most learning theories assume that reinforcement that has been received recently influences behavior more strongly than reinforcement that was received longer ago (e.g., Camerer & Ho, 1999a, b; Erev & Roth, 1998; Estes, 1976; Sutton & Barto, 1998). This implies that the expectancy of a cognitive strategy declines over time and that a strategy becomes unlikely to be selected if it does not receive any reinforcement. Accordingly, a *forgetting parameter*, can be incorporated into SSL by modifying the updating rule (3). The forgetting parameter determines how strongly previous expectancies affect new expectancies. The "forgetting model" predicts an accelerated learning process in comparison to SSL, since the forgetting process quickly wipes out initial strategy preferences in favor of the best-performing strategy. In addition, due to forgetting, strategies' expectancies can converge to the minimum allowed value, so that the preferred strategy will be more or less selected exclusively.

The idea that people imagine strategies' performances goes back to theories of "fictitious play" (Brown, 1951). Through an imagination process, people might realize that alternative strategies could have solved whatever problem they were facing more adequately. Therefore, not only the selected strategy, but unselected strategies as well, could receive reinforcement when people imagine their outcomes (cf. Camerer & Ho, 1999a, b; Cheung & Friedman, 1997). To incorporate such an imagination process into SSL the updating rule (3) is modified with an *imagination parameter*. Hence, the selected strategy receives its reinforcement, and unselected strategies receive their reinforcement multiplied by the imagination parameter. If the imagination parameter equals one, all strategies receive reinforcement as if they had been selected; values between zero and one allow alleviated reinforcement for unselected strategies. The "imagination model" can predict particular learning effects: First, an accelerated learning process at the beginning of a learning situation compared to SSL results, since the strategy that is not preferred by the decision maker will also receive reinforcement. Second, the strategies' expectancies will converge to a constant ratio; so that, contrary to SSL, the model predicts that the learning process does not lead to an exclusive selection of the best-performing strategy even after sufficient learning; yet rather to a selection probability that depends on the ratio of the strategies' performances.

### *Exemplar-Based Inferences*

The central aim of this approach is to propose a computational theory for the strategy repertoire approach. However, there are alternative approaches that could predict people's inferences. For instance, models that have been proposed for the domain of categorizations could also be applied to inferential choices. The models include, among others, neural network models (e.g., Gluck & Bower, 1988; Shanks, 1991; Sieck & Yates, 2001), exemplar models (Lamberts, 2000; Medin & Schaffer, 1978; Nosofsky, 1986; Nosofsky & Johansen, 2000), and combinations of both (Kruschke, 1992; Nosofsky *et al.*, 1992). Gluck and Bower (1988) proposed a neural network model for categorization processes that, in a nutshell, claims that people integrate the information of objects' dimensions (cues), and due to learning the weights of the dimensions change. The neural network model shares some properties with

SSL, as it also assumes that people use a strategy to make inferences, namely, a compensatory strategy. Contrary to SSL, the model assumes that this compensatory strategy is modified due to learning, whereas SSL assumes that strategies are "modified" by switching to different strategies. Despite this difference, both models make similar learning predictions. The fundamentally different exemplar-based approach claims that objects are categorized by comparing them with memorized category representations. In general, exemplar models have been successfully applied in various domains, for example, memory (Hintzman, 1988), automatization (Logan, 1988), social cognition (Smith & Zarate, 1992), likelihood judgments (Dougherty *et al.*, 1999), and attention (Logan, 2002).

Juslin and Persson (2002, see also Juslin, Jones, *et al.*, 2003; Juslin *et al.*, 2003) have proposed an exemplar model for the inferential choice task that is the decision problem focused here. According to the exemplar-based approach, inferences in an inference situation (the probe) are made by searching for similar inference situations (the exemplars) in memory. The inference is made according to the best responses that were memorized for these exemplars. Thus, people do not learn to select abstract strategies that they apply to an inference situation, however instead learn "stimulus–outcome associations." In addition, exemplar models differ from SSL in the type of learning assumed: Exemplar models require feedback about whether a decision was correct or incorrect, thus representing forms of supervised learning (Sutton & Barto, 1998, p. 4). In contrast, because SSL only receives feedback about a decision's reward, but not whether it was correct or whether a different decision would lead to a better outcome, SSL represents unsupervised reinforcement learning (although the decision's reward, sometimes – as in Study 6 and 7 – yet not always, allows the inference that there could have been a better decision). Since exemplar models have been applied successfully as an "all-purpose inference machine" (Juslin, Jones *et al.*, 2003, p. 925) and offer a fundamentally different explanation of how inferences are made, they are strong and interesting competitors for SSL.

In the following, a modified version of the exemplar-based model (EBM) proposed by Juslin, Jones *et al.* (2003) is used. According to EBM, when making inferences, individuals compare the choice situation with previous choices between alternatives. Contrary to Juslin, Jones, *et al.* (2003), it is assumed that during such a retrieval process the whole choice situation containing both alternatives is retrieved, not single alternatives. Each alternative is described by a vector of cue values that can be positive, negative, or unknown. A pair of alternatives, representing an exemplar can then be described by a "cue configuration." For each cue in this configuration, nine possible combinations of cue values are possible (i.e., positive-positive, positive-negative, positive-unknown, negative-positive, etc.). When making inferences, the cue configuration of the present pair of alternatives (probe) is compared with the configuration of previous pairs (exemplars) by determining the similarity between the configurations. Attention weights represent the subjective importance of cues; the smaller the value the greater the impact on the perceived similarity. The number of parameters equals the number of cues. The probability that the first alternative $a$ of the alternative pair $\{a, b\}$ is chosen is defined by the sum reached over all exemplars $j$ where the first alternative $a$ was the correct choice, whereas the index $j \in b$ denotes that the sum is reached over all exemplars $j$ where the second alternative $b$ was the correct choice. Note that a particular exemplar for alternative $a$ was the correct choice could have identical cue values as another exemplar for alternative $b$ was the correct choice. Thus, with respect to categorization research, the choice situation is "ill defined" (Medin *et al.*, 1984), since for choice situations with identical available information, the correct responses can differ.

In the following studies, participants made inferences in different environment conditions when provided with outcome feedback. These studies were designed to explore the three main questions: Do people select different strategies? Do they learn to select the strategy that performs best? Finally, can SSL predict the learning process? To evaluate SSL, the theory is compared pair-wise with its competitors. In principle, the goal is to select the model that best captures the underlying cognitive process. Therefore, the model with the highest generalizability is searched for, that is, a model's ability to "fit all data samples generated by the same cognitive process, not just the currently observed sample" (Pitt & Myung, 2002, p. 422). From the different model selection techniques available (Pitt *et al.*, 2002), the Akaike information criterion is used that trades the model's fit against the model's complexity (see Akaike, 1973; Bozdogan, 2000; Burnham & Anderson, 1998) when estimating a model's generalizability (Browne, 2000). Akaike information criterion is an appropriate model selection criterion for nested models (Myung & Pitt, 1997); it applies to SSL in comparison to the three alternative learning models. To compare SSL with EBM, we consider the models' fits (neglecting the models' complexities) and additional qualitative predictions of the models.

## 5.2. Company Selection in Different Environments (Study 6)

First, Study 6 examines whether people improve their decisions when they repeatedly make inferences with feedback about their performance and the study explores how well TTB and WADD are able to predict the inferences. Second, Study 6 tests SSL's learning prediction that people learn to select the best-performing strategy, and it compares SSL with its competitors. For this test, participants made decisions in two differently constructed environment conditions: In the first "compensatory environment," the application of the compensatory strategy WADD led to the highest performance, defined as the received payoff, whereas in the second "noncompensatory environment," the application of the noncompensatory strategy TTB led to the highest performance.

### 5.2.1. Method

Forty people (23 women and 17 men) with an average age of 25 participated in the experiment. The computerized task was conducted in individual sessions, lasting approximately one hour. The participants were mainly students (85%) from various departments at the Free University of Berlin. Participants received their payoffs in the experiment as a payment for their participation; the average payment was around €14 ($21).

Participants were instructed: from two unnamed companies, they had to select the more creditworthy company (i.e., the company that would pay back a loan), and that only one company was the correct choice. For each decision they made, they had to pay 15 cents (22.5 pennies); described as a "handling fee" and, for each correct decision, they earned a payoff of 30 cents (45 pennies). In this payoff structure, participants who randomly chose between the companies netted a payment of zero. Each company was described by six cues and their validities. The companies' cue values could be either positive or negative, were presented in random order in matrix form using a computerized information board (see Figure 5.1). The information board shows the cue values for both alternatives that could be acquired by clicking on the boxes. The cue values were concealed in boxes that had to be opened by clicking on the box. Once a box was opened the cue values remained visible until a choice was made. The received payoffs were presented at the bottom of the screen.

The importance of the six cues was explained by means of their validities, and presented next to the names of the cues. The cues (and the cue validities given to the participants) were 'efficiency' (0.90), 'financial resources' (0.85), 'financial flexibility' (0.78), 'capital structure' (0.75), 'management' (0.70), and 'qualifications of employees' (0.60). All cues are common for assessing companies' creditworthiness (Rommelfanger & Unterharnscheid, 1985).

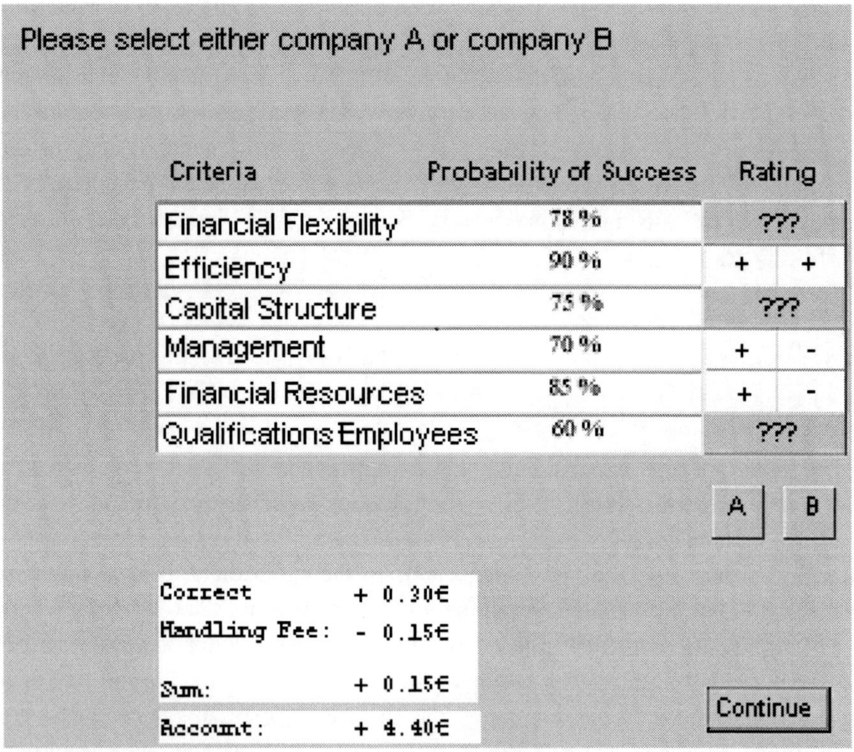


Figure 5.1. Decision situation

In both experimental conditions, participants made 171 choices without any time constraints. These 171 items consisted of three initial items to familiarize participants with the task, followed by seven blocks, each consisting of the same set of 24 items. The items within each trial block were randomly ordered, and the position of the two companies for each item (left or right on the screen) varied randomly. To examine participants' potential initial preferences for one of the two strategies for solving the task, no feedback was provided in the first trial block. In the following trial blocks, outcome feedback on the decisions' correctness was provided to allow for learning.

For all items, the strategies WADD and TTB always made an unambiguous prediction of which of the two companies to choose; therefore, their predictions never relied on random choice. In the compensatory environment, the item set was constructed such that WADD reached an accuracy of 92% (i.e., 22 correct of a possible 24 predictions) compared to TTB with an accuracy of 58% (i.e., 14 correct predictions out of 24). In the noncompensatory environment, the strategies' accuracies were reversed such that WADD reached an accuracy of 58% compared to TTB with an accuracy of 92%. It is important that the inferior strategy still leads to accuracy above chance, otherwise an adaptive selection of a strategy would be to choose the opposite of the strategy's prediction. To infer which strategy had been selected based on the participant's choices, it was crucial to construct a decision problem where strategies' predictions differed substantially. Therefore, in addition to the specific accuracy levels of the strategies, the items were so constructed that for both environment conditions, strategies' predictions differed for 12 of the 24 items. All items were created from a set of 50 companies for which the validities of the cues were determined. However, due to the necessary properties of the item set; that is, the strategies' performances and the separability of the strategies' predictions, the validities of the selected item set in the experiment deviated from those told to the participants (the deviations ranged between 0.05 and 0.43).

The experimental design has two factors: environment (between subjects; compensatory vs. noncompensatory environment), and trial block, with seven repetitions of the item set (within subjects). Study 6 tests the learning prediction that the best-performing strategy of the strategy set should reach a higher fit in predicting participants' choices after sufficient learning opportunity. In addition, Study 6 tests whether SSL is the best model to describe a potential learning process.

### 5.2.2. Results

Before evaluating the learning models, we first have to look for learning effects, that is, whether participants improved their decisions through feedback.

Participants were able to increase their payoff substantially across the seven trial blocks, illustrating a strong learning effect. Figure 5.2 shows the average payoffs (in Euros) received by the participants across the seven trial blocks in Study 6 in the compensatory and noncompensatory environment conditions. A repeated measurement analysis of variance (ANOVA) was conducted with the average obtained payoff as the dependent variable, the trial block as a within-subjects factor, and the environment as a between-subjects factor. The average payoff of €1.36 (SD = 0.78) in the first trial block increased significantly to an average payoff of €2.50 (SD = 0.67) in the last trial block, $F(6, 33) = 12.5$, $p = .001$, $\eta^2 = 0.69$. Additionally, there was an environment effect, since participants did better, with an average total payoff of €15.88 (SD = 2.84), in the compensatory environment than in the noncompensatory environment, €12.41 (SD = 3.94); $F(1) = 10.2$, $p = .003$, $\eta^2 = 0.21$. There was no interaction between the trial block and the environment.

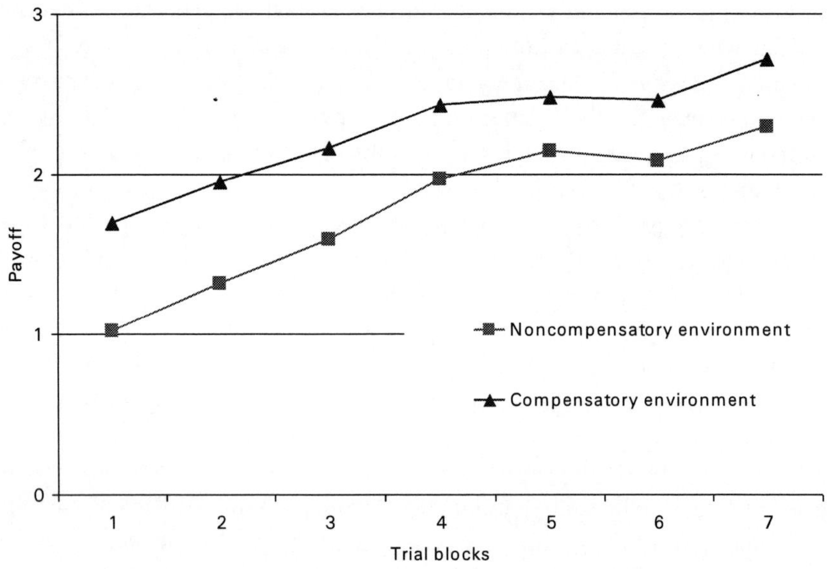


Figure 5.2. Learning curves in different environments

What strategy do people select for making their inferences? To answer this question, the percentages of predicted choices by TTB and WADD were determined for the items of each block where the strategies made different predictions. Figure 5.3 shows the percentage of choices predicted by the better-performing strategy for each environment condition. This is the percentage of predicted choices by the best-performing strategy in the compensatory (A) and the noncompensatory (B) environment conditions of Study 6 (only for those items where the strategies made different predictions). Additionally, Figure 5.3 shows the predicted probability by the different learning models with which the best-performing strategy is selected. SSL's prediction differed from the percentage of predicted choice by the best-performing strategy with a mean square error (MSE) of 0.23%. The fit for the exponential selection model was MSE = 0.22%, for the forgetting model it was MSE = 0.31%, and for the imagination model it was MSE = 0.16%.

At the beginning of the task, WADD was better at predicting participants' choices regardless of the environment condition. This indicated an initial preference for integrating all available information when making an inference. It also explained why participants received a higher payoff in the compensatory environment compared to the noncompensatory environment, since the initially preferred compensatory strategy led to a higher payoff in the compensatory environment. After the first trial block, this preference changed depending on the environment condition. For the compensatory environment, the fit of WADD increased over the trial blocks. In contrast, for the noncompensatory environment, TTB's fit increased, implying a decrease for WADD's fit. These results support the hypothesis that people select different strategies for inferences and that they learn to select the best-performing strategy. In the last trial block, WADD predicted 88% of all choices in the compensatory environment and TTB predicted 71% of all choices in the noncompensatory environment (for all items with differing predictions of the strategies). Since the validities told to the participants differed from those of the item set used in the experiment, participants might have learned the validities of the item set for the strategies they used. However, a WADD strategy using the validities of the item set predicted only 64% of all choices in the compensatory environment compared to a fit of 88% for WADD using the validities told to the participants. Likewise, a TTB strategy for the noncompensatory environment using the rank order of the validities of the item set predicted only 53% of all choices compared to 76% for TTB using the rank order of the validities told to the participants. Alternatively, a WADD strategy using the validities of the item set predicted only 56% of all choices in the noncompensatory environment. As strategies with the presented validities produced the best outcome, the usage of these validities rather than a learning of the actual validities of the item set can be assumed.

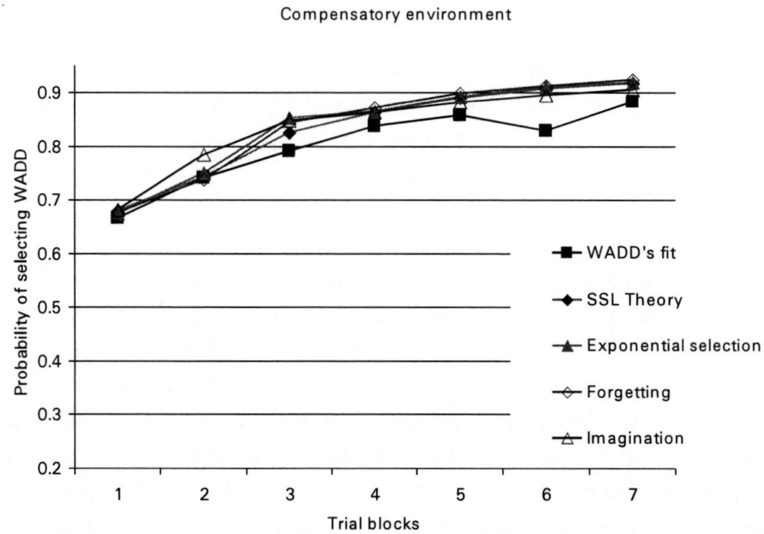


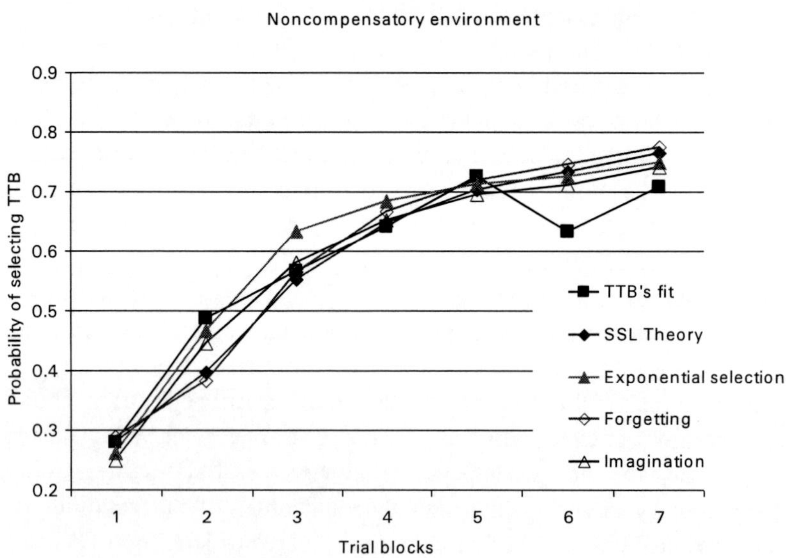


Figure 5.3. Predicted choices for Study 6

The accuracies of the models' predictions for each trial were evaluated by determining the likelihood of the observed choice, and a model's overall fit was assessed by determining the sum of the log likelihood for all choices across the 168 trials. As a goodness-of-fit, we use the $G^2$ measurement (Burnham & Anderson, 1998) defined in Equation 11, for which $f(y \mid \theta, t\text{-}1)$ is the likelihood function that denotes the probability of choice y given the model's parameter set $\theta$ and all information from the preceding trial $t$-1.

$$G^2 = -2\sum_{t=1}^{168} \ln(f(y \mid \theta, t-1)) \tag{6}$$

Applying maximum likelihood estimation for each model and individual, the parameter values that minimized $G^2$ were searched for. Reasonable parameter values were first selected by a grid-search; thereafter, the best-fitting grid values were used as a starting point for subsequent optimization using the simplex method (Nelder & Mead, 1965). For all models the initial association parameter was restricted to $0.0002 \leq w \leq 20$. This optimization procedure was applied to each of the 40 participants. SSL captured the choices with an average probability of .79, with an average predicted probability of .82 (with SD = .04 across the seven blocks) for the compensatory environment and of .77 (SD = .02) for the noncompensatory environment. When ignoring the probability prediction and considering only whether the alternative SSL predicted as most likely was chosen by the participants, SSL could predict 88% of all choices. Thus, SSL obtained a good fit by taking the dynamics of the inference process into account. Consistent with the results shown in Figure 5.3, the average initial preference parameter of $\beta_{TTB} = .30$ obtained, expressed a preference for WADD at the beginning of the task. In fact, for only 5 of 40 participants was an optimized initial preference value for TTB above .50 obtained. The average obtained value of the application error parameter of $\varepsilon = .05$ demonstrated that the assumed set of strategies was reasonable; in fact for only two participants was the value above .20, indicating a relatively error-prone strategy application.

How well did SSL compete against the alternative learning models? SSL is compared pair-wise with each alternative learning model by considering, for each participant, whether SSL or the alternative model had the higher generalizability. The generalizability of the models was evaluated by their Akaike information criterion values (Akaike Information Criterion defined as AIC = $G^2$-$2k$ with $k$ as the number of parameters). The fits of the models were also compared by a generalized likelihood ratio test (Wickens, 1989, pp. 100-103). For each model, the sum of $G^2$ values for all 40 participants was determined (each participant's $G^2$ value is computed according to Equation 6). The difference of the sums is approximately $\chi^2$ distributed with $df = 40$ (the degrees of freedom result from one additional free parameter for each of the 40 participants for the more general models). For the purpose of model selection, SSL was compared pair-wise with the more general four-parameter models. The percentage of participants for which the more general model reached a smaller (better) AIC value was determined. When compared with the general models, SSL obtained a better AIC value for the majority of participants (*p* according to a sign test). SSL reached a higher generalizability for the majority of participants in the comparison with the forgetting model and the imagination model. When compared with the exponential selection model, SSL reached a higher generalizability for only 52.5% of the participants (see Table 5.1).

**Table 5.1. Optimized parameter values for Study 6**

| | Learning model | | | |
|---|---|---|---|---|
| | SSL | Exponential selection model | Forgetting model | Imagination model |
| Initial association *w* | 7 ($SD$ = 7) | 3 ($SD$ = 6) | 9 ($SD$ = 8) | 4 ($SD$ = 6) |
| Initial preference $\beta_{TTB}$ | .30 ($SD$ = .15) | .26 ($SD$ = .22) | .31 ($SD$ = .15) | .28 ($SD$ = 0.18) |
| Application error $\varepsilon$ | .05 ($SD$ = .07) | .05 ($SD$ = .07) | .05 ($SD$ = .07) | .05 ($SD$ = .07) |
| Additional parameter | -- | $\mu$ = 1.5 ($SD$ = 2.8) | $\phi$ = 0.05 ($SD$ = 0.11) | $\delta$ = 0.12 ($SD$ = 0.11) |
| Predicted probability of choices | .791 | .797 | .793 | .792 |
| Sum of $G^2$ values | $G^2$ = 4439 | $G^2$ = 4357 ($\chi^2(40)$ = 82, $p$ = .001) | $G^2$ = 4419 ($\chi^2(40)$ = 20, $p$ = .997) | $G^2$ = 4405 ($\chi^2(40)$ = 33, $p$ = .758) |
| Median AIC | 113 | 115 | 115 | 115 |
| Participants with AIC improvement for more general model | -- | 47.5% ($p$ = .875) | 7.5% ($p$ = .001) | 22.5% ($p$ = .001) |

Besides describing the choice behavior, can SSL also explain the adaptive selection of cognitive strategies? The percentage of choices predicted by the strategies TTB and WADD, respectively, can be taken as an approximation of participants' strategy selection and can be compared to the probability with which SSL predicts this selection per trial block (see Figure 5.3). For both environments the probability SSL predicted for the selection of the best-performing strategy accurately matched the percentage of choices predicted by the best-performing strategy. The three alternative models did not obtain substantially better fits. This good match is surprising considering that the models' parameters were fitted with respect to participants' choices and not to the strategies' predictions.

The exemplar model proposed by Juslin, Jones *et al.* (2003) does not aim to describe the initial learning process. Instead, it focuses on how people make inferences after they have learned exemplars. Thus, to determine a fair test of SSL, EBM was used only to predict the choices of the last two blocks. For each of these 48 choices, a prediction was made by comparing the cue configuration of the pair of alternatives with the cue configuration of the pairs in all subsequent trials excluding the first block of 24 trials, for which no feedback was provided. For instance, when making a prediction for the last trial, EBM determined the similarity of that pair of alternatives (probes) to the previous 143 pairs (exemplars) starting with the inference of the 25th trial and ending with the 167th trial. Since each block repeated the same 24 items, the similarity of a probe to identical exemplars was frequently determined. Therefore, in contrast to Juslin, Jones, *et al.* (2003), here a frequency-sensitive form of EBM (Nosofsky, 1988) is used.

The model predicts the probability with which a participant will choose either company *a* or *b*. To assess the model's overall fit for a given individual and set of parameters, the $G^2$ measurement was determined for the last 48 choices. The six free attention-weight parameters, which were restricted for all three studies to $0.001 \leq s_m \leq 0.999$, were fitted separately to each individual's data. Reasonable parameter values were first selected by a grid-search technique; thereafter, the best-fitting grid values were used as a starting point for subsequent optimization. The average optimized parameter values were, in decreasing order of the cues according to their validities: $s_1 = .10$, $s_2 = .40$, $s_3 = .50$, $s_4 = .09$, $s_5 = .32$, and $s_6 = .66$ for the compensatory environment and $s_1 = .11$, $s_2 = .51$, $s_3 = .85$, $s_4 = .29$, $s_5 = .62$, and $s_6 = .31$ for the noncompensatory environment. Thus, the attention weights did not correlate substantially with cue validities; only the attention weight of the most valid cue obtained a high attention weight relative to the other cues.

EBM predicted the choices with an average probability of .76 for the two environments. SSL reached a better fit as it predicted the choices in the last two blocks with an average probability of .86 for the compensatory environment, and .78 for the noncompensatory environment. However, SSL's predictions were derived from fitting the model to all blocks, and its fit could be improved when fitted to the last two blocks only as was done for EBM. Simply comparing SSL with EBM for each participant model's fit in predicting the choices and thereby ignoring the models' complexity, since AIC is not appropriate for non-nested models (see also Roberts & Pashler, 2000). SSL had a better fit compared to EBM for 60% of all participants ($p = .268$ according to a sign test), although SSL had only three free parameters compared to EBM with six free parameters. Thus, SSL was slightly more appropriate than the exemplar-model to predict the choices when only considering the fit of the models and neglecting their complexities.

### 5.2.3. Discussion

Study 6 demonstrated that when people repeatedly make probabilistic inferences their performance improves. In addition, it showed that people apparently select different strategies for the inference task. In the first trial block with no feedback, WADD predicted more choices in comparison to TTB, indicating that WADD is the strategy people initially prefer to select. This is what one would expect in an unfamiliar task when the information is provided without any costs and does not need to be retrieved from memory (for the difference between inference "from memory" and inference "from givens" see Gigerenzer & Goldstein, 1996; Bröder & Schiffer, 2003). The initial preference for WADD also explains why participants perform better (i.e., reach a higher payoff) in the compensatory environment, because by selecting WADD in the compensatory environment, they select the strategy that produces the higher payoff right from the beginning. However, the initial preference for a particular strategy changes as a result of feedback. After sufficient experience, a person is likely to select a different strategy. Study 6 suggested that people learn to select the strategy that performs best in the environment.

The standard cost-benefit approach (e.g., Payne *et al.*, 1988) predicts that people select strategies depending on the experimental conditions. Accordingly, WADD should predict more choices in the compensatory environment and TTB should predict more choices in the noncompensatory environment. The results support this prediction. However, the cost-benefit approach does not specify how the strategy selection process changes over time due to learning. SSL fills this gap and describes how strategy selection changes adaptively. In particular, the shift from the selection of one strategy to another in the noncompensatory environment can only be explained by a learning approach. SSL is the best learning model when compared with the three competing learning models. The additional mechanisms that are captured by the more general learning models do not appear to be essential for predicting the observed learning process. Only when SSL is compared with the exponential selection model do both models perform equally well according to their generalizability. The obtained average sensitivity parameter for the exponential selection model was 1.5. Thus it is possible to predict a relatively high probability with which a strategy is selected compared to SSL, even for relatively small expectancy differences of the strategies. The exponential selection model is thereby able to predict an accentuated learning rate at the beginning of the learning process (in particular in the noncompensatory environment), which gives the model – for some participants – a better fit than does SSL. The following studies explore whether this advantage holds for other situations.

We derive these conclusions from a strategy repertoire perspective. Is this perspective justified based on the comparison of it with the exemplar-based perspective? The results of the comparison of SSL with EBM suggest that the answer is yes. First, although SSL has only three free parameters compared to EBM, with six free parameters, it still reached a better fit for the majority of the participants. Second, there is a qualitative prediction that SSL makes, depending on the strategies' predictions that speaks in its favor. When the strategies select the same alternative, then SSL predicts the choice of this alternative with a relatively high probability compared with situations in which the strategies select different alternatives. Consistently, participants' choices matched SSL's prediction more frequently when the strategies' predictions coincided. Contrastingly, the exemplar model does not predict this difference. Nevertheless, participants' choices were more in line with EBM's prediction for items where the strategies select the same alternative – a result that cannot be explained by the exemplar model. In summary, for Study 6's probabilistic inference task, SSL provided the best account of people's inference processes. However, this conclusion needs to be restricted, since Study 6's inference situation was not advantageous to an exemplar-based inference process. The learning phase was relatively short given the large number of exemplars. In many studies where exemplar models were tested (e.g., Juslin, Jones, *et al.*, 2003), only a few exemplars were presented in a relatively long learning phase; so that people have the opportunity to acquire a good memory representation of the exemplars against which new instances can later be compared. In Study 6, the learning phase could have been too short for participants to memorize exemplars and this may explain EBM's lower fit. Nevertheless, participants were still successful in making their choices and we observed a strong learning effect. Thus, although EBM potentially could be a better model when more opportunity for learning exists, with the limited learning opportunity given in Study 6, the strategy repertoire perspective provides a better account of people's inferences. For an inference task with a relatively small learning opportunity, individuals seem to rely on an abstraction; that is, the application of a cognitive strategy, rather than on comparing inference situations with previously made inferences. Study 7 will further test the generalizability of these conclusions in a different inference situation.

## 5.3. Company Selection with Memory Costs (Study 7)

One important criticism of the inference situation of Study 6 is that participants were provided with cue validities. There are situations where people have knowledge about the validity of the information they use, however they often have to learn how good cues are for making inferences, and these validities have to be retrieved from memory. Such a situation is examined in Study 7. In addition, the demands on memory in Study 7 are increased by instituting a more active information search, so that the available pieces of information are never visually presented simultaneously. Instead, the cue values have to be acquired sequentially. Increased cognitive demands for applying a cognitive strategy might make it more likely that people rely on memorized exemplars to solve inference problems. Thus, Study 7 tested whether the results and conclusions of Study 6 can be generalized to a situation with increased cognitive demands.

### 5.3.1. Method

Forty people (17 women and 23 men) with an average age of 24 participated in the experiment. The computerized task was conducted in individual sessions and lasted approximately one and a half hours. The participants were mainly students (88%) from various departments at the Free University of Berlin. Payments depended on the participants' performance; the average payment was €22 ($33).

As in Study 6, participants were instructed to select the more creditworthy of two unnamed companies that were described by six cues, presented on a computerized information board (with one company being the correct choice). Contrary to Study 6, the experimental session started with a validity-learning phase that took, on average 40 min and included 70 items. Each item contained the information of three discriminating cues randomly selected from the set of six cues, so that each cue was presented 35 times. After a participant made a choice, he or she was informed as to which company was correct without receiving any payoffs or paying any costs. Thereafter, a histogram was presented that showed, for all cues, how often each cue was successful versus unsuccessful in predicting the correct choices for all items viewed up to that point. By presenting three cues simultaneously, the learning process was reinforced, because participants were required to compare the cues, making the validity differences between them more salient. Restricting the number to three cues implied that participants were hindered in learning cognitive strategies for solving the task. The cues (and their validities) in the learning phase were 'efficiency' (.77), 'financial resources' (.71), 'financial flexibility' (.66), 'capital structure' (.60), 'management' (.57), and 'qualifications of employees' (.54). These validities for the learning phase were essentially the same as for those in the subsequent inference phase, with a maximum deviation of 0.015.

At the end of the validity-learning phase the participants had to estimate the cue validities: Participants were asked for each cue separately, "How often, out of 100 decisions, does this cue make a correct prediction, given that one company has a positive cue value and the other company has a negative cue value?" Participants could earn a maximum bonus of about €2.00 ($3) when they made perfect estimates; in the case of the worst possible estimates they would have received nothing, as the estimates were evaluated by the quadratic scoring rule (Yates, 1990). The scoring rule was not explained in detail; instead participants were told that the better their estimates were the higher their bonus would be. The validity-learning phase was quite successful, since the average correlation between estimated validities and real validities was $r$ = .88 (SD = .17, Median = .94, and for more than 70% of all participants, the correlation was above .90). However, because the estimated validities deviated from the real validities, each participant's individually estimated validities were used for the predictions of the cognitive strategies and subsequently for the learning models' predictions. In fact, the whole analysis was repeated by using the objective cue validities, which did not substantially affect the results and did not change the conclusion. However, using the subjective estimated validities describes a more conservative method by not making potentially unjustified assumptions about the success of the cue-validity learning phase.

After the validity-learning phase, participants proceeded with the inference phase with 185 choices. For each choice, the cue information could be acquired by clicking on information boxes. In contrast to Study 6, only one information box could be opened at a time, so that when another information box was opened, the previously opened box automatically closed. The 185 items consisted of three initial items to familiarize participants with the task, followed by seven trial blocks, each consisting of the same set of 26 items. For all items, the strategies always led to unambiguous predictions of which of the two companies to choose, and for 50% of the items, they led to different predictions (to construct the item set and determine strategies' predictions, the actual cue validities were employed). As in Study 6, no feedback was provided in the first trial block, followed by six blocks with outcome feedback. For each choice they made, participants paid 20 cents (14 pence); they then received 40 (28 pence) cents for a correct choice.

Study 7 had two experimental factors: environment (between subjects; compensatory vs. noncompensatory environment) and trial block (within subjects). In the compensatory environment condition, the item set was constructed such that WADD reached an accuracy of 88% compared to TTB with an accuracy of 61%. In the noncompensatory environment condition, the strategies' accuracies were reversed.

### 5.3.2. Results

A repeated measurement ANOVA was conducted with the average obtained payoff as the dependent variable, the trial block as a within-subjects factor, and environment as a between-subjects factor. Again a strong learning effect is documented, since the average obtained payoff of €2.32 (SD = 0.84) in the first block increased substantially across the seven blocks to a payoff of €3.21 (SD = 0.80) in the last block, $F(6, 33) = 9.8$, $p = .001$, $\eta^2 = 0.64$. Participants received an average total payoff of €21 (SD = 3.8) in the compensatory environment compared to a payoff of €19 (SD = 3.2) in the noncompensatory environment, $F(1, 38) = 2.6$, $p = .112$, $\eta^2 = 0.06$. No interaction between trial block and environment occurred. Figure 5.4 shows the payoff development across the seven trial blocks for both environment conditions. Here the average payoffs (in Euros) received by the participants across the seven trial blocks in the compensatory and noncompensatory environment conditions are shown for Study 7.

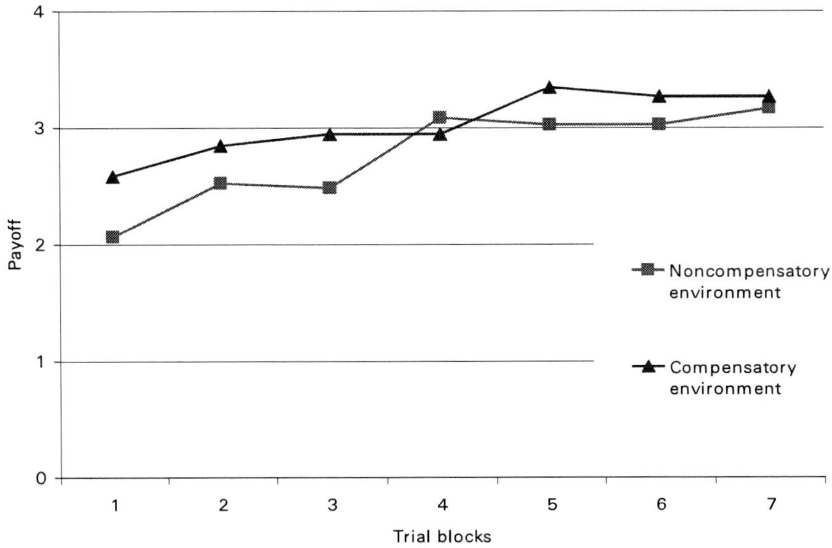


Figure 5.4. Learning curves for the different environments with memory costs

How well do the two strategies predict participants' choices? Figure 5.5 shows the percentage of choices predicted by the best-performing strategy. The percentage of predicted choices by the best-performing strategy in the compensatory (A) and the noncompensatory (B) environment conditions of Study 7 (only for those items where the strategies made different predictions), and the predicted probability of the best-performing strategy by SSL theory and the three alternative learning models are shown. SSL's prediction differed from the percentage of predicted choice by the best-performing strategy with a mean square error of 0.20%. The fit for the exponential selection model was MSE = 0.12%, for the forgetting model it was MSE = 0.20%, and for the imagination model it was MSE = 0.16%.

For both environments, WADD and TTB predicted a similar proportion of choices for the first trial block. Thus, in contrast to Study 6, no initial preference for integrating the available information according to WADD was observed. However, again, the learning prediction that people learn an environment's best-performing strategy is supported. The WADD's and TTB's fits increased in the respective compatible environments across the seven trial blocks. In the last trial block, WADD predicted on average, 77% of all choices in the compensatory environment; and TTB predicted an average of 68% of all choices in the noncompensatory environment, when considering all choices where the two strategies made different predictions.

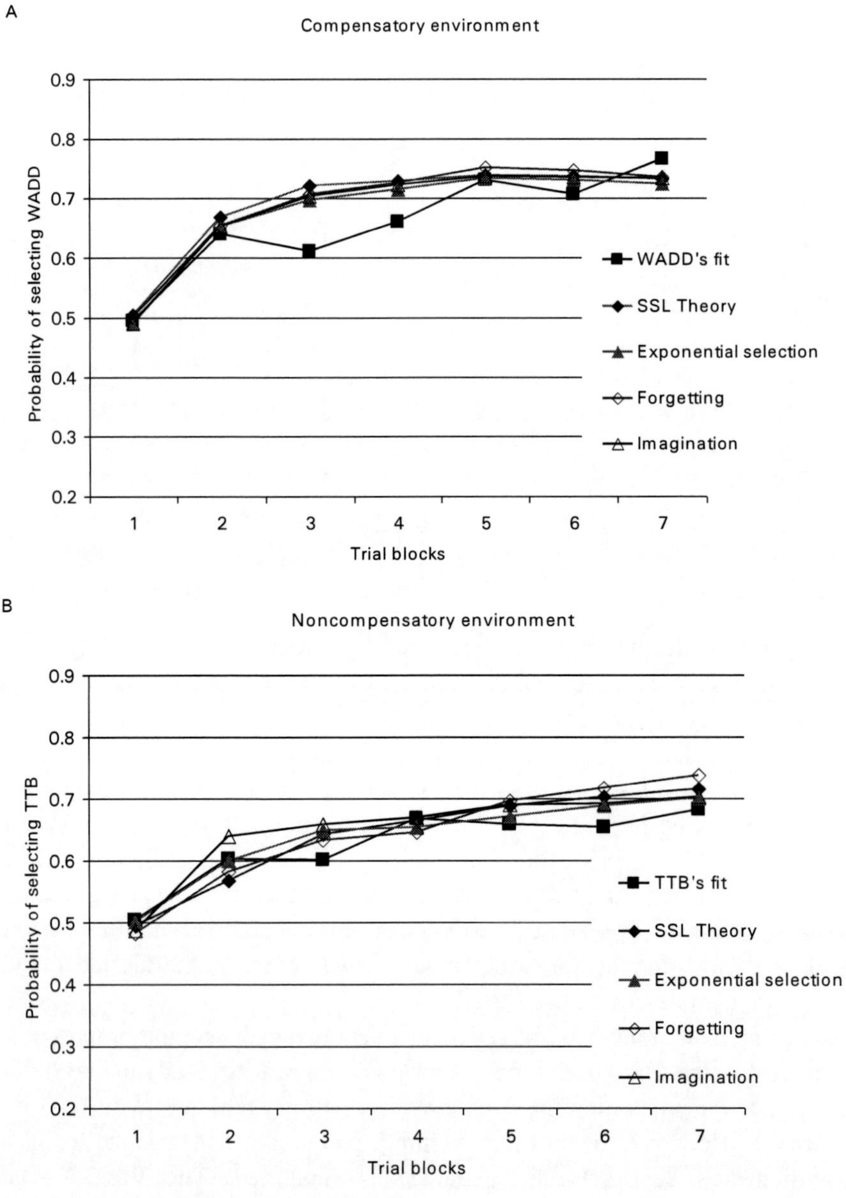


Figure 5.5. Predicted choices for Study 7

Similar to Study 6, each learning model was fitted to the participants individually to obtain 40 sets of optimal parameter estimates (see Table 5.2).

SSL captured the choices with an average probability of .74 for both environment conditions. When only considering if the alternative most likely predicted by SSL was chosen by the participants, SSL could predict 81% of all choices. Consistent with the results presented in Figure 5.5, the average initial preference parameter of $\beta_{TTB}$ = .50 for SSL expresses no preference for WADD at the beginning of the task. The average obtained value for the application error parameter ($\varepsilon$ = .07) is slightly greater in comparison to that of Study 6 and, again, only two participants had a value above 0.20. Therefore, it can be concluded that an adequate set of strategies was assumed. To compare SSL against the alternative learning models, each model was evaluated according to its estimated generalizability. In all three pair comparisons, SSL reached a higher generalizability for at least 70% of all participants (see Table 5.2). In sum, SSL obtained a good fit by taking the dynamics of the inference process into account.

**Table 5.2. Optimized parameter values for Study 7**

| | **Learning model** | | | |
|---|---|---|---|---|
| | **SSL** | **Exponential selection model** | **Forgetting model** | **Imagination model** |
| Initial association $w$ | 9 (*SD* = 9) | 6 (*SD* = 8) | 11 (*SD* = 9) | 6 (*SD* = 8) |
| Initial preference $\beta_{TTB}$ | .50 (*SD* = .14) | .52 (*SD* = .25) | .49 (*SD* = .15) | .50 (*SD* = 0.15) |
| Application error $\varepsilon$ | .07 (*SD* = .07) | .07 (*SD* = .07) | .07 (*SD* = .07) | .07 (*SD* = .07) |
| Additional parameter | -- | $\mu$ = 1.4 (*SD* = 2.3) | $\phi$ = 0.04 (*SD* = 0.09) | $\delta$ = 0.39 (*SD* = 0.42) |
| Predicted probability of choices | .742 | .744 | .744 | .743 |
| Sum of $G^2$ values | $G^2$ = 5803 | $G^2$ = 5742 ($\chi^2(40)$ = 61, $p$ = .017) | $G^2$ = 5778 ($\chi^2(40)$ = 25, $p$ = .97) | $G^2$ = 5776 ($\chi^2(40)$ = 27, $p$ = .94) |
| Median AIC | 146 | 148 | 147 | 148 |
| Participants with AIC improvement for more general model | -- | 30% ($p$ = .017) | 10% ($p$ = .001) | 15% ($p$ = .001) |

To predict the selection of the cognitive strategies, TTB's and WADD's percentages of predicted choices are taken as an approximation of strategy selection and compared with the probability of SSL predicting this selection (see Figure 5.5). For both environments, SSL's predicted selection probabilities accurately match the percentage of predicted choices by the best-performing strategy. This again is an impressive match between strategy selection predicted by SSL and the choices predicted by the cognitive strategies.

Identical to Study 6, EBM was used only to predict the inferences of the last two blocks. For each of these 52 inferences, a prediction was made by comparing the cue configuration of a pair of alternatives with the configuration of all previous pairs excluding the first block. The six attention-weight parameters of EBM were fitted separately for each individual, using the same optimization procedure as in Study 6. For the six attention weights, the optimized parameter values, in decreasing order of the cues according to their validity, were: $s_1 = .18$, $s_2 = .23$, $s_3 = .63$, $s_4 = .72$, $s_5 = .30$, and $s_6 = .76$ for the compensatory environment; and $s_1 = .25$, $s_2 = .21$, $s_3 = .20$, $s_4 = .70$, $s_5 = .40$, and $s_6 = .56$ for the noncompensatory environment. As in Study 6, the attention weights did not correlate substantially with the cue validities.

EBM predicted the choices with an average probability of .78 for the compensatory environment and with an average of .74 for the noncompensatory environment. In comparison, SSL predicted the choices of the last two blocks with an average probability of .75 for both environment conditions. To compare SSL with EBM, we simply determine which model had a better fit for each participant, ignoring the model's complexity. According to the $G^2$ fit criterion, SSL and EBM did not differ, as SSL had a better fit for 47.5% of all participants.

### 5.3.3. Discussion

Study 7 again demonstrates that people improve the accuracy of their decisions when they receive outcome feedback. Even in a situation where cue validities have to be learned, people learn to select the strategy that performs best for the inference situation. In contrast to Study 6, in Study 7 we observed no initial preference for WADD. This seems to be the result of the increased cognitive demands of Study 7. The validities had to be retrieved from memory and the cue values had to be remembered, which seem to make the selection of a noncompensatory heuristic preferable. The larger cognitive demands of Study 7 might have also made the inference process more complicated, since the best-performing strategies had a lower fit in predicting choices in the last trial block compared to Study 6. Possibly, the remembered validities and cue values are more vulnerable to error, so that a person's inference process deviates frequently from the strategies' predictions. This conjecture is supported by an on average higher value for the application error obtained for

SSL. When comparing SSL with the more general learning models, it described the learning process more accurately. In particular, SSL reached a higher generalizability compared to the exponential selection model, which reached a similar generalizability as in Study 6. The learning effect at the beginning of the experiment was less pronounced when compared with Study 6, and this moderate learning effect could be equally well predicted by SSL. Thus, the additional learning mechanisms of the more general learning models are not essential for predicting the learning process.

The adaptive behavior in Study 6 and Study 7 was observed under conditions of substantial accuracy differences between the two strategies. Whereas the best-performing strategy reached an accuracy of approximately 90%, the worst-performing strategy reached an accuracy of approximately 60%. Such large accuracy differences between strategies might not be common in real-world situations (Martignon & Laskey, 1999). Therefore, Study 8 tested whether the results and conclusions of Study 6 and Study 7 can be generalized to a situation in which the accuracy differences between strategies are smaller.

## 5.4. Company Selection with Information Costs (Study 8)

Simple noncompensatory strategies often reach accuracies that are similar in level to those of more complex strategies that integrate the available information. The so-called flat maximum phenomenon states that the optimal set of weights in a linear model can often be replaced by many other sets of weights without losing much accuracy (Dawes & Corrigan, 1974; Wainer, 1976). This provides one explanation of why simple heuristics can work well. Generally, heuristics often have two advantages. Besides their robust accuracy levels, they possess low application costs, as they require a small amount of information that is easy to process. In Study 8, strategies' costs will be made explicit by introducing information acquisition costs.

According to SSL, strategies are selected proportional to their expectancies, and these depend on the gains and losses the strategies produce. Gains and losses are explicitly defined in monetary terms; however, in principle, they could also include non-monetary aspects, for instance, the cognitive costs of processing information (for the distinction between information acquisition and processing costs, see Johnson & Payne, 1985).

Study 8 tests whether people are able to learn the best-performing strategies for an inference task for which the strategies' performance, defined by the strategies' payoffs, differ mainly because of different information acquisition costs. Can the previous conclusions, that people adapt their strategy selection based on strategies' performances, be generalized to yet another plausible inference situation?

One might argue that EBM is less suited to the inference situation of Study 8, since the model predicts that individuals memorize only the correct choice for an exemplar and it does not predict how individuals also evaluate and memorize an adequate amount of information for making an inference. However, in principle, this missing property does not restrict the application of EBM. Individuals following an exemplar-based inference process might decide from the beginning only to look up a constant subset of information to reduce costs. Then, they memorize exemplars on the basis of the acquired information and compare new instances with these stored exemplars. Thus, the way people search for information is not predicted by EBM, but this does not restrict its application.

### 5.4.1. Method

Forty people (23 women and 17 men) with an average age of 25 participated in the experiment. The computerized task, which was conducted in individual sessions, lasted approximately one hour. The participants were mainly students (78%) from various departments at the Free University of Berlin. Payments depended on the participants' performance; the average payment was €8 ($12).

The instructions were similar to those in Study 6. Participants had to select the more creditworthy company of two unnamed companies, described by six cues with given cue validities. The 171 items consisted of three initial items to familiarize participants with the task, followed by seven trial blocks, each consisting of the same set of 24 items, presented in random order. Feedback was provided after the first trial block to allow learning. The two strategies made unambiguous predictions for all items and for 50% of the items they made different predictions. The validities told to the participants were the same as in Study 6. Again, due to the necessary properties of the item set – the performances required and possible separability of the strategies – the validities of the selected item set in the experiment deviated from the ones told to the participants (with deviations varying between 0.14 and 0.38).

The experimental design had two factors: environment (between subjects) and trial block (within subjects). In the compensatory environment, WADD reached an accuracy of 79% (i.e., 19 correct predictions of 24) compared to TTB with an accuracy of 71%. In the noncompensatory environment, the strategies' accuracies were reversed. In the compensatory environment, participants earned 75 cents (50 pence) for a correct decision, but paid 37.5 cents (25 pence) for each decision. For each acquired cue, an additional three cents (4.5 pennies) had to be paid, so that the cost of acquiring one cue relative to the possible gain of a correct decision was 8%. For this payoff structure, the application of TTB led to a payoff of €15.50 ($23) compared to WADD with a payoff of €6.50 ($10) for all 168 items. In the noncompensatory environment, participants earned 35 cents (50 pennies) for a correct decision and paid 17.5 cents (25 pennies) for each decision. For each acquired cue, an additional 0.5 cents (0.7 pennies) had to be paid, implying relative information costs to gains of 3%. The application of TTB led to a payoff of €15.40 ($22) compared to WADD with a payoff of €7.20 ($11). Thus, in both environment conditions, TTB's performance, defined as the overall payoff produced by a strategy, was higher than WADD's performance, due to lower information costs. Therefore, SSL predicts that people will learn to select TTB in both environment conditions.

## 5.4.2. Results

In Study 8, participants did not improve their payoffs across the seven trial blocks as much as was observed in Study 6 or Study 7. Average payoffs (in Euros) received by the participants across the seven trial blocks in Study 8 in the compensatory and noncompensatory environment conditions are shown in Figure 5.6.

For both environments, WADD and TTB predicted a similar proportion of choices for the first trial block. Thus, in contrast to Study 6, no initial preference for integrating the available information according to WADD was observed. However, again, the learning prediction that people learn an environment's best-performing strategy is supported. The WADD's and TTB's fits increased in the respective compatible environments across the seven trial blocks. In the last trial block, WADD predicted on average, 77% of all choices in the compensatory environment; and TTB predicted an average of 68% of all choices in the noncompensatory environment, when considering all choices where the two strategies made different predictions.

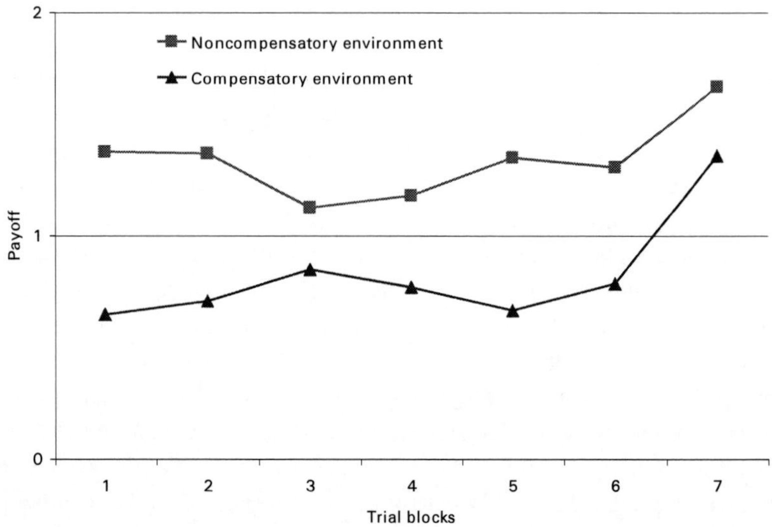


Figure 5.6. Learning curve in the different environments with information costs

The repeated measurement ANOVA, with the average obtained payoff as the dependent variable, trial block as a within-subjects factor, and environment as a between-subjects factor shows a weak learning effect: The average obtained payoff of €1.01 in the first block (SD = 0.93) increased to an average payoff of €1.51 (SD = 0.85) in the last block, $F(6, 33) = 2.2$, $p = .065$, $\eta^2 = 0.28$. Participants did worse in the compensatory environment with an average payoff of €5.77 (SD = 4.65) compared to an average payoff of €9.37 (SD = 4.15) in the noncompensatory environment, $F(1, 38) = 6.6$, $p = .014$, $\eta^2 = 0.15$. Participants searched on average for too much information, which explains why they received a lower payoff in the compensatory environment, with relatively high information search costs, compared to the noncompensatory environment. No interaction between trial block and environment occurred.

Figure 5.7 shows the percentage of choices predicted by TTB, the best-performing strategy in both environments. Here the percentage of predicted choices by the best-performing strategy in the compensatory (A) and the noncompensatory (B) environment conditions of Study 8 are shown only for those items where the strategies made different predictions.

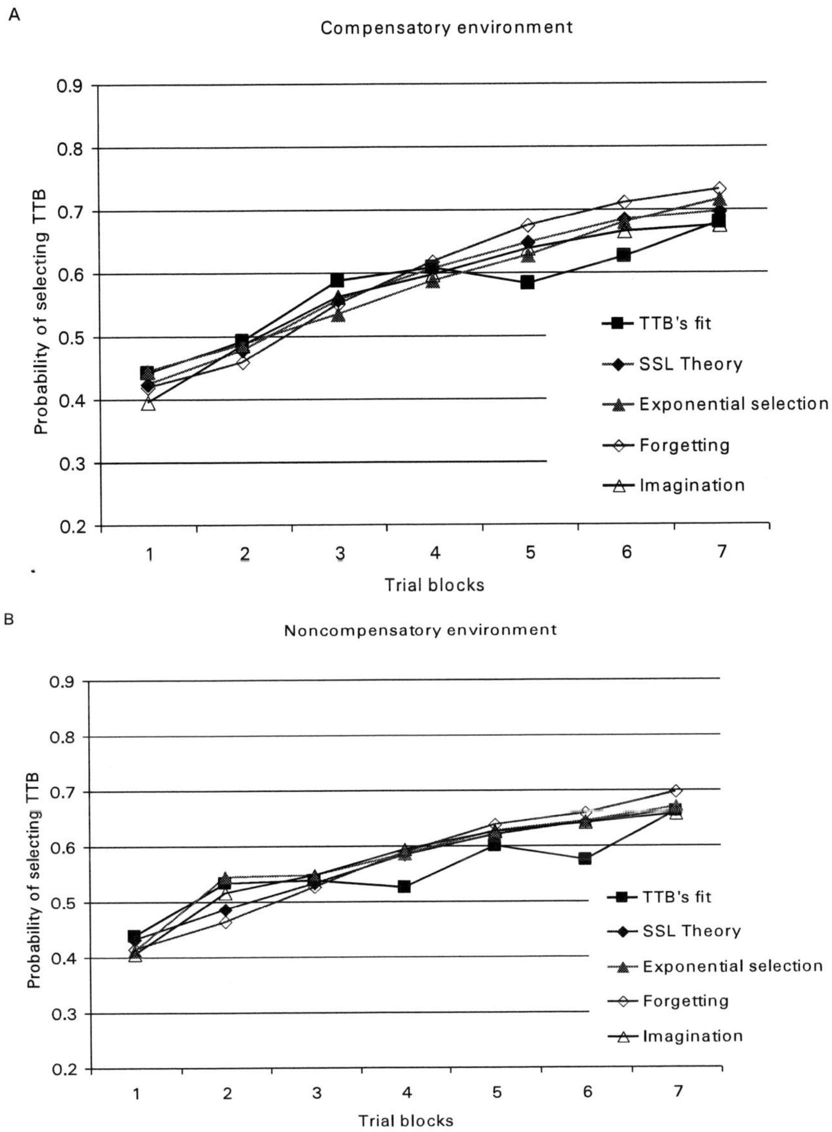


Figure 5.7. Predicted choices for Study 8

Additionally, the figure shows the predicted probability with which the best-performing strategy is selected by SSL and the three alternative learning models. SSL's prediction differed from the percentage of predicted choice by the best-performing strategy with a mean square error of 0.15%. The fit for the exponential selection model was MSE = 0.14%, for the forgetting model it was MSE = 0.29%, and for the imagination model it was MSE = 0.14%. At the beginning of the task with no feedback (first trial block), WADD predicted more choices than TTB, regardless of the environment. This again indicates an initial preference for WADD, similar to yet weaker than in Study 6. After the first trial block, this weak preference changed. For both environments the fit of WADD decreased in favor of an increasing fit of TTB, again supporting the prediction that the participants learned to select the best-performing strategy. In the last block, TTB predicted 68% of the choices in the compensatory environment and 66% of the choices in the noncompensatory environment when considering only items for which the two strategies make diverse predictions. Since the validities told to the participants differed from those of the item set used in the experiment, participants might have learned the validities of the item set for the strategies they used. However, a TTB strategy using the rank order of the validities of the item set predicted only 70% (67%) of all choices of the compensatory (noncompensatory) environment compared with TTB using the rank order of the validities told to the participants, which predicted 75% (74%) of all choices for the compensatory (noncompensatory) environment. A WADD strategy using the validities of the item set predicted 65% (66%) of all choices for the compensatory (noncompensatory) environment. Again, as strategies with the presented validities produced the best outcome, the usage of these validities rather than a learning of the actual validities of the item set can be assumed.

Analogously to Studies 6 and 7, each learning model was fitted separately to each individual's data (see Table 5.3). SSL captured the choices with an average probability of .75, with an average predicted probability of .76 for the compensatory environment and of .74 for the noncompensatory environment. When only considering whether the alternative that was most likely predicted by SSL was chosen by the participants, SSL could predict 82% of all choices. SSL obtained a good fit by taking the dynamics of the decision process into account. The average obtained initial preference parameter of $\beta_{TTB}$ = .43 for SSL reflects a slight preference for the selection of WADD at the beginning of the task. The average obtained application error parameter of $\varepsilon$ = .07 is only slightly larger in comparison to Study 6 and identical to that of Study 7, and for only four participants was a value above .20 obtained. Thus, an adequate set of strategies was assumed.

**Table 5.3. Optimized parameter values for Study 8**

| | **Learning model** | | | |
|---|---|---|---|---|
| | **SSL** | **Exponential selection model** | **Forgetting model** | **Imagination model** |
| Initial association $w$ | 11 ($SD$ = 9) | 6 ($SD$ = 8) | 14 ($SD$ = 8) | 9 ($SD$ = 8) |
| Initial preference $\beta_{TTB}$ | .43 ($SD$ = .28) | .40 ($SD$ = .31) | .42 ($SD$ = .26) | .40 ($SD$ = 0.29) |
| Application error $\varepsilon$ | .07 ($SD$ = .10) | .07 ($SD$ = .10) | .07 ($SD$ = .10) | .07 ($SD$ = .10) |
| Additional parameter | -- | $\mu$ = 2.3 ($SD$ = 3.2) | $\phi$ = 0.02 ($SD$ = 0.04) | $\delta$ = 0.54 ($SD$ = 0.45) |
| Predicted probability of choices | .751 | .756 | .753 | .752 |
| Sum of $G^2$ values | $G^2$ = 5069 | $G^2$ = 4963 ($\chi^2(40)$ = 105, $p$ = .001) | $G^2$ = 5034 ($\chi^2(40)$ = 34, $p$ = .72) | $G^2$ = 5037 ($\chi^2(40)$ = 31, $p$ = .84) |
| Median AIC | 125 | 125 | 127 | 126 |
| Participants with AIC improvement for more general model | -- | 40% ($p$ = .268) | 10% ($p$ = .001) | 20% ($p$ = .001) |

How well did SSL compete against the alternative learning models? SSL's estimated generalizability was better for the majority of participants when compared with the alternative models, although SSL did not significantly outperform the exponential selection model, since SSL reached a better AIC value for 60% of the participants ($p$ = .268 according to a sign test, for details see Table 5.3).

Again, the percentages of predicted choices by TTB and WADD were taken as an approximation of participants' strategy selection and were compared with the probability that SSL predicts the selection (see Figure 5.7). For both environments, the probability predicted by SSL for the best-performing strategy accurately matches the percentage of predicted choices by this strategy. The three alternative models did not obtain substantially better fits.

Identical with Studies 6 and 7, EBM was used to predict the inferences of the last two blocks on the basis of the preceding inferences excluding the first block. EBM's parameters were fitted separately to each individual's data using the $G^2$ measurement as a goodness-of-fit criterion. For the six attention weights, the optimized parameter values, in decreasing order of the cues according to their validity, were: $s_1$ = .28, $s_2$ = .33, $s_3$ = .85, $s_4$ = .35, $s_5$ = .21, and $s_6 = .52$ for the compensatory environment; and $s_1 = .07$, $s_2 = .12$, $s_3 = .65$, $s_4 = .65$, $s_5 = .53$, and $s_6 = .66$ for the noncompensatory environment. As in Studies 6 and 7, the attention weights did not correspond with the cue validities, and only to a small extent did cues with a higher validity have larger attention weight values.

EBM predicted the choices with an average probability of .64 for the compensatory environment and of .67 for the noncompensatory environment. In comparison, SSL predicted the choices of the last two blocks with an average probability of .79 (.75) for the compensatory (noncompensatory) environment. SSL was compared with EBM by determining which model had a better fit according to the $G^2$ measurement, disregarding the model's complexity. SSL had a better fit for all 40 participants. Thus, in Study 8, SSL clearly outperformed EBM in predicting participants' choices.

### 5.4.3. Discussion

Study 8 provides further support for the adaptive view of strategy selection. As in Studies 6 and 7, participants in Study 8 apparently learned to select the best-performing strategy. In both environments, the strategy initially selected was discarded in favor of TTB. However, the learning effect observed, measured by the payoff, was weaker than in the previous two studies. Apparently, the inference task is more difficult here. In Studies 6 and 7, participants could focus solely on the strategies' accuracy, which determined the strategies' performance, ignoring the number of cues they needed to look up. In Study 8, the strategies' performances depended on their accuracy and on their costs, namely, on the number of looked-up cues. Thus, participants had to trade off strategies' accuracy against their information search costs, making learning more complicated. Additionally, this trade-off produced costs: When deciding which strategy to select, all information had first to be acquired to compare TTB's and WADD's performances. Only after a preference in favor of TTB was developed could participants search for a smaller amount of information, which would then no longer allow them to see whether WADD would perform better. In contrast, in Studies 6 and 7, participants always had the possibility of acquiring additional information to check WADD's performance. Obviously, these differences make Study 8's inference task more difficult and impede the learning process.

Nevertheless, SSL again represents a good account of the observed learning process of strategy selection. SSL not only predicts that TTB will reach a higher fit in predicting participants' choices compared to WADD, it also provides a prediction of how the strategy selection process changes by learning. In this, it goes beyond a cost–benefit framework. As in the previous two studies, SSL outperformed the more general learning models in terms of their generalizability, although the difference to the exponential selection model was not significant. For a substantial proportion of participants, the exponential selection model reached an advantage in comparison to SSL, due to its ability to predict an accelerated initial learning process.

When comparing SSL with EBM, the former reached a better fit in predicting the choices for all participants. Moreover, SSL again made different predictions for incongruent and congruent items (where TTB and WADD lead to different or identical choices), consistent with the experimental results. EBM could predict these differences only to a small degree. In Study 8, EBM was least suitable when compared with SSL in describing participants' inferences.

The introduction of search costs emphasizes SSL's advantage as a reinforcement model of unsupervised learning. Although in Study 8, feedback was given on whether a decision was correct or incorrect, no information on whether the participants could have done better by searching for fewer cues was provided. SSL is suitable for such a situation, since this information is not required for a reinforcement model. Correct inferences based on less information simply provide greater reinforcement and can thus lead to a reduced information search if this search was sufficient for making good inferences.

## 5.5. Process Modeling

Do people select different strategies in different environments? Do they learn to select the strategy that performs best? How can we predict the learning process? These are the main questions asked in this section of performance prediction and guide the following discussion.

### 5.5.1. Strategies for Inferences

What strategies underlie people's inferences? Studies by Bröder (2000, 2003), Bröder and Schiffer (2003), Newell and Shanks (2003), Newell, Weston, and Shanks (2003), and Rieskamp and Hoffrage (1999, 2003) provide experimental evidence that TTB out-competes other strategies in predicting peoples' inferences when the costs of applying compensatory strategies are high or its application is cognitively demanding. In contrast, compensatory strategies are better in predicting inferences when information search is not costly and when integrating available information leads to a good performance. The results support this conclusion. In Study 6, information about cue values and cue validities was easily accessible, promoting the selection of compensatory strategies. Consistently, in the first trial block (without feedback), the compensatory strategy WADD was best at predicting participants' choices. This result is important as it indicates that in an unfamiliar inference situation, where people do not know strategies' performance and application costs can be neglected; people prefer to select compensatory strategies, presumably because they expect compensatory strategies to perform well. In fact, in a study on preferences (Chu & Spires, 2003) participants gave the highest ratings to WADD and relatively low ratings to a lexicographic heuristic when judging which of the several strategies would "choose the best alternative."

However, application costs can rarely be ignored. In Study 7, the application of a compensatory strategy required greater memory demands and participants had no initial preference for the compensatory strategy. Likewise, in Study 8 where explicit information acquisition costs were introduced, the initial preference for the compensatory strategy was less strong when compared with Study 6. From previous studies examining explicit information costs, one could have expected an initial preference for noncompensatory strategies in Study 8. Presumably such a preference was not observed because the search costs were relatively low: even in the compensatory environment condition with the largest search costs, the costs relative to the gain of a correct decision (above the gain expected from random choice) were approximately 8%. In contrast, Bröder (2000, Experiments 3 and 4) used relative information costs of 20% and Newell and Shanks (2003) used relative information costs of 40% in their high search costs conditions, so that the performance of WADD was even below that of random choice. This makes it less surprising that a preference for WADD was not observed in their studies, especially as participants received outcome feedback from the beginning of the task. However, here we did not, primarily, examine the factors, such as search costs, that influence initial strategy selection; instead we focused on the question of whether people adaptively change the strategies they select on the basis of feedback.

According to a cost-benefit framework, people trade strategies' costs against their benefits. The current three choice studies provide examples of how strategies' costs and accuracies favor different strategies. According to the accuracy-effort framework (Payne *et al.*, 1993), people anticipate the accuracy and effort of a strategy when selecting a strategy. Several task characteristics can influence this selection process. SSL incorporates this initial selection process by initial strategy preferences. Consistently in the three studies, we obtained different initial preferences. Whereas in Study 6 participants had an initial preference for applying WADD, this preference was less pronounced in Study 8 and was not observed in Study 7. In Study 6, this preference might be ascribed to low anticipated costs of information search and information processing. However, initial strategy preferences are not sufficient, since taking a learning process into account can explain how participants' preferences for strategies change and thereby can lead to better predictions of the inferences. We can assume that learning is the key feature for solving the strategy selection problem. In all three reported studies, feedback apparently led to the selection of the best-performing strategy. According to SSL, people produce an initial evaluation of strategies, which changes continuously through feedback when making inferences, leading to a dynamic strategy selection process. In this way, unsuccessful strategies become less likely to be selected. A conscious cost–benefit trade-off of strategy selection could mimic such a learning process. Therefore, this learning approach does not contradict the cost–benefit approach. On the contrary, this supplements it with a computational theory of how the strategy selection process could be accomplished.

However, the effect of feedback will naturally depend on the strategies' performances, in particular on strategies' differences in performance. This could explain why people often do not learn to integrate information according to a normative standard (Brehmer, 1980). If alternative strategies do not lead to substantially different performances, why should people change their inference strategy according to the normative standard? Likewise, Smith and Walker (1993, p. 245) argue that if people do not follow a normative standard, this can be "attributed to low opportunity cost of deviations from the rational prediction." In all the company choice studies, the opportunity costs of selecting the lower-performing strategy were high, explaining substantial learning effects. Only in the difficult inference situation of Study 8, in which participants needed to restrict their information search as early as possible to receive high payoffs, did weaker learning effects occur. Thus learning effects seem to depend on the gains of "optimal" behavior.

### 5.5.2. Strategy Selection Learning

Starting with work by Restle (1962), the idea that the outcome of learning is a strategy that specifies how the individual reacts to a specific situation has gained growing interest. Most of this work has been accumulated in the domain of probabilistic categorization and focuses on the question of how people adjust a parameter (such as a cut-off value, etc.) for the application of a single strategy (for a review see Kubovy & Healy, 1980). More recently, Busemeyer and Myung (1992) have extended this work by proposing a theory that additionally assumes a learning process of selection among strategies. For the domain of experimental games Stahl (1996, 2000) and Erev and Roth (2001) have proposed learning theories that assume a selection process among strategies. Strategy learning has also attracted attention in the domain of skill acquisition (e.g., Anderson, 1993; Newell & Simon, 1972; Taatgen & Wallach, 2002). According to the so-called "ACT-R theory" (Anderson, 1993; Anderson & Lebiere, 1998), the aim of reinforcement is the development of production rules. A heuristic like TTB can be represented as a sequence of production rules (Nellen, 2003), an idea similarly proposed by Johnson and Payne (1985) and Huber (1980).

SSL extends the idea that people learn to select between cognitive strategies in the domain of probabilistic inferences. SSL assumes that people have varying initial expectancies of the strategies they possess. Only when a strategy has been applied does it receive reinforcement, thereby changing its expectancies. Contrary to many recent learning theories (e.g., Erev & Roth, 1998; Camerer & Ho, 1999a; Rieskamp *et al.*, 2003), SSL does not assume that the object of reinforcement is observable action. Such direct reinforcement that is also claimed by EBM, appears unreasonable for an inference situation in which the number of cue configurations can be extremely large. Here lies SSL's advantage: generalizations to different cue configurations, in particular to new unobserved configurations, are easy to accomplish.

The three choice studies demonstrate that SSL can accurately describe the strategy selection process and that it outperforms all alternative learning models with respect to their estimated generalizability. The exponential strategy selection rule is able to increase the selection probability of the best-performing strategy, even for small expectancy differences. In particular, the exponential strategy selection rule is capable of predicting an accelerated learning process at the beginning of the inference situation. This possibility was useful in Studies 6 and 8, where the exponential selection model obtained a higher estimated generalizability in comparison to SSL for a substantial proportion of participants. However, when considering the participants of all three studies, the model's estimated generalizability was not larger and because the exponential selection model is the more complex model, SSL appears to be preferable. The second mechanism considered is 'a forgetting process' that leads to a decline of expectancies over time, which was not very useful in predicting the learning process. This result is surprising considering that many models incorporate such a process (e.g., Camerer & Ho, 1999a, b ; Erev & Roth, 1998; Estes, 1976). The assumption that people imagine the outcomes of unselected strategies, the third additional learning mechanism considered, does not seem to be essential for describing the learning process. Summing up the results, none of the three additional learning mechanisms appears necessary to describe the observed learning processes.

However, this conclusion needs to be limited to the situations studied; there are different inference situations where these mechanisms might be important. For instance, in a domain where strategies perform rather badly and produce losses, an exponential selection model that can deal with negative expectancies might be preferable to SSL. Moreover, in a dynamic environment where the performance of strategies changes, a forgetting process becomes adaptive as it gives lower weight to reinforcement received long ago. Likewise, a dynamic environment could also favor a process of imagination of unselected strategies, and would more quickly detect when alternative strategies outperform the preferred strategy.

A basic assumption of SSL is that people learn to select strategies from an already existing set. The decisions to include which strategies in this strategy set has to be carefully considered and should be based on prior empirical evidence. When a set is assumed that is too large or too small, this could complicate or inhibit strategy identification. TTB and WADD have been shown to work well for predicting individuals' probabilistic inferences (e.g., Bröder, 2000; Rieskamp & Hoffrage, 2003) and are reasonable candidates for the strategy set. They can be regarded as prototypes for compensatory and noncompensatory strategies; people might apply variations, but these would be captured with the proposed strategies. For instance, if a linear model is applied with somewhat different weights than the used validities, this variant would presumably come up with predictions similar to WADD. However, SSL could also be applied with different or larger strategy sets. Whether an enlarged set would also pay off in a substantially better fit is an empirical question. Moreover one could argue that people generate new strategies instead of selecting existing strategies. That WADD was already successful in predicting participants' choices in the first trial block of Studies 6 and 7 speaks against a generation process. Likewise, Rieskamp and Hoffrage (1999, 2003) showed that TTB is best in predicting people's choices under time pressure, again in a situation without feedback. These results indicate that people already possess – and do not generate – strategies that are at least similar to WADD and TTB.

### 5.5.3. Predicting Inferences

The focus here is on the strategy repertoire approach to inferences about companies. A computational model is proposed of how people select among cognitive strategies and we interpret the experimental results from a strategy-repertoire perspective. Although this perspective is supported by the experimental evidence, it needs further tests against alternative approaches.

In the domain of categorization, memory-based categorization processes have been proposed as an alternative approach to strategy-based categorization processes (for discussions see, for instance, Erickson & Kruschke, 1998; Nosofsky *et al.*, 1989; Nosofsky & Johansen, 2000; Smith *et al.*, 1998). Theorists have argued that for well-defined categories, strategies were more likely applied, whereas for ill-defined categories, memory-based inference processes would prevail (for a discussion and limitations of this view, see Nososfky, 1992). When applying this argument to the task of probabilistic inferences, we should find that people are more likely to rely on a memory-based inference process, since the correct choices for the inference's situation are ill-defined. For testing the strategy repertoire approach against the memory-based inference approach, we tested SSL against a modified version of the exemplar model (EBM) proposed by Juslin, Jones *et al.* (2003).

Did this comparison reveal a clear winner? When the results of all three studies are taken together with respect to the models' fit, the models' complexity, and the models' different predictions for items with diverse or identical predictions of the strategies; the answer is yes: SSL outperformed EBM substantially in predicting individuals' inferences. In particular, in Studies 6 and 8, SSL was better at predicting the inferences. Although EBM was also partly able to predict the inferences, when one considers EBM's complexity with six parameters that were fitted to predict the inference of only the last two blocks, SSL with only three parameters appears preferable. In particular, the results of Study 8 support a strategy approach, presumably for two reasons. First, the introduction of search costs leads participants to limit their information search and to consider strategies that enable inferences without much information. Second, when one assumes that the information search process includes a substantial amount of variability, this implies that even for identical pairs of alternatives; participants could have acquired different information, which could have distorted EBM's prediction. In contrast, the higher cognitive demands for applying cognitive strategies in Study 7 might have fostered a memory-based inference process as described by EBM.

### 5.5.4. Adaptive Strategy Selection

The main aim was not to show the superiority of the strategy repertoire approach in comparison to the exemplar-based approach. Instead this highlights that in many domains, researchers claim that cognition can be understood by assuming that people possess a repertoire of cognitive strategies. Following this assumption, the necessity to provide a computational theory of how people select strategies from their repertoire is evident. SSL is proposed as such a theory. The experimental results and the comparison of SSL with the exemplar model shows that SSL represents an adequate description of how people select strategies from their repertoire to make inferences about companies.

In inference situations where memorizing the situation and the correct responses is cognitively demanding, we can expect that SSL provides a better account than EBM for probabilistic inferences. However, it should be emphasized that these conclusions are restricted to the inference problem considered here. As Study 7 indicates, there might be inference situations where people could switch to a memory-based inference process. Thus, people might frequently rely on a memory-based inference process when the number of exemplars is relatively small, contrary to these choice studies here, as discussed earlier. Moreover, there are many situations where the assumption that people learn to select among cognitive strategies does not appear reasonable. Instead, people might simply learn direct actions in response to decision situations without comparing the situation to memorized situations. For instance, Erev and Roth (1998) demonstrated that simple reinforcement learning models appropriately describe how people learn to choose actions in constant-sum games. Thus, there is no single best model to predict people's inferences, but each model might work best in particular domains and one needs to "understand why different models are required to deal with different situations" (Estes, 1976, p. 39). It is an interesting enterprise to explore in which domain a particular theory is most appropriate.

What are the underlying cognitive mechanisms of people's inferences about states of the world? Among others, Gigerenzer *et al.* (1999) have argued that people possess a set of strategies for the judgment and decision-making problems they face. Based on the findings here, people's reasoning seems to be ruled by a flexible selection of cognitive strategies. Contrary to the single-purpose mechanism view, different strategies seem to be applied in different situations. Furthermore, people appear to select their strategies adaptively, such that strategies that perform well become more likely to be selected. Thus, the present three studies support the perspective of an "adaptive decision maker" who selects strategies according to the environment. SSL provides a computational theory that describes how this strategy selection process could take place. By following the traditional roots of psychology in learning, the strategy selection problem receives a promising answer and might also lead to a better understanding of financial decisions even beyond personal company evaluations.

*Chapter 6*

# GENERAL DISCUSSION

The work introduces a variety of new methods for the evaluation of financial behavior. In general this documents a new perspective for the understanding of financial behavior. The results illustrate a variety of strategies used in different financial domains. Financial strategies strongly differ within the domain. Spending behavior shows systematic variations over the way people pursue their individual goals. Saving behavior strongly differs in how commonly shared saving aims are followed up individually with regard to different self-control mechanisms. The evaluation of companies has a shared semantic basis and different investment strategies can be learned dependent on the incentive structure of the domain. In general, adaptive learning processes are assumed to account for the observed differences over and within decision domains.

First, we discuss this postulation of alternative models that are grounded in cognitive functioning. Second, the variability in financial behavior is striking and in concert with the financial personality aspect the behavior of the market is discussed. Third, the relation to economic theory is outlined in the conclusion.

## 6.1. CHARACTERIZING MENTAL PROCESSES

Diuturnal in cognitive sciences is the discussion on how mental mechanisms can be represented (Anderson, 1978; Pylyshyn, 1980). To which degree can mental mechanism be captured and illustrated? How can we assume that specific mental models are valid given that someone always can come up with an alternative explanation? This is one reason why fundamental questions, like the specificity versus universality of mental processes or to what degree the behavior is "learned", are continuously discussed and can not be solved conclusively. These questions are also of importance for financial decisions and for a foundation of cognitive finance. Spending, saving, and investing can thus, be evaluated under the paradigm of different mental processes. One distinction can be made between domain specificity and universality of cognitive mechanisms, another one between learning and individual variation in financial behavior. In both cases different explanations are provided for the observed processes of financial behavior.

### 6.1.1. Domain Specificity versus Universal Mechanisms

One could ask how far spending, saving, and investing patterns in the real world are a function of general cognitive mechanisms or whether they can only be understood in terms of specific environmental constraints and socially structured financial provisions. To proclaim a more domain specific approach here is mainly to derive the regularities within one domain as a basis for generalizations as a second step. This approach is rare in financial decisions. Thus, as we have seen in other domains of choices under uncertainty, there are specific behavioral tendencies in place which strongly depend upon the framing of the decision. Only if we take this decision frame seriously, can we derive a fundamental explanation of behavioral variation. Financial decisions like spending, saving, or investing can be seen as such a decision frame, which activates context specific behavior. This approach brings as a downside the limited predictability of behavior. On the one hand, if the research domain is too specific, a useful interpretation of the underlying processes appears arbitrary. On the other hand, if common grounds between domains are explored and regularities are found, this could bring a real advantage for the understanding of the usage of different strategies. Then general conditions for the behavioral variation into one or the other direction are revealed. This focus is illustrated in Chapter 4, where general mechanisms are sought for. If we can explain how domain specific behavior evolves, we can derive behavioral regularities from this end. SSL is an example of this. Also the observed peculiarities in spending and saving strategies must be understood from this angle of general mechanisms in domain specific strategy usage. Only if regularities and universal principles across domains are the focus of the research, is a domain specific approach useful to bring us closer to a discovery of the underlying mental processes and we are able to answer questions like how stable mental processes in cognitive finance are. Then it will become possible to reveal more general principles without only referring to experimental abstractions that always are in danger of being ecologically invalid.

### 6.1.2. Learning and Intra-/Interindividual Variation

The field of psychology breaks apart into two fields that stress differently the importance of nature versus nurture. In cognitive sciences the focus is more on general mechanisms although learning can play a huge part. How can we thus explain the variation in behavior? One possibility is to assume that we are equipped with a set of strategies and that we just learn to use one or the other strategy more frequently. This approach is supported by Tooby and Cosmides (1990b) stressing the advantage of a coexistence of different strategies in a population. Then individual adaptation is just part of a learning process. Alternatively, individual learning on its own; without referring to a set of universal psychological adaptations, accounts for the observed differences in financial behavior. In contrast, Wilson (1994) argues for a genetic polymorphism leading to individual variation. In this work we cannot discriminate between genetic or phenotypic adaptations and mainly stress the variation in observed strategies. If we knew to what degree their proportion changes over time and to what extent they are individually stable, we would have a better answer to this question. So far based on the observed strong differences, I only assume a reason for the variation which itself has to be further explored.

## 6.2. Financial Personality

A strongly neglected area in finances is the evaluation of individual differences. To some degree these variations have been documented here. They make the assumption plausible that there exists something like a financial personality analogous to other dimensions of personality.

### 6.2.1. Demand Variation

When regarding spending, saving, and investment strategies people show strong differences in their behavior. Possible reasons for this variation have been discussed. To take these variations as givens appears to be a reasonable conclusion. *De gustibus non est disputandum.* The term financial personality conceptualizes these behavioral variations to make them scientifically applicable. It stands for the differences in the financial demands people have.

Research regarding individual differences in financial behavior mainly regards general risk taking attitudes (Bromley & Curley, 1992; Dulebohn, 2002). For example women appear more risk averse in retirement allocations (Jianakoplos & Bernasek, 1998; Powell & Ansic, 1997) and men appear to be more prone to excessive trading in investment decisions due to overconfidence (Barber & Odean, 2001). My work here documents that risk attitude is only one facet of the individual differences in financial behavior and that the underlying financial motives might be much more diverse than assumed. Given that the decision space is restricted, only within the interaction of suitable products can these demands sufficiently be elaborated.

### 6.2.2. Tailored Products

If heuristics and biases are taken seriously, then accordingly suitable products can be demanded. A first development into this direction was made by Thaler and colleagues (Benartzi & Thaler, 2002; Thaler, 1994; Thaler & Benartzi, 2004; Sunstein & Thaler, 2003; Thaler & Sunstein, 2003). Their "libertarian paternalism" agenda shows examples of how individual behavior can be improved. The work presented here goes beyond a simple manipulation of reference points or default levels and asks for the underlying cognitive mechanisms for providing a better understanding. By tailoring these mechanisms this could lead to the development of better products in general, as well on an individual level. In a similar vein, Laibson *et al.* (1998) argue about easing penalties on early withdrawals from saving plans (compare Farkas & Johnson, 1997), for an acknowledgment of individual differences for giving up control. The general overestimation by economists of peoples' understanding of their personal financial situation, as well as, the misalignment between intention and action demand more tailored products. Here the individual perspective with support mechanisms and commitment features, including illiquid assets, helps to develop self-control devices in line with cognitive mechanisms which are also psychologically appealing.

From a service perspective, behavioral variations can directly serve to improve saving, spending, and investment tools. Currently the huge variation in financial products on the global market is mainly based on cultural and regional differences, but not oriented to the different demands within a local market. Product engineering is a common practice in most large industries, where for example sound, electronic devices, etc. are adjusted to the demands of the customer. It is surprising that similar research activities are not observed in financial industries.

## 6.3. Economic Evaluation

Economists always have known that strong rationality assumptions are incorrect for individual agents, but assumed that rational models still lead to good aggregates of economic behavior. However, this assumption has been increasingly thrown into doubt and many economic phenomena may be fundamentally psychological in origin. Moreover, research in judgment and decision making has developed theories that successfully connect with analysis in economics to produce valid behavioral models. Over the last years, economic theorists increasingly became aware of the empirical shortcomings that can be seen as a crisis in economics that has to be solved. How a shift will look like is difficult to predict. Weber and Camerer (2006, pp. 187-188) see the task of behavioral research as follows:

"Importantly, most behavioral economists have the goal, not of developing an alternative to economic theory and methods, although instead to incorporate new assumptions and methods into mainstream economic research. Thus, the goal of behavioral economists is not to develop a 'behavioral economic theory' but instead to improve economic theory so that it is also 'behavioral'."

This asks for a simple expansion of the standard economic model without a paradigm shift.

### 6.3.1. Gains and Losses

If behavioral results are simply seen as 'an add on' to the standard economic model, the development of new theories is bounded by existing assumptions. But from a standard research theory perspective (Popper, 1934), only the same acceptance of new models fecundate the research progress.

The goal of informing and developing economic theory has to be taken seriously. The development of new methods for the understanding of economic behavior can be seen as a huge advantage of behavioral research. How the generated results can be incorporated into economic theory is difficult to say. If the standard model can cope with a strong inflow of contradicting evidence this would speak for a strong theory. Important is that new methods generate a better understanding of the problem. If heterogeneity, i.e., variation over individuals, is informative for the general understanding of the phenomenon, these results cannot be neglected. An example in standard economic research for individual variation comes from the stock market where noise traders, as agents with a specific behavioral characteristic, are assumed to form the overall market behavior (DeLong *et al.*, 1990; Shleifer & Summers, 1990).

Behavioral observations will in any case influence theory developments in the future. A common scientific understanding (Ockham's Razor) is that if models just increase in complexity, nothing much is gained and fundamental changes have to take place.

## 6.3.2. Future Perspectives

The opening of the field of finance for behavioral questions provides a huge potential and clearly asks for necessary developments. Three points appear important for the future. First, finance theory will be able to acknowledge empirical findings in its theoretical development. Second, it provides the opportunity for interdisciplinary research. And third, a behaviorally grounded decision model could facilitate knowledge transfer to practical questions in finance.

### *Empirical Foundation*

The incorporation of behavioral results could strengthen the economic model and its acceptance as a core research discipline. This must be a sensible process in order not to loose ground to informality. It is not useful to give up the strong homogeneity of finance theory with its advantage of consistency. Only if behavioral results can improve the understanding of basic questions in finance research, does a change appear demandable. Current movements in behavioral analysis try to achieve just this and can be seen as a huge chance for bringing finance theory back to the world. If the understanding to use different strategies for financial decisions is fundamental for the prediction of behavior, taking these results into account cannot be avoided. This use of different financial strategies can result in naturally occurring observations of behavioral sophistication and computational limitations alike. Analogously, cognitive correlates can be provided systematically in the future, an empirical but also cognitively sound theory of financial behavior becomes possible.

### *Interdisciplinarity*

Combining theory and methods from different disciplines is often demanded to improve the research progress. Historically, this often led to new approaches with a highly reputative research practice. A recent convincing example is the merging of chemistry and biology into cell genetics.

The linkage between economics and other fields like anthropology, psychology, and neurology is a radical prospect. If this leads to new advances in the overlap between social and natural sciences, I think more can be gained than lost. Recent examples show that this exchange already led to promising studies in anthropology (i.e., Henrich et al., 2001), in psychology (i.e., Hertwig & Ortmann, 2001), and neurology (i.e., Glimcher & Rustichini, 2004).

The development of new ideas appears to be crucial for the improvement of economic theory. The recruiting of other disciplines appears to be a useful approach.

### *Practical Importance*

Research can always be measured by its practical applicability and its value for improving issues of societal importance. If financial theory is based on actual observable behavior and underlying cognitive functioning, a transfer to everyday solutions becomes much easier to achieve.

A couple of research possibilities are introduced here for behavioral specifics in different financial domains. Direct examples of applications are provided or can easily be derived. Segmentation, product development, and performance prediction are just a few examples. Many other applications can be developed under this framework and a broad area opens up for practical derivations.

Key areas of interest with practical implications is that the actual decision process matters; where the way decisions are reached and the variables influencing this decision process are of significant importance. Also, the individual variation of behavior can be captured and used for practical applications. Further on, if mental accounting is so common, even in well organized organizations, could it not just be rational to keep apart different categories and structure our environment accordingly?

Cognitive processes play the key role in every decision. A better understanding and modeling of these processes can improve performance in many ways. Thus, the acknowledgment of cognitive finance and of respective differences in financial personality cannot only provide strong economic advantages but societal improvements in general.

# ACKNOWLEDGEMENTS

My projects with Decision Technology and discussions within this team were useful to sharpen and develop the different ideas presented here. Thanks to Henry Stott, Greg Davies, and Richard Lewis for their useful inspirations. I also would like to thank Jörg Rieskamp for his support and his contributions regarding the specification of the learning models in Chapter 5. This work taught me much and supported a meaningful and important theory development for me.

Besides this, the publication reviews for the different parts of this work are highly appreciated and many thanks to the reviewers for their detailed responses. The work of Chapter 2 resulted in an article published in the Journal of Retailing and Consumer Services (Otto *et al.* 2009). Chapter 3 led to a publication in the Global Business and Economics Review special edition on "Behavioral Economics, Business Decision-Making, and Applied Policy Analysis" (Otto *et al.*, 2007). The work presented in Chapter 5 contributed to the publication in the Journal of Experimental Psychology: General on the "Strategy Selection Learning Theory" (Rieskamp & Otto, 2006).

The ESRC is thanked for their flexible financial support and assistance for this thesis at the University College London. And finally a big thanks to my supervisors: Nick Chater who provided me with good ideas and important feedback throughout the process, and David Shanks for giving useful comments in the final stages of getting this project published.

# REFERENCES


Aaker, J. L. (1997). Dimensions of brand personality. *Journal of Marketing Research, 34*(3), 347-356.

Abelson, R. P., & Levi, A. (1985). Decision making and decision theory. In G. Lindzey & E. Aronson (Eds.), *Handbook of social psychology: Theory and method* (Vol. 1, pp. 231-309). New York: Erlbaum.

Allais, M., (1953). Le comportement de l'homme rationnel devant le risque: Critique des postulats et axiomes de l'école Américaine. *Econometrica, 21*, 503-546.

Ainslie, G. (1975). Specious reward: A behavioral theory of impulsiveness and impulse control. *Psychological Bulletin, 82*(4), 463-496.

Ainslie, A., & Rossi, P. E. (1998). Similarities in choice behaviour across product categories. *Marketing Science, 17*(2), 91-106.

Akaike, H. (1973). Information theory as an extension of the maximum likelihood principle. In B. N. Petrov & F. Csaki (Eds.), *Proceedings of the Second International Symposium on Information Theory* (pp. 267-281). Budapest: Akademiai Kiado.

Ameriks, J., Caplin, A., & Leahy, J. (2003). Wealth accumulation and the propensity to plan. *The Quarterly Journal of Economics, 118*(3), 1007-1048.

Anderson, J. R. (1978). Arguments concerning representations for mental imagery. *Psychological Review, 85*(4), 249-277.

Anderson, J. R. (1991). Is human cognition adaptive? *Behavioral and Brain Sciences, 14*, 471-517.

Anderson, J. R. (1993). *Rules of the mind.* Hillsdale, NJ: Erlbaum.

Anderson, J. R., & Lebiere, C. (1998). *The atomic components of thought.* Mahwah, NJ: Erlbaum.

Ando, A., & Modigliani, F. (1963). The life cycle hypothesis of saving: Aggregate implications and tests. *The American Economic Review, 53*(1), 55-84.

Angeletos, G.-M., Laibson, D., Repetto, A., Tobacman, J., & Weinberg, S. (2001). The hyperbolic consumption model: Calibration, simulation, and empirical evaluation. *Journal of Economic Perspectives, 15*(3), 47-68.

Ashby, F. G., & Maddox, W. T. (1992). Complex decision rules in categorization: Contrasting novice and experienced performance. *Journal of Experimental Psychology: Human Perception and Performance, 18*, 50-71.

Ashby, F. G., & Maddox, W. T. (1993). Relations between prototype, exemplar, and decision bound models of categorization. *Journal of Mathematical Psychology, 37*, 372-400.

Axelrod, R., & Hamilton, W. D. (1981). The evolution of cooperation. *Science, 211*(4489), 1390-1396.

Ball, C. T., Langholtz, H. J., Auble, J., & Sopchak, B. (1998). Resource-allocation strategies: A verbal protocol analysis. *Organizational Behavior and Human Decision Processes, 76*, 70-88.

Balzer, W. K., Doherty, M. E., & O'Connor, R. (1989). Effects of cognitive feedback on performance. *Psychological Bulletin, 106*, 410-433.

Bandura, A. (1977). Self-efficacy: Towards a unifying theory of behavioral change. *Psychological Review, 84*(2), 191-215.

Bandura, A., & Schunk, D. H. (1981). Cultivating competence, self-efficacy, and intrinsic interest through proximal self-motivation. *Journal of Personality and Social Psychology, 41*(3), 587-598.

Barber, B. M., & Odean, T. (2001). Boys will be boys: Gender, overconfidence, and common stock investment. *The Quarterly Journal of Economics, 116*(1), 261-292.

Baumeister, R. F. (2002). Yielding to temptation: Self-control failure, impulsive purchasing, and consumer behavior. *Journal of Consumer Research, 28*(March), 670-676.

Baumeister, R. F., & Heatherton, T. F. (1996). Self-regulation failure: An overview. *Psychological Inquiry, 7*(1), 1-15.

Beach, L. R., & Mitchell, T. R. (1978). A contingency model for the selection of decision strategies. *Academy of Management Review, 3,* 439-449.

Becker, G. S., & Murphy, K. M. (1988). A theory of rational addiction. *The Journal of Political Economy, 96*(4), 675-700.

Benartzi, S., & Thaler, R. H. (2001). Naive diversification strategies in defined contribution saving plans. *The American Economic Review, 91*(1), 79-98.

Benartzi, S., & Thaler, R. H. (2002). How much is investor autonomy worth? *Journal of Finance, 57*(4), 1593-1616.

Benhabib, J., & Bisin, A. (2005). Modeling internal commitment mechanisms and self-control: A neuroeconomics approach to consumption-saving decisions. *Games and Economic Behavior,* 52(2), 460-492.

Bernheim, B. D. (1995). Do households appreciate their financial vulnerabilities? An analysis of actions, perceptions, and public policy. *Tax policy for economic growth in the 1990s* (pp. 1-30). Washington, DC: American Council for Capital Formation.

Bernheim, B. D., & Rangel, A. (2004). Addiction and cue-triggered decision processes. *The American Economic Review, 94*(5), 1558-1590.

Bernheim, B. D., Skinner, J., & Weinberg, S. (2001). What accounts for the variation in retirement wealth among U.S. households. *The American Economic Review, 91*(4), 832-857.

Bernoulli, D. (1738). Speciman theoriae novae de mensura sortis [Exposition of a new theory on the measurement of risk]. *Commentarii Academiae Scientiatum Imperalas Petropolitanae, 5*, 175-192.

Bertaut, C. C., & Haliassos, M. (2001). Debt revolvers for self control. *University of Cyprus Working Paper, 0208.*

Birnbaum, M. H. (2000). *Psychological experiments on the internet.* London: Academic Press.

Börgers, T., & Sarin, R. (1997). Learning through reinforcement and replicator dynamics. *Journal of Economic Theory, 77*, 1-14.

Bozdogan, H. (2000). Akaike's information criterion and recent developments in information complexity. *Journal of Mathematical Psychology, 44*, 62-91.

Brehmer, B. (1980). In one word: Not from experience. *Acta Psychologica, 45*, 223-241.

Bröder, A. (2000). Assessing the empirical validity of the "Take-The-Best" Heuristic as a model of human probabilistic inference. *Journal of Experimental Psychology: Learning, Memory, and Cognition, 26*(5), 1332-1346.

Bröder, A. (2003). Decision making with the "adaptive toolbox": Influence of environmental structure, intelligence, and working memory load. *Journal of Experimental Psychology: Learning, Memory, and Cognition, 29*, 611-625.

Bröder, A., & Schiffer, S. (2003). "Take The Best" versus simultaneous feature matching: Probabilistic inferences from memory and effects of representation format. *Journal of Experimental Psychology: General, 132*, 277-293.

Bromley, P., & Curley, S. P. (1992). Individual differences in risk taking. In J. F. Yates (Ed.), *Risk-taking behavior* (pp. 87-132). New York: Wiley.

Brown, G. W. (1951). Iterative solutions of games by fictitious play. In T. C. Koopmans (Ed.), *Activity analysis of production and allocation* (pp. 374-376). New York: Wiley.

Brown, N. R. (1995). Estimation strategies and the judgment of event frequency. *Journal of Experimental Psychology: Learning, Memory, and Cognition, 21*, 1539-1553.

Brown, N. R., Cui, X., & Gordon, R. D. (2002). Estimating national populations: Cross-cultural differences and availability effects. *Applied Cognitive Psychology, 16*, 811-827.

Browne, M. W. (2000). Cross-validation methods. *Journal of Mathematical Psychology, 44*, 108-132.

Bucklin, R. E., & Gupta, S. (1992). Brand choice, purchase incidence, and segmentation: An integrated modeling approach. *Journal of Marketing Research, 29*(May), 201-215.

Burnham, K. P., & Anderson, D. R. (1998). *Model selection and multimodel inference*. New York: Springer.

Burns, B. D. (2004). Heuristics as beliefs and as behaviors: The adaptiveness of the "hot hand". *Cognitive Psychology, 48*(3), 295-331.

Busemeyer, J. R. (1993). Violations of the speed-accuracy tradeoff relation: Decreases in decision accuracy with increases in decision time. In O. Svenson & A. J. Maule (Eds.), *Time pressure and stress in human judgment and decision making* (pp. 181-193). New York: Plenum Press.

Busemeyer, J. R., & Myung, I. J. (1992). An adaptive approach to human decision making: Learning theory, decision theory, and human performance. *Journal of Experimental Psychology: General, 121*, 177-194.

Busemeyer, J. R., & Stout, J. C. (2002). A contribution of cognitive decision models to clinical assessment: Decomposing performance on the Bechara gambling task. *Psychological Assessment, 14*, 253-262.

Bush, R. R., & Mosteller, F. (1955). *Stochastic models of learning*. New York: Wiley.

Camerer, C., & Ho, T.-H. (1999a). Experienced-weighted attraction learning in games: Estimates from weak-link games. In D. V. Budescu & I. Erev (Eds.), *Games and human behavior: Essays in honor of Amnon Rapoport* (pp. 31-51). Mahwah, NJ: Erlbaum.

Camerer, C., & Ho, T.-H. (1999b). Experienced-weighted attraction learning in normal form games. *Econometrica, 67*(4), 827-874.

Campbell, J. Y., & Mankiw, N. G. (1990). Permanent income, current income, and consumption. *Journal of Business and Economic Statistics, 8*(3), 265-279.

Carrillo, J. D., & Mariotti, T. (2000). Strategic ignorance as a self-disciplining device. *The Review of Economic Studies, 67*(3), 529-544.

Carroll, C. D. (1997). Buffer-stock saving and the life cycle/permanent income hypothesis. *The Quarterly Journal of Economics, 112*(1), 1-55.

Cattell, R. B. (1965). *The scientific study of personality*. Baltimore: Penguin Books.

Cattell, R.B. (1966). The scree test for the number of factors. *Multivariate Behavioral Research, 1*, 245-276.

Chater, N. (2000). How smart can simple heuristics be? *Behavioral and Brain Science, 23*(5), 745-746.

Cheung, Y.-W., & Friedman, D. (1997). Individual learning in normal form games: Some laboratory results. *Games and Economic Behavior, 19*, 46-76.

Chlopan, B. E., McCain, M. L., Carbonell, J. L., & Hagen, R. L. (1985). Empathy: Review of available measures. *Journal of Personality and Social Psychology, 48*(3), 635-653.

Choi, J. J., Laibson, D., Madrian, B. C., & Metrick, A. (2002). Defined contribution pensions: plan rules, participant choices, and the path of least resistance. *Tax Policy and the Economy, 16*, 67-113.

Christensen-Szalanski, J. J. (1978). Problem solving strategies: A selection mechanism, some implications, and some data. *Organizational Behavior and Human Performance, 22*, 307-323.

Chu, P. C., & Spires, E. E. (2003). Perception of accuracy and effort of decision strategies. *Organizational Behavior and Human Decision Processes, 91*, 203-214.

Connolly, T. & Gilani, N. (1982). Information search in judgment tasks: A regression model and some preliminary findings. *Organizational Behavior and Human Performance, 30*, 330-350.

Connolly, T., & Wholey, D. R. (1988). Information mispurchase in judgment tasks: A task-driven causal mechanism. *Organizational Behavior and Human Decision Processes, 42*, 75-87.

Cooksey, R. W. (1996). The methodology of social judgment theory. *Thinking and Reasoning, 2*, 141-173.

Coombs, C. H. (1975). Portfolio theory and the measurement of risk. In M. F. Kaplan & S. Schwartz (Eds.), *Human judgment and decision* (pp. 63-68). New York: Academic Press.

Cordes, J. J. (1990). Socio-economic perspectives on household saving behavior. *The Journal of Behavioral Economics, 19*(3), 273-284.

Cosmides, L. (1989). Evolutionary psychology and the generation of culture: A computational theory of social exchange. *Ethology and Sociobiology, 10*(1-3), 51-97.

Coughlan, A. T. (1985). Competition and cooperation in marketing channel choice: Theory and application. *Marketing Science, 4*(2), 110-129.

Covey, J. A., & Lovie, A. D. (1998). Information selection and utilization in hypothesis testing: A comparison of process-tracing and structural analysis techniques. *Organizational Behavior and Human Decision Processes, 75*(1), 56-74.

Coyle, T. R., Read, L. E., Gaultney, J. F., & Bjorklund, D. F. (1998). Giftedness and variability in strategic processing in a multitrial memory task: Evidence for stability in gifted cognition. *Learning and Individual Differences, 10(4)*, 273-290.

Creyer, E. H., Bettman, J. R., & Payne, J. W. (1990). The impact of accuracy and effort feedback and goals on adaptive decision behavior. *Journal of Behavioral Decision Making, 3*, 1-16.

Dawes, R. M., & Corrigan, B. (1974). Linear models in decision making. *Psychological Bulletin, 81*, 95-106.

DeLong, J. B., Shleifer, A., Summers, L. H., & Waldmann, R. J. (1990). Positive feedback investment strategies and destabilizing rational speculation. *Journal of Finance, 45*(2), 379-395.

Dewan, R., Freimer, M., & Seidmann, A. (2000). Organizing distribution channels for information goods on the internet. *Management Science, 46*(4), 483-495.

Dougherty, M. R. P., Gettys, C. F., & Ogden, E. E. (1999). MINERVA-DM: A memory process model for judgments of likelihood. *Psychological Review, 106*(1), 180-209.

Dretske, F. (1993). Mental events as structuring causes of behavior. In J. Heil & A. Mele (Eds.), *Mental causation* (pp. 121-136). New York: Oxford University Press.

Dreze, J. H., & Modigliani, F. (1972). Consumption decisions under uncertainty. *Journal of Economic Theory, 5*(3), 308-335.

Dulebohn, J. H. (2002). An investigation of the determinants of investment risk behavior in employer-sponsored retirement plans. *Journal of Management, 28*(1), 3-26.

Edwards, W. (1954). The theory of decision making. *Psychological Bulletin, 51*, 380-417.

Einhorn, H. J. (1970). The use of nonlinear, noncompensatory models in decision making. *Psychological Bulletin, 73*, 221-230.

Einhorn, H. J. (1971). Use of nonlinear, noncompensatory models as a function of task amount of information. *Organizational Behavior and Human Performance, 6*, 1-27.

Eisenberg, P., & Becker, C. A. (1982). Semantic context effects in visual word recognition, sentence processing, and reading: Evidence for semantic strategies. *Journal of Experimental Psychology: Human Perception and Performance, 8*, 739-756.

Elster, J. (1979). *Ulysses and the sirens.* Cambridge: Cambridge University Press.

Epstein, S. (1977). Traits are alive and well. In D. Magnusson & N. S. Elder (Eds.), *Personality at the crossroad* (pp. 83-98). Hilsdale, NJ: Lawrence Erlbaum Associates.

Erev, I. (1998). Signal detection by human observers: A cutoff reinforcement learning model of categorization decisions under uncertainty. *Psychological Review, 105*, 280-298.

Erev, I., & Roth, A. E. (1998). Predicting how people play games: Reinforcement learning in experimental games with unique, mixed strategy equlibria. *The American Economic Review, 88*, 848-881.

Erev, I., & Roth, A. E. (2001). Simple reinforcement learning models and reciprocation in the prisoner's dilemma game. In G. Gigerenzer & R. Selten (Eds.), *Bounded rationality: The adaptive toolbox* (pp. 215-231). Cambridge, MA: MIT Press.

Erickson, M. A., & Kruschke, J. K. (1998). Rules and exemplars in category learning. *Journal of Experimental Psychology: General, 127*, 107-140.

Ericsson, K. A., & Lehmann, A. C. (1996). Expert and exceptional performance: Evidence of maximal adaptation to task constraints. *Annual Review of Psychology, 47,* 273-305.

Eriksson, K., & Vaghult, A. L. (2000). Customer retention, purchasing behavior, and relationship substance in professional services. *Industrial Marketing Management, 29*, 363-372.

Estes, W. K. (1950). Towards a statistical theory of learning. *Psychological Review, 57*, 94-107.

Estes, W. K. (1976). The cognitive side of probability learning. *Psychological Review, 83*, 37-64.

Estes, W. K., Campbell, J. A., Hatsopoulos, N., & Hurwitz, J. B. (1989). Base-rate effects in category learning: A comparison of parallel network and memory storage-retrieval models. *Journal of Experimental Psychology: Learning, Memory, and Cognition, 15*, 556-571.

Evans, J. S. T. (2003). In two minds: dual-process accounts of reasoning. *Trends in Cognitive Sciences, 7*(10), 454-459.

Eysenck, H. J., & Eysenck, M. W. (1985). *Personality and individual differences: A natural sciences approach.* New York: London.

Farkas, S., & Johnson, J. (1997). *Miles to go: A status report on American' plans for retirement.* New York: Public Agenda.

Fechner, G. T. (1860). *Elemente der Psychophysik [Elements of psychphysics].* Leipzig: Breitkopf und Härtel.

Fishbein, M., & Ajzen, I. (1975). *Belief, attitude, intention, and behavior.* Reading, MA: Addison-Wesley.

Fiske, A. P. (1992). The four elementary forms of sociality: Framework for a unified theory of social relations. *Psychological Review, 99*(4), 689-723.

Ford, J. K., Schmitt, N., Schechtman, S. L., Hults, B. M., & Doherty, M. L. (1989). Process tracing methods: Contributions, problems, and neglected research questions. *Organizational Behavior and Human Decision Processes, 43*, 75-117.

Fox, C. R., & Tversky, A. (1998). A belief-based account of decision under uncertainty. *Management Science, 44*(7), 879-895.

Freud, S. (1911). Formulations on the two principles of mental functioning. In J. Strachey & A. Freud (Eds.), *The standard edition of the complete psychological works of Sigmund Freud* (Vol. 12, pp. 213-226). London: Hogarth.

Friedman, M. (1957). *A theory of the consumption function.* Princeton, NJ: Princeton University Press.

Friedman, M., & Savage, L. J. (1948). The utility analysis of choices involving risk. *Journal of Political Economy, 56*(4), 279-304.

Geeroms, N., Vermeir, I., Kenhove, P. V., & Hendrickx, H. (2005). A taxonomy of consumer motives through preferred brand personality: Empirical findings for 11 countries. *Ghent University Belgium Working Paper Series, 05/346.*

Gelman, S. A. (1988). The development of induction within natural kind and artifact categories. *Cognitive Psychology, 20*(1), 65-95.

Gigerenzer, G. & Goldstein, D. G. (1996). Reasoning the fast and frugal way: Models of bounded rationality. *Psychological Review, 103*(4), 650-669.

Gigerenzer, G., & Goldstein, D. G. (1999). Betting on one good reason: The take the best heuristic. In G. Gigerenzer, P. M. Todd, & the ABC Research Group (Eds.), *Simple heuristics that make us smart* (pp. 75-95). New York: Oxford University Press.

Gigerenzer, G., Todd, P. M., & the ABC Research Group (1999). *Simple heuristics that make us smart*. New York: Oxford University Press.

Gilovich, T., Griffin, D., & Kahneman, D. (2002). *Heuristics and biases: The psychology of intuitive judgment*. New York: Cambridge University Press.

Ginossar, Z., & Trope, Y. (1987). Problem solving in judgment under uncertainty. *Journal of Personality and Social Psychology, 52*, 464-474.

Glimcher, P. W., & Rustichini, A. (2004). Neuroeconomics: The consilience of brain and decision. *Science, 306*(5695), 447-452.

Gluck, M. A., & Bower, G. H. (1988). From conditioning to category learning: An adaptive network model. *Journal of Experimental Psychology: General, 117*(3), 227-247.

Godin, S. (1999). *Permission marketing: Turning strangers into friends and friends into customers*. New York: Simon and Schuster.

Gollwitzer, P. M. (1999). Implementation intentions. *American Psychologist, 54*(7), 493-503.

Goodhardt, G. J., Ehrenberg, A. S. C., & Chatfield, C. (1984). The dirichlet: A comprehensive model of buying behavior. *Journal of the Royal Statistical Society Series (A-Statistics in Society), 147*, 621-655.

Goodwin, C. (1991). Privacy: Recognition of a consumer right. *Journal of Public Policy and Marketing, 12*(1), 106-119.

Gould, S. J. (1997). The use of psychographics by advertising agencies: An issue of value and knowledge. In L. R. Kahle & L. Chiagouris (Eds.), *Values, lifestyles, and psychographics* (pp. 217-229). New Jersey: LEA.

Gourville, J. T. (1998). Pennies-a-day: The effect of temporal reframing on transaction evaluation. *Journal of Consumer Research, 24*(4), 395-408.

Gourville, J. T., & Soman, D. (1998). Payment depreciation: The behavioral effects of temporally separating payments from consumption. *Journal of Consumer Research, 25*(2), 160-174.

Griffiths, T., & Steyvers, M. (2004). Finding scientific topics. *Proceedings of the National Academy of Sciences, 101*(suppl.1), 5228-5235.

Groenland, E. A. G., Bloem, J. G., & Kuylen, A. A. A. (1996). Prototypicality and structure of the saving concept for customers. *Journal of Economic Psychology, 17*, 691-708.

Gross, D. B., & Souleles, N. S. (2002). Do liquidity constraints and interest rates matter for consumer behavior? Evidence from credit card data. *The Quarterly Journal of Economics, 117*, 149-185.

Gul, F., & Pesendorfer, W. (2001). Temptation and self-control. *Econometrica, 69*(6), 1403-1435.

Gul, F., & Pesendorfer, W. (2004). Self-control and the theory of consumption. *Econometrica, 72*(1), 119-158.

Hakansson, N. H. (1970). Optimal investment and consumption strategies under risk for a class of utility functions. *Econometrica, 38*(5), 587-607.

Haliassos, M., & Reiter, M. (2006). Credit card debt puzzles. *CFS Working Paper, 2005/26.*

Hammond, K. R. (1955). Probabilistic functioning and the clinical method. *Psychological Review, 62*, 255-262.

Hammond, K. R., & Summers, D. A. (1972). Cognitive control. *Psychological Review, 79*, 58-67.

Harley, C. B. (1981). Learning the evolutionary stable strategy. *Journal of Thoeretical Biology, 89*, 611-633.

Harris, C., & Laibson, D. (2001). Dynamic choices of hyperbolic customers. *Econometrica, 69*(4), 935-957.

Hartmann, T. (1985). A concept-specific semantic differential for the rating of German 1st and 2nd names. *Journal of Social Psychology, 125*(6), 787-788.

Heath, C., & Soll, J. B. (1996). Mental budgeting and consumer decisions. *Journal of Consumer Research, 23*(1), 40-52.

Heise, D. R. (1970). The semantic differential and attitude research. In G. F. Summers (Ed.), *Attitude measurement* (pp. 235-253). Chicago: Rand McNally.

Henrich, J., Boyd, R., Bowles, S., Camerer, C., Fehr, E., Gintis, H., & McElreath, R. (2001). In search of Homo economicus: Behavioral experiments in 15 small-scale societies. *The American Economic Review, 91*(2), 73-78.

Hertwig, R., & Ortmann, A. (2001). Experimental practices in economics: A methodological challenge for psychologists? *Behavioral and Brain Sciences, 24*(3), 383-451.

Hintzman, D. L. (1988). Judgment of frequency and recognition memory in a multiple-trace memory model. *Psychological Review, 95*, 528-551.

Hirschman, E. C. (1984). Experience seeking: A subjectivist perspective of consumption. *Journal of Business Research, 12*(1), 115-136.

Hirschman, E. C., & Holbrook, M. B. (1982). Hedonic consumption: Emerging concepts, methods and propositions. *Journal of Marketing, 46*(3), 92-101.

Hoch, S., & Loewenstein, G. F. (1991). Time-inconsistent preferences and consumer self-control. *Journal of Consumer Research, 17*(4), 492-507.

Holbrook, M. B., & Hirschman, E. C. (1982). The experiential aspects of consumption: Consumer fantasies, feelings, and fun. *Journal of Consumer Research, 9*(2), 132-140.

Homer (900-600 B.C). *The Odyssey*. [online translation by Samuel Butler: http://classics.mit.edu/homer/odyssey.html].

Horioka, C. Y., & Watanabe, W. (1997). Why do people save? A micro-analysis of motives for household saving in Japan. *The Economic Journal, 107*(May), 537-552.

Hsu, S. H., Chuang, M. C., & Chang, C. C. (2000). A semantic differential study of designers' users' product form perception. *International Journal of Industrial Ergonomics, 25*(4), 375-391.

Huber, O. (1980). The influence of some task variables on cognitive operations in an information-processing decision model. *Acta Psychologica, 45*, 187-196.

Hustad, T. P., & Pessemier, E. A. (1974). The development and application of psychographic life style and associated activity and attitude measures. In W. D. Wells (Ed.), *Life styles and psychographics* (pp. 31-70). Chicago: AMA.

Jeuland, A. P., & Shugan, S. M. (1983). Managing channel profits. *Marketing Science, 2*(3), 239-272.

Jianakoplos, N. A., & Bernasek, A. (1998). Are women more risk averse? *Economic Inquiry, 36*(4), 620-630.

Johnson, E. J., & Payne, J. W. (1985). Effort and accuracy in choice. *Management Science, 31*, 394-414.

Juslin, P., Jones, S., Olsson, H., & Winman, A. (2003). Cue abstraction and exemplar memory in categorization. *Journal of Experimental Psychology: Learning, Memory, and Cognition, 29*(5), 924-941.

Juslin, P., Olsson, H., & Olsson, A.-C. (2003). Exemplar effects in categorization and multiple-cue judgment. *Journal of Experimental Psychology: General, 132*, 133-156.

Juslin, P., & Persson, M. (2002). PROBabilities from EXemplars (PROBEX): A "lazy" algorithm for probabilistic inference from generic knowledge. *Cognitive Science, 26*, 563-607.

Juster, F. T. (1966). Consumer buying intentions and purchase probability: An experiment in survey design. *Journal of the American Statistical Association, 61*(315), 658-696.

Kahneman, D., Slovic, P., & Tversky, A. (1982). *Judgment under uncertainty: Heuristics and biases*. Cambridge, UK: Cambridge University Press.

Kahneman, D., & Tversky, A. (1979). Prospect theory: Analysis of decision under risk. *Econometrica, 47*(2), 263-291.

Kahneman, D., & Tversky, A. (2000). *Choices, values, and frames*. New York: Cambridge University Press and the Russell Sage Foundation.

Kamakura, W. A., Mela, C. F., Ansari, A., Bodapati, A., Fader, P., Iyengar, R., Naik, P., Neslin, S., Sun, B., Verhoef, P. C., Wedel, M., & Wilcox, R. (2005). Choice models and customer relationship management. *Marketing Letters, 16*(3-4), 279-291.

Kamakura, W. A., & Wedel, M. (2000). Factor analysis and missing data. *Journal of Marketing Research, 37*(4), 490-498.

Katz, J., Aakhus, M., Kim, H. D., & Turner, M. (2002). Young user's attitudes towards ICTs: A comparative semantic differential study of the mobile telephone. *Annals of Telecommunications, 57*(3-4), 225-237.

Kelly, G. A. (1955). *The psychology of personal constructs*. (Vol. 1). New York: Norton.

Keynes, J. M. (1936). *The general theory of employment, interest, and money*. London: Macmillan.

Kivetz, R., & Simonson, I. (2002). Self-control for the righteous: Towards a theory of pre-commitment to indulgence. *Journal of Consumer Research, 29*(2), 199-217.

Klayman, J. (1988). On the how and why (not) of learning from outcomes. In B. Berndt & C. R. B. Joyce (Eds.), *Human judgment: The SJT view* (pp. 115-162). New York: Elsevier.

Koehler, D. J. (2000). Probability judgment in three-category classification learning. *Journal of Experimental Psychology: Learning, Memory, and Cognition, 26*, 28-52.

Kruschke, J. K. (1992). ALCOVE: An exemplar-based connectionist model of category learning. *Psychological Review, 99*, 22-44.

Kubovy, M., & Healy, A. F. (1980). Process models of probabilistic categorization. In T. S. Wallsten (Ed.), *Cognitive processes in choice and decision behavior* (pp. 239-262). Hillsdale, NJ: Erlbaum.

Laibson, D. I. (1996). *Hyperbolic discount functions, undersaving, and saving policy* (NBER working paper series 5635). Cambridge, MA: National Bureau of Economic Research.

Laibson, D. I. (1997). Golden eggs and hyperbolic discounting. *The Quarterly Journal of Economics, 112*(2), 443-477.

Lamberts, K. (2000). Information-accumulation theory of speeded categorization. *Psychological Review, 107*, 227-260.

Laibson, D. I., Repetto, A., Tobacman, J., Hall. R. E., Gale, W. G., & Akerlof, G. A. (1998). Self-control and saving for retirement. *Brooking Papers on Economic Activity, 1,* 91-196.

Landahl, H. D. A. (1938). Centroid orthogonal transformation. *Psychometrika, 3*, 219-223.

Landauer, T. K., & Dumais, S. T. (1997). A solution to Plato's problem: The Latent Semantic Analysis theory of the acquisition, induction, and representation of knowledge. *Psychological Science, 104*, 211-240.

Lemaire, P., & Siegler, R. S. (1995). Four aspects of strategic change: Contributions to children's learning of multiplication. *Journal of Experimental Psychology: General, 124*, 83-97.

Lesser, J. A., & Hughes, M. A. (1986). The generalizability of psychographic market segments across geographic locations. *Journal of Marketing, 50*(1), 18-27.

Levin, L. (1998). Are assets fungible? Testing the behavioral theory of life-cycle savings. *Journal of Economic Behavior & Organization, 36*(1), 59-83.

Lewin, S. B. (1996). Economics and Psychology: Lessons for our own day from the early twentieth century. *Journal of Economic Literature, 34*(3), 1293-1323.

Lichtenstein, S., & Slovic, P. (1971). Reversals of preference between bids and choices in gambling decisions. *Journal of Experimental Psychology, 89*(1), 46-55.

Lievens, F., & Highhouse, S. (2003). The relation of instrumental and symbolic attributes to a company's attractiveness as an employer. *Personnel Psychology, 56*, 75-102.

Likert, R. (1932). A technique for the measurement of attitudes. *Archives of Psychology, 140*, 1-55.

Lin, Q.-Y., Chen, Y.-L., Chen, J.-S., & Chen, Y.-C. (2003). Mining inter-organizational retailing knowledge for an alliance formed by competitive firms. *Information and Management, 40*, 431-442.

Lindqvist, A. (1981). A note on determinants of household saving behavior. *Journal of Economic Psychology, 1*, 39-57.

Lipshitz, R. (2000). Two cheers for bounded rationality. *Behavioral and Brain Sciences, 23*, 756-757.

Lockshin, L. S., Spawton, A. L., & Macintosh, G. (1997). Using product, brand, and purchasing involvement for retail segmentation. *Journal of Retailing and Consumer Services, 4*(3), 171-183.

Loewenstein, G. F. (1987). Anticipation and the valuation of delayed consumption. *The Economic Journal, 97*(Sept.), 666-684.

Loewenstein, G. F. (1988). Frames of mind in intertemporal choice. *Management Science, 34*(2), 200-214.

Loewenstein, G. F. (1996). Out of control: Visceral influences on behavior. *Organizational Behavior and Human Decision Processes, 65*(3), 272-292.

Loewenstein, G. F. (2000). Emotions in economic theory and economic behavior. *The American Economic Review, 90*(2), 426-432.

Loewenstein, G. F., & Prelec, D. (1992). Anomalies in intertemporal choice: Evidence and an interpretation. *The Quarterly Journal of Economics, 107*(2), 573-597.

Loewenstein, G. F., & Prelec, D. (1993). Preferences for sequences of outcomes. *Psychological Review, 100*(1), 91-108.

Logan, G. D. (1988). Towards an instance theory of automatization. *Psychological Review, 95*(4), 492-527.

Logan, G. D. (2002). An instance theory of attention and memory. *Psychological Review, 109*(2), 376-400.

Loomes, G., & Sugden, R. (1982). Regret theory: An alternative theory of rational choice under uncertainty. *Economic Journal, 92*(368), 805-824.

Luce, R. D. (1959). *Individual choice behavior*. New York: Wiley.

Macmillan, I. C., Siegel, R., & Narasimha, P. N. S. (1985). Criteria used by venture capitalists to evaluate new venture proposals. *Journal of Business Venturing, 1*(1), 119-128.

MacQueen, J. B. (1967). Some methods for classification and analysis of multivariate observations. In L. M. LeCam & J. Neyman (Eds.), *Proceedings 5th Berkeley Symposium on Mathematical Statistics and Probability* (pp. 282-297). London: Cambridge University Press.

Madrian, B. C., & Shea, D. F. (2001). The power of suggestion: Inertia in 401(k) participation and savings behavior. *The Quarterly Journal of Economics, 116*(4), 1149-1187.

Manuck, S. B., Flory, J. D., Muldoon, M. F., & Ferrell, R. E. (2003). A neurobiology of intertemporal choice. In G. Loewenstein, D. Read, & R. Baumeister (Eds.), *Time and decision* (pp. 139-172). New York: Russel Sage Foundation.

Martignon, L., & Laskey, K. (1999). Bayesian benchmarks for fast and frugal heuristics. In G. Gigerenzer, P. M. Todd, & the A.BC Reserch Group

(Eds.), *Simple heuristics that make us smart* (pp. 169-188). New York: Oxford University Press.

Massaro, D. W., & Friedman, D. (1990). Models of integration given multiple sources of information. *Psychological Review, 97*, 225-252.

McClure, S. M., Laibson, D. I., Loewenstein, G., & Cohen, J. D. (2004). Separate neural systems value immediate and delayed monetary rewards. *Science, 306*(5695), 503-507.

Medin, D. L., Altom, M. W., & Murphy, T. D. (1984). Given versus induced category representations: Use of prototype and exemplar information in classification. *Journal of Experimental Psychology: Learning, Memory, and Cognition, 10*, 333-352.

Medin, D. L., & Schaffer, M. M. (1978). Context theory of classification learning. *Psychological Review, 85*, 207-238.

Mele, A. R. (1995). *Autonomous agents*. New York: Oxford University Press.

Metcalfe, J., & Mischel, W. (1999). A hot/cool-system analysis of delay of gratification: Dynamics of willpower. *Psychological Review, 106*(1), 3-19.

Miller, G. A. (1956). The magical number seven, plus or minus two: some limits on our capacity for processing information. *Psychological Review, 63*(2), 81-97.

Milne, G. R. (2000). Privacy and ethical issues in database/interactive marketing and public policy. *Journal of Public Policy and Marketing, 19*(1), 1-6.

Milne, G. R., & Boza, M.-E. (1998). *Trust and concern in consumers' perception of marketing information management practices*. (Vol. 98-117). Cambridge, MA: Marketing Science Institute.

Mirman, L. J. (1971). Uncertainty and optimal consumption decisions. *Econometrica, 39*(1), 179-185.

Modigliani, F. (1966). The life cycle hypothesis of saving, the demand for wealth, and the supply of capital. *Social Research, 33*(2), 160-217.

Modigliani, F. (1986). Life cycle, individual thrift and the wealth of nations. *The American Economic Review, 76*(3), 297-313.

Modigliani, F., & Brumberg, R. (1954). Utility analysis and the consumption function: An interpretation of cross section data. In K. K. Kurihara (Ed.), *Post-Keynesian economics* (pp. 388-436). New Brunswick: Rutgers University Press.

Mondragon, S., Company, P., & Vergara, M. (2005). Semantic differential applied to the evaluation of machine tool design. *International Journal of Industrial Ergonomics, 35*(11), 1021-1029.

Moon, P., Keasey, K., & Duxbury, D. (1999). Mental accounting and decision making: The relationship between relative and absolute savings. *Journal of Economic Behavior and Organization, 38*, 145-153.

Murphy, G. (2002). *The big book of concepts*. Cambridge, MA: MIT Press.

Myung, I. J., & Pitt, M. A. (1997). Applying Occam's razor in modeling cognition: A Bayesian approach. *Psychonomic Bulletin and Review, 4*, 79-95.

Nelder, J. A., & Mead, R. (1965). A simplex method for function minimization. *Computer Journal, 7*, 308-313.

Nellen, S. (2003). The use of the "Take The Best" heuristic under different conditions, modeled with ACT-R. *Paper presented at the Fifth International Conference on Cognitive Modeling,* Bamberg, Germany.

Newell, A., & Simon, H. A. (1972). *Human problem solving*. Englewood Cliffs, NJ: Prentice-Hall.

Newell, B. R., & Shanks, D. R. (2003). Take the best or look at the rest? Factors influencing "one-reason" decision making. *Journal of Experimental Psychology: Learning, Memory, and Cognition, 29*, 53-65.

Newell, B. R., Weston, N. J., & Shanks, D. R. (2003). Empirical tests of a fast-and-frugal heuristic: Not everyone "takes-the-best". *Organizational Behavior and Human Decision Processes, 91*(1), 82-96.

Nosofsky, R. M. (1986). Attention, similarity, and the identification-categorization relationship. *Journal of Experimental Psychology: General, 115*, 39-57.

Nosofsky, R. M. (1988). Similarity, frequency, and category representations. *Journal of Experimental Psychology: Learning, Memory, and Cognition, 14*, 54-65.

Nosofsky, R. M. (1992). Exemplars, prototypes, and similarity rules. In A. F. Healy, S. M. Kosslyn, & R. Shiffrin (Eds.), *Essays in honor of William K. Estes* (pp. 149-167). Hillsdale, NJ: Erlbaum.

Nosofsky, R. M., Clark, S. E., & Shin, H. J. (1989). Rules and exemplars in categorization, identification, and recognition. *Journal of Experimental Psychology: Learning, Memory, and Cognition, 15*, 282-304.

Nosofsky, R. M., Kruschke, J. K., & McKinley, S. C. (1992). Combining exemplar-based category representations and connectionist learning rules. *Journal of Experimental Psychology: Learning, Memory, and Cognition, 18*, 211-233.

Nosofsky, R. M., & Johansen, M. K. (2000). Exemplar-based accounts of "multiple-system" phenomena in perceptual categorization. *Psychonomic Bulletin & Review, 7*, 375-402.

O'Donoghue, T., & Rabin, M. (2003). Self awareness and self control. In G. Loewenstein, D. Read, & R. F. Baumeister (Eds.), *Time and decision: Economic and psychological perspectives on intertemporal choice* (pp. 217-243). New York: Russell Sage Foundation.

O'Guinn, T. C., & Faber, R. (1989). Compulsive buying: A phenomenological exploration. *Journal of Consumer Research, 16*(September), 147-157.

Ohnishi, S., Shinkawa, A., Katto, M., Hamanaka, F., Kurioka, Y., Kawasaki, M., & Takashima, Y. (1996). Evaluation of odor quality using a semantic differential method for five odrants of a T&T olfactometer: The case for using concrete adjectives. *Chemical Senses, 21*(1), 34-34.

Oliveira-Castro, J. M., Foxall, G. R., & Schrezenmaier, T. C. (2006). Consumer brand choice: Individual and group analyses of demand elasticity. *Journal of the Experimental Analysis of Behavior, 85*(2), 147-166.

Osgood, C. E. (1962). Studies of the generality of affective meaning systems. *American Psychologist, 17*(1), 10-28.

Osgood, C. E., Tannenbaum, P. H., & Suci, G. J. (1957). *The measurement of meaning*. Urbana: University of Illinois Press.

Otto, P. E., Davies, G. B., & Chater, N. (2007). Note on ways of saving: Mental mechanisms as tools for self-control? *Global Business and Economics Review, 9*(2-3), 227-254.

Otto, P. E., Davies, G. B., Chater, N., & Stott, H. (2009). From spending to understanding: Analyzing customers by their spending behavior. *Journal of Retailing and Consumer Services, 16*, 10-18.

Oyama, T., Yamada, H., & Iwasawa, H. (1998). Synthetic tendencies as the basis of sensory symbolism: A review of series of experiments by means of semantic differential. *Psychologia, 41*(3), 203-215.

Papke, L. E. (2003). Individual financial decisions in retirement saving plans: The role of participant-direction. *Journal of Public Economics, 88*, 39-61.

Patalano, A. L., Smith, E. E., Jonides, J., & Koeppe, R. A. (2001). PET evidence for multiple strategies of categorization. *Cognitive, Affective, and Behavioral Neuroscience, 1*, 360-370.

Payne, J. W. (1976). Task complexity and contingent processing in decision making: An information search and protocol analysis. *Organizational Behavior and Human Performance, 16*, 366-370.

Payne, J. W., Bettman, J. R., & Johnson, E. J. (1988). Adaptive strategy selection in decision making. *Journal of Experimental Psychology: Learning, Memory, and Cognition, 14*(3), 534-552.

Payne, J. W., Bettman, J. R., & Johnson, E. J. (1993). *The adaptive decision maker*. New York: Cambridge University Press.

Pernica, J. (1974). The second generation of market segmentation studies: An audit of buying motivations. In W. D. Wells (Ed.), *Life style and psychographics* (pp. 297-313). Chicago: AMA.

Phelps, J., Nowak, G., & Ferrell, E. (2000). Privacy concerns and consumer willingness to provide personal information. *Journal of Public Policy and Marketing, 19*(1), 27-41.

Pitt, M. A., & Myung, I. J. (2002). When a good fit can be bad. *Trends in Cognitive Sciences, 6*, 421-425.

Pitt, M. A., Myung, I. J., & Zhang, S. (2002). Towards a method of selecting among computational models of cognition. *Psychological Review, 109*, 472-491.

Plummer, J. T. (1971). Life style patterns and commercial bank credit card usage. *Journal of Marketing, 35*(2), 35-41.

Plummer, J. T. (1974). The concept and application of life style segmentation. *Journal of Marketing, 38*(1), 33-37.

Popper, K. R. (1934). *Logik der Forschung [The logic of scientific discovery]*. Vienna: Springer.

Poterba, J. M., Venti, S. F., & Wise, D. A. (1996). How retirement saving programs increase saving. *Journal of Economic Perspectives, 10*(4), 91-112.

Powell, M., & Ansic, D. (1997). Gender differences in risk behaviour in financial decision-making: An experimental analysis. *Journal of Economic Psychology, 18*(6), 605-628.

Prelec, D., & Loewenstein, G. (1998). The red and the black: Mental accounting of savings and debt. *Marketing Science, 17*(1), 4-28.

Pylyshyn, Z. W. (1980). Computation and cognition: Issues in the foundations of cognitive science. *Behavioral and Brain Sciences, 3*(1), 111-132.

Rachlin, H. (1995). Self-control: Beyond commitment. *Behavioral and Brain Sciences, 18*, 109-159.

Rapoport, A., & Wallsten, T. S. (1972). Individual decision behavior. *Annual Review of Psychology, 23*, 131-176.

Reinartz, W., & Kumar, V. (2002). The mismanagement of customer loyalty. *Harvard Business Review, 80*(7), 86-94.

Reisch, L. A., & Røpke, I. (2004). *Ecological economic consumption*. Cheltenham, UK: Edward Elgar Publications.

Restle, F. (1962). The selection of strategies in cue learning. *Psychological Review, 69*, 329-343.

Rieskamp, J., Busemeyer, J. R., & Laine, T. H. (2003). How do people learn to allocate resources? Comparing two learning theories. *Journal of Experimental Psychology: Learning, Memory, and Cognition, 29*, 1066-1081.

Rieskamp, J., & Hoffrage, U. (1999). When do people use simple heuristics and can we tell. In G. Gigerenzer, P. Todd, & the ABC Research Group (Eds.), *Simple heuristics that make us smart* (pp. 141-167). New York: Oxford University Press.

Rieskamp, J., & Hoffrage, U. (2003). The use of simple heuristics: Inferences and preferences under time pressure. *Submitted for publication.*

Rieskamp, J., & Otto, P. E. (2006). SSL: A theory of how people learn to select strategies. *Journal of Experimental Psychology: General, 135*(2), 207-236.

Roberts, S., & Pashler, H. (2000). How persuasive is a good fit? A comment on theory testing. *Psychological Review, 107*, 358-367.

Roe, R. M., Busemeyer, J. R., & Townsend, J. T. (2001). Multialternative decision field theory: A dynamic connectionist model of decision making. *Psychological Review, 108*(2), 370-392.

Romal, J. B., & Kaplan, B. J. (1995). Differences in self-control among spenders and savers. *Psychology: A Quarterly Journal of Human Behavior, 32*(2), 8-17.

Rommelfanger, H., & Unterharnscheid, D. (1985). Entwicklung einer Hierarchie gewichteter Bonitätskriterien [Development of a hierarchy of credit-worthiness criteria]. *Österreichisches Bankarchiv, 12*, 419-427.

Rook, D. W., & Fisher, R. J. (1995). Normative influences on impulsive buying behavior. *Journal of Consumer Research, 22*(3), 305-313.

Rosenbaum, M. (1980). A schedule for assessing self-control behaviors: Preliminary findings. *Behavior Therapy, 11*, 109-121.

Rossi, P. E., McCulloch, R. E., & Allenby, G. M. (1996). The value of purchase history data in target marketing. *Marketing Science, 15*(4), 321-340.

Rotter, J. B. (1966). Generalized expectancies for internal versus external control of reinforcement. *Psychological Monographs, 80*(1), Whole No. 609.

Schelling, T. C. (1980). *The strategy of conflict.* Cambridge, MA: Harvard University Press.

Schelling, T. C. (1984). Self-command in practice, in policy, and in a theory of rational choice. *The American Economic Review, 74*(2), 1-11.

Schoenblacher, D. D., & Gordon, G. L. (2002). Mulit-channel shopping: Understanding what drives channel choice. *Journal of Consumer Marketing, 19*(1), 42-53.

Schunn, C. D., & Reder, L. M. (1998). Strategy adaptivity and individual differences. In D. L. Medin (Ed.), *The psychology of learning and motivation: Advances in research and theory* (Vol. 38, pp. 115-154). San Diego, CA: Academic Press.

Shanks, D. R. (1991). Categorization by a connectionist network. *Journal of Experimental Psychology: Learning, Memory, and Cognition, 17*, 433-443.

Shefrin, H. M., & Statman, M. (2000). Behavioral portfolio theory. *Journal of Financial and Quantitative Analysis, 35*(2), 127-151.

Shefrin, H. M., & Thaler, R. H. (1988). The behavioral life-cycle hypothesis. *Economic Enquiry, 26*, 609-643.

Shefrin, H. M., & Thaler, R. H. (1992). Mental accounting, saving, and self-control. In G. Loewenstein & J. Elster (Eds.), *Choice over time* (pp. 287-330). New York: Russell Sage Foundation.

Shleifer, A., & Summers, L. H. (1990). The noise trader approach to finance. *Journal of Economic Perspectives, 4*(2), 19-33.

Sieck, W. R., & Yates, J. F. (2001). Overconfidence effects in category learning: A comparison of connectionist and exemplar memory models. *Journal of Experimental Psychology: Learning, Memory, and Cognition, 27*, 1003-1021.

Siegler, R. S. (1999). Strategic development. *Trends in Cognitive Science, 3*, 430-435.

Simon, H. A. (1955). A behavioral model of rational choice. *The Quarterly Journal of Economics, 69*(1), 99-118.

Simon, H. A. (1956). Rational choice and the structure of the environment. *Psychological Review, 63*, 129-138.

Simonson, I., & Tversky, A. (1992). Choice in context: Trade-off contrast and extremeness aversion. *Journal of Marketing Research, 29*(3), 281-295.

Skinner, J. (1992). Individual retirement accounts: A review of the evidence. *Tax Notes, 54*(2), 200-212.

Slama, M. E., & Tashchian, A. (1985). Selected socioeconomic and demographic characteristics associated with purchasing involvement. *Journal of Marketing, 49*(1), 72-82.

Slaughter, J. E., Zickar, M. J., Highhouse, S., & Mohr, D. C. (2004). Personality trait inferences about organizations: Development of a measure and assessment of construct validity. *Journal of Applied Psychology, 89*(1), 85-103.

Sloman, S. A. (1996). The empirical case for two systems of reasoning. *Psychological Bulletin, 119*(1), 3-22.

Sloman, S. A., & Malt, B. C. (2003). Artifacts are not ascribed essences, nor are they treated as belonging to kinds. *Language and Cognitive Processes, 18*, 563-582.

Smedslund, J. (1955). *Multiple probability learning.* Oslo, Norway: Oslo University Press.

Smith, E. E., Patalano, A. L., & Jonides, J. (1998). Alternative strategies of categorization. *Cognition, 65*, 167-196.

Smith, E. R., & Zarate, M. A. (1992). Exemplar-based model of social judgment. *Psychological Review, 99*, 3-21.

Smith, V. L., & Walker, J. M. (1993). Monetary rewards and decision cost in experimental economics. *Economic Inquiry, 31*, 245-261.

Soman, D. (1998). The illusion of delayed incentives: Evaluating future effort-money transactions. *Journal of Marketing Research, 35*(Nov.), 427-437.

Soman, D. (2001). Effects of payment mechanism on spending behavior: The role of rehearsal and immediacy of payments. *Journal of Consumer Research, 27*(4), 460-474.

Soman, D., & Cheema, A. (2002). The effect of credit on spending decisions: The role of the credit limit and credibility. *Marketing Science, 21*(1), 32-53.

Soman, D., & Gourville, J. T. (2001). Transaction decoupling: How price bundling affects the decision to consume. *Journal of Marketing Research, 38*(Feb.), 30-44.

Stahl, D. O. (1996). Bounded rational rule learning in a guessing game. *Games and Economic Behavior, 16*, 303-330.

Stahl, D. O. (2000). Rule learning in symmetric normal-form games: Theory and evidence. *Games and Economic Behavior, 32*, 105-138.

Stern, P., & Hammond, K. (2004). The relation between customer loyalty and purchase incidence. *Marketing Letters, 15*(1), 5-19.

Stewart, N., Chater, N., & Brown, G. D. A. (2006). Decision by sampling. *Cognitive Psychology, 53*(1), 1-26.

Stewart, N., Chater, N., Stott, H. P., & Reimers, S. (2003). Prospect relativity: How choice options influence decision under risk. *Journal of Experimental Psychology: General, 132*(1), 23-46.

Strotz, R. H. (1955). Myopia and inconsistency in dynamic utility maximization. *The Review of Economic Studies, 23*(3), 165-180.

Sunstein, C. R., & Thaler, R. H. (2003). Libertarian paternalism is not an oxymoron. *University of Chicago Law Review, 70*(4), 1159-1202.

Sutton, R. S., & Barto, A. G. (1998). *Reinforcement learning: An introduction.* Cambridge, MA: MIT Press.

Svenson, O. (1979). Process descriptions of decision making. *Organizational Behavior and Human Performance, 23*, 86-112.

Svenson, O. (1992). Differentiation and consolidation theory of human decision making: A frame of reference for the study of pre and post-decision processes. *Acta Psychologica, 80*, 143-168.

Taatgen, N. A., & Wallach, D. (2002). Whether skill acquisition is rule or instance based is determined by the structure of the task. *Cognitive Science Quarterly, 2*(2), 163-204.

Tessarolo, M. (1981). The musical experience: The semantic differential as a research instrument. *International Review of Aesthetics and Sociology of Music, 12*(2), 153-153.

Thaler, R. H. (1980). Towards a positive theory of consumer choice. *Journal of Economic Behavior and Organization, 1*, 39-60.

Thaler, R. H. (1985). Mental accounting and consumer choice. *Marketing Science, 4*(3), 199-214.

Thaler, R. H. (1994). Psychology and savings policies. *The American Economic Review, 84*(2), 186-192.

Thaler, R. H. (1999). Mental accounting matters. *Journal of Behavioral Decision Making, 12*(3), 183-206.

Thaler, R. H., & Benartzi, S. (2004). Save More Tomorrow (TM): Using behavioral economics to increase employee saving. *Journal of Political Economy, 112*(1), S164-S187.

Thaler, R. H., & Shefrin, H. M. (1981). An economic theory of self-control. *Journal of Political Economy, 89*(2), 392-406.

Thaler, R. H., & Sunstein, C. R. (2003). Libertarian paternalism. *The American Economic Review, 93*(2), 175-179.

Thorndike, E. (1898). On the law of effect. *Journal of the experimental analysis of behavior, 13*, 243-266.

Thurstone, L. L. (1930). The learning function. *Journal of General Psychology, 3*, 469-493.

Tobin, J. (1959). On the predictive value of consumer intentions and attitudes. *The Review of Economics and Statistics, 41*(1), 1-11.

Tooby, J., & Cosmides, L. (1990a). The past explains the present: Emotional adaptations and the structure of ancestral environments. *Ethology and Sociobiology, 11*(4-5), 375-424.

Tooby, J., & Cosmides, L. (1990b). On the universality of human-nature and the uniqueness of the individual: The role of genetics and adaptation. *Journal of Personality, 58*(1), 17-67.

Trivedi, M. (1998). Distribution channels: An extension of exclusive retailership. *Management Science, 44*(7), 896-909.

Trope, Y., & Fishbach, A. (2000). Counteractive self-control in overcoming temptation. *Journal of Personality and Social Psychology, 29*(4), 493-506.

Trope, Y., & Liberman, N. (2003). Temporal Construal. *Psychological Review, 110*(3), 403-421.

Tversky, A., & Kahneman, D. (1974). Judgment under uncertainty: Heuristics and biases. *Science, 185*(4157), 1124-1131.

Tversky, A., & Kahneman, D. (1983). Extensional versus intuitive reasoning: The conjunction fallacy in probability judgment. *Psychological Review, 90*(4), 293-315.

Tversky, A., & Kahneman, D. (1992). Advances in prospect theory: Cumulative representation of uncertainty. *Journal of Risk and Uncertainty, 5*(4), 297-323.

Tversky, A., Slovic, P., & Kahneman, D. (1990). The causes of preference reversal. *The American Economic Review, 80*(1), 204-217.

Usher, M., & McClelland, J. L. (2004). Loss aversion and inhibition in dynamic models of multialternative choice. *Psychological Review, 11*(3), 757-769.

Veldhoven, G. M. v., & Groenland, E. A. G. (1993). Exploring saving behaviour: A framework and a research agenda. *Journal of Economic Psychology, 14*, 507-522.

Venti, S. F., & Wise, D. A. (1987). *Have IRAs increased U.S. saving? Evidence from consumer expenditure surveys* (NBER working paper series 2217). Cambridge, MA: National Bureau of Economic Research.

Wahlund, R., & Gunnarsson, J. (1996). Mental discounting and financial strategies. *Journal of Economic Psychology, 17*, 709-730.

Wainer, H. (1976). Estimating coefficients in linear models: It don't make no nevermind. *Psychological Bulletin, 83*, 213-217.

Wallsten, T. S. (1968). Failure of predictions from subjectively expected utility theory in a Bayesian decision task. *Organizational Behavior and Human Decision Processes, 3*, 239-252.

Ward, L. M., & Russell, J. A. (1981). The psychological representation of molar physical environments. *Journal of Experimental Psychology, 110*, 121-152.

Weber, E. U., Blais, A. R., & Betz, N. E. (2002). A domain-specific risk-attitude scale: Measuring risk perceptions and risk behaviors. *Journal of Behavioral Decision Making, 15*(4), 263-290.

Weber, R. A., & Camerer, C. F. (2006). “Behavioral experiments” in economics. *Experimental Economics, 9*(3), 187-192.

Wedel, M., & Kamakura, W.A., (2000). *Market segmentation: Conceptual and methodological foundations*. Dordrech: Kluwer.

Weinberg, P., & Gottwald, W. (1982). Impulsive consumer buying as a result of emotions. *Journal of Business Research, 10*(1), 43-57.

Wells, W. D. (1975). Psychographics: A critical review. *Journal of Marketing Research, 12*(May), 196-213.

Wertenbroch, K. (1998). Consumption self-control by rationing purchase quantities of virtue and vice. *Marketing Science, 17*(4), 317-337.

Wickens, T. D. (1989). *Multiway contingency tables analysis for the social sciences*. Hillsdale, NJ: Erlbaum.

Wilson, D. S. (1975). Theory of group selection. *Proceedings of the National Academy of Sciences of the United States of America, 72*(1), 143-146.

Wilson, D. S. (1994). Adaptive genetic-variation and human evolutionary psychology. *Ethology and Sociobiology, 15*(4), 219-235.

Wilson, D. S., & Sober, E. (1994). Reintroducing group selection to the human behavioral-sciences. *Behavioral and Brain Sciences, 17*(4), 585-608.

Wind, Y. (1978). Issues and advances in segmentation research. *Journal of Marketing Research, 15*(August), 317-337.

Yates, J. F. (1990). *Judgment and decision making*. Old Tappan, NJ: Prentice-Hall.

Zacharakis, A. L., & Meyer, G. D. (1998). A lack of insight: Do venture capitalists really understand their own decision process? *Journal of Business Venturing, 13*(1), 57-76.

Zuckerman, M. (1971). Dimensions of sensation seeking. *Journal of Consulting and Clinical Psychology, 36*(1), 45-52.

Zuckerman, M. (1984). Sensation seeking: A comparative approach to a human trait. *Behavioral and Brain Sciences, 7*(3), 413-434.

Zuckerman, M. (1994). *Behavioral expressions and biosocial basis of sensation seeking*. Cambridge: Cambridge University Press.

# APPENDIX

## Appendix A: Derived Saving Structures

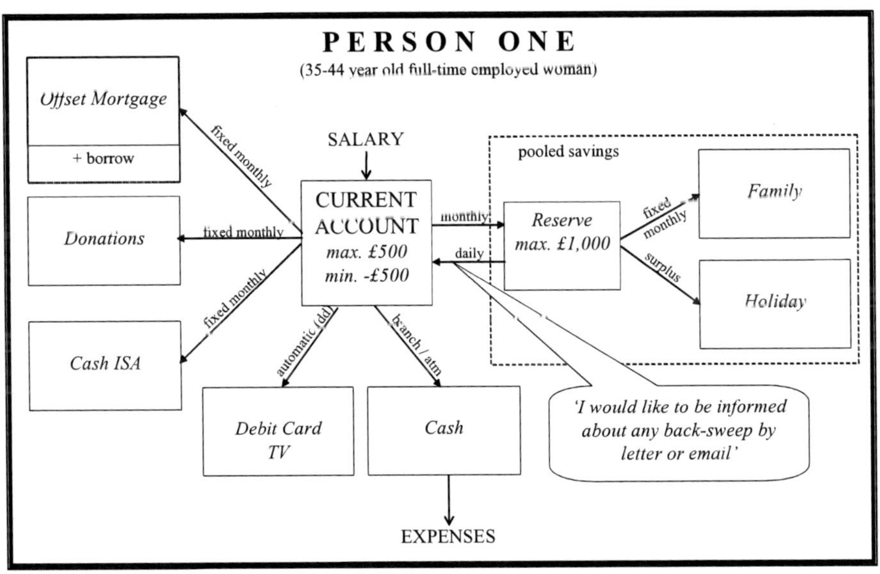

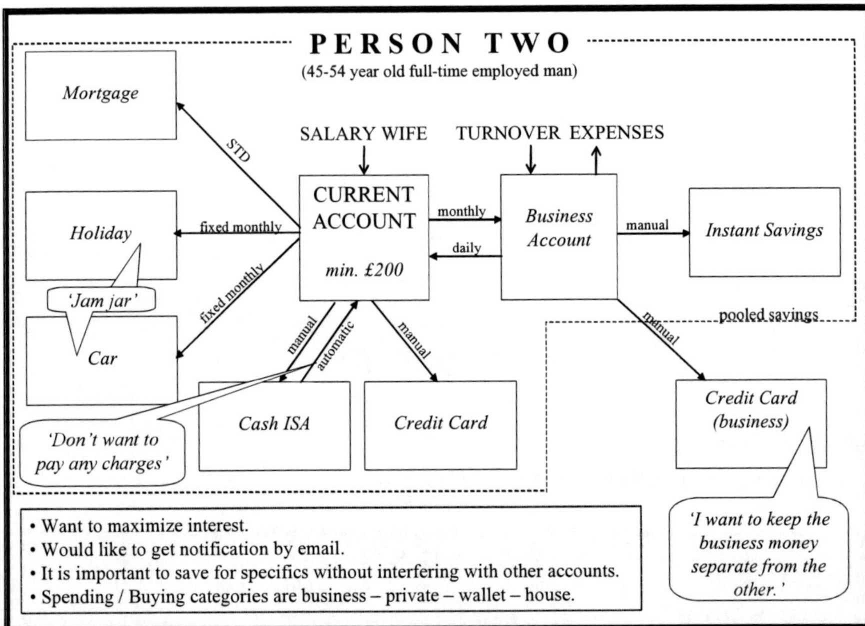
PERSON TWO
(45-54 year old full-time employed man)
Mortgage
STD
SALARY WIFE
TURNOVER
EXPENSES
CURRENT ACCOUNT
min. £200
monthly
daily
Business Account
manual
Instant Savings
Holiday
fixed monthly
'Jam jar'
fixed monthly
Car
manual
automatic
manual
manual
pooled savings
Cash ISA
Credit Card
Credit Card (business)
'Don't want to pay any charges'
• Want to maximize interest.
• Would like to get notification by email.
• It is important to save for specifics without interfering with other accounts.
• Spending / Buying categories are business – private – wallet – house.
'I want to keep the business money separate from the other.'

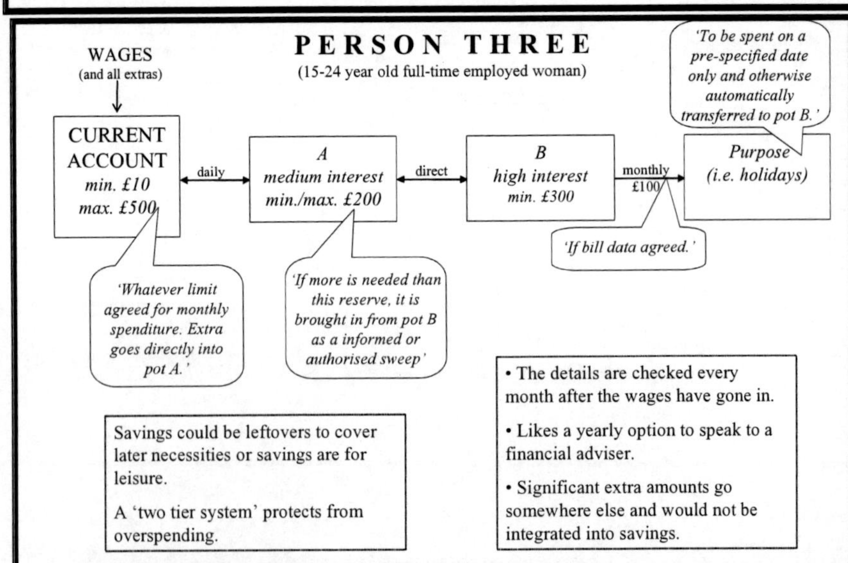
PERSON THREE
(15-24 year old full-time employed woman)
WAGES
(and all extras)
'To be spent on a pre-specified date only and otherwise automatically transferred to pot B.'
CURRENT ACCOUNT
min. £10
max. £500
daily
A
medium interest
min./max. £200
direct
B
high interest
min. £300
monthly
£100
Purpose
(i.e. holidays)
'If bill data agreed.'
'Whatever limit agreed for monthly spenditure. Extra goes directly into pot A.'
'If more is needed than this reserve, it is brought in from pot B as a informed or authorised sweep'
• The details are checked every month after the wages have gone in.
• Likes a yearly option to speak to a financial adviser.
• Significant extra amounts go somewhere else and would not be integrated into savings.
Savings could be leftovers to cover later necessities or savings are for leisure.
A 'two tier system' protects from overspending.

## PERSON FOUR

(55-64 year old full-time employed woman)

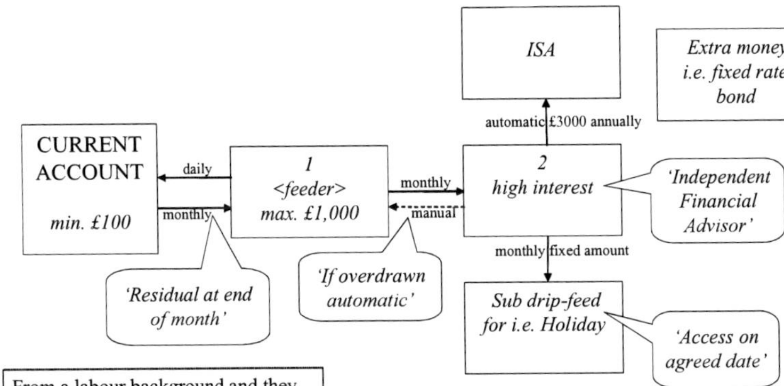


From a labour background and they tended to put money away on a regular basis into a building society: 'You did save!' or 'the rainy-day syndrome'. Besides this habit save for specific items.

- Like to fall directly on the money if needed.
- The system should be secured 'by the computer'. But you are still responsible for your money although you sometimes need penalties to get hold of it.

## PERSON FIVE

(65 years or older retired woman)

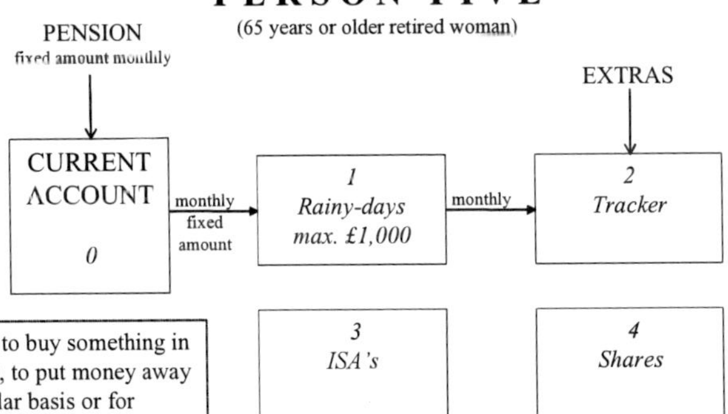


Saving is to buy something in particular, to put money away on a regular basis or for something unexpected.

- All other transfers are made manually. I.e if I need money for the holidays I put that specific amount from the 'Tracker Pot' into the Current Account.
- If overdrawn then a little more careful the next months.
- Would like to have financial advice on income as a whole to move money accordingly. Don't want to loose money.
- Don't want too many accounts.

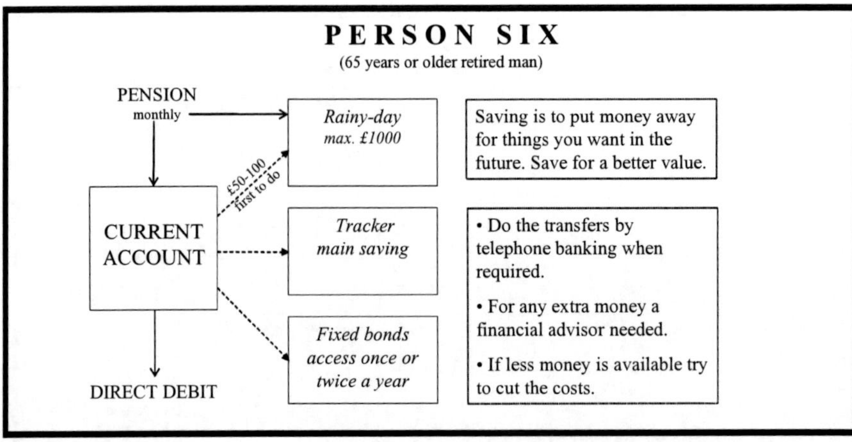
PERSON SIX
(65 years or older retired man)
PENSION
monthly
Rainy-day
max. £1000
Saving is to put money away for things you want in the future. Save for a better value.
£50-100
first to do
CURRENT ACCOUNT
Tracker
main saving
• Do the transfers by telephone banking when required.
• For any extra money a financial advisor needed.
• If less money is available try to cut the costs.
Fixed bonds
access once or twice a year
DIRECT DEBIT

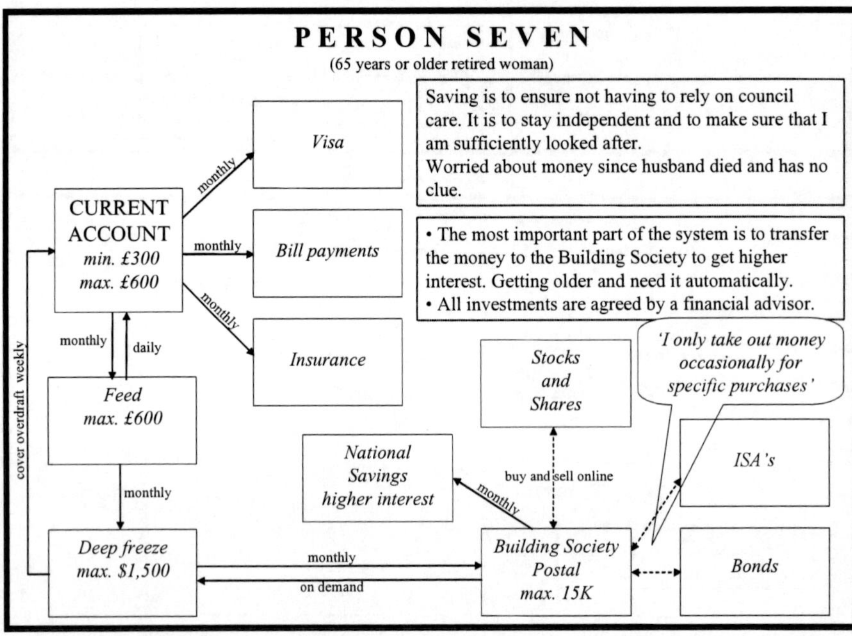
PERSON SEVEN
(65 years or older retired woman)
Saving is to ensure not having to rely on council care. It is to stay independent and to make sure that I am sufficiently looked after.
Worried about money since husband died and has no clue.
Visa
monthly
CURRENT ACCOUNT
min. £300
max. £600
monthly
Bill payments
• The most important part of the system is to transfer the money to the Building Society to get higher interest. Getting older and need it automatically.
• All investments are agreed by a financial advisor.
monthly
Insurance
monthly
daily
cover overdraft weekly
Feed
max. £600
Stocks
and
Shares
'I only take out money occasionally for specific purchases'
National
Savings
higher interest
buy and sell online
ISA's
monthly
monthly
Deep freeze
max. $1,500
monthly
on demand
Building Society
Postal
max. 15K
Bonds

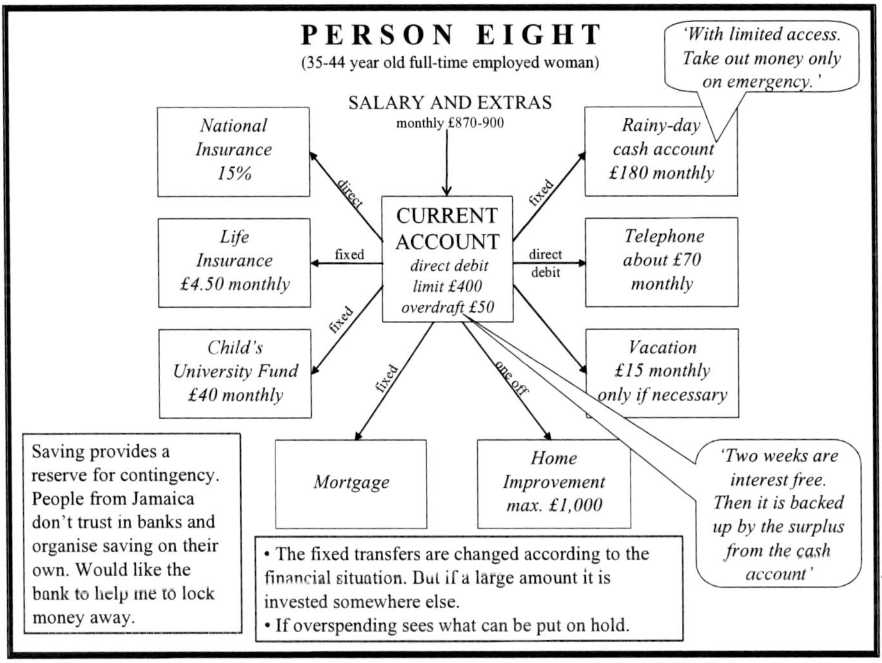
PERSON EIGHT
(35-44 year old full-time employed woman)
SALARY AND EXTRAS
monthly £870-900
'With limited access. Take out money only on emergency.'
National Insurance 15%
direct
Rainy-day cash account £180 monthly
fixed
CURRENT ACCOUNT direct debit limit £400 overdraft £50
Life Insurance £4.50 monthly
fixed
direct debit
Telephone about £70 monthly
fixed
Child's University Fund £40 monthly
Vacation £15 monthly only if necessary
fixed
one off
Mortgage
Home Improvement max. £1,000
'Two weeks are interest free. Then it is backed up by the surplus from the cash account'
Saving provides a reserve for contingency. People from Jamaica don't trust in banks and organise saving on their own. Would like the bank to help me to lock money away.
• The fixed transfers are changed according to the financial situation. But if a large amount it is invested somewhere else.
• If overspending sees what can be put on hold.

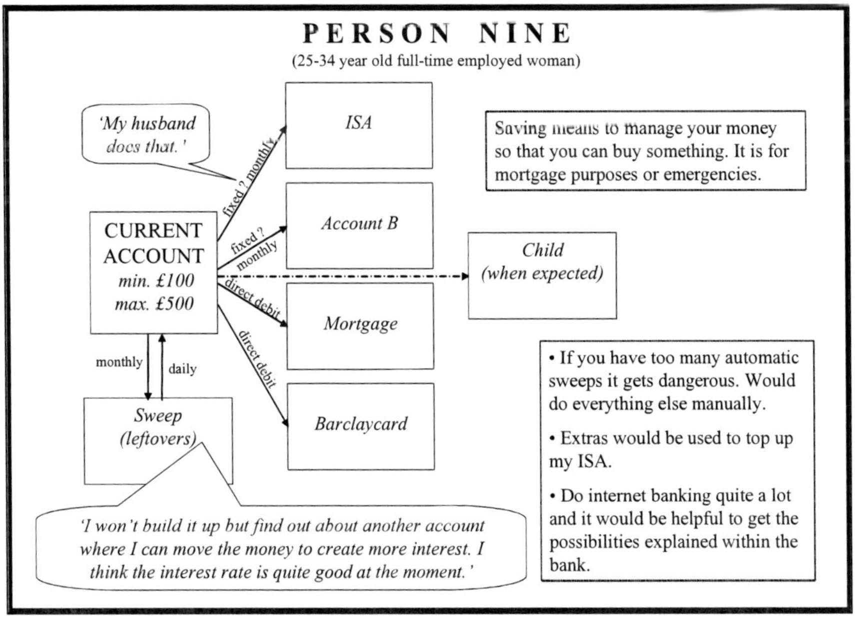
PERSON NINE
(25-34 year old full-time employed woman)
'My husband does that.'
ISA
fixed ? monthly
Saving means to manage your money so that you can buy something. It is for mortgage purposes or emergencies.
CURRENT ACCOUNT min. £100 max. £500
fixed ? monthly
Account B
Child (when expected)
direct debit
Mortgage
direct debit
Barclaycard
monthly
daily
Sweep (leftovers)
• If you have too many automatic sweeps it gets dangerous. Would do everything else manually.
• Extras would be used to top up my ISA.
• Do internet banking quite a lot and it would be helpful to get the possibilities explained within the bank.
'I won't build it up but find out about another account where I can move the money to create more interest. I think the interest rate is quite good at the moment.'

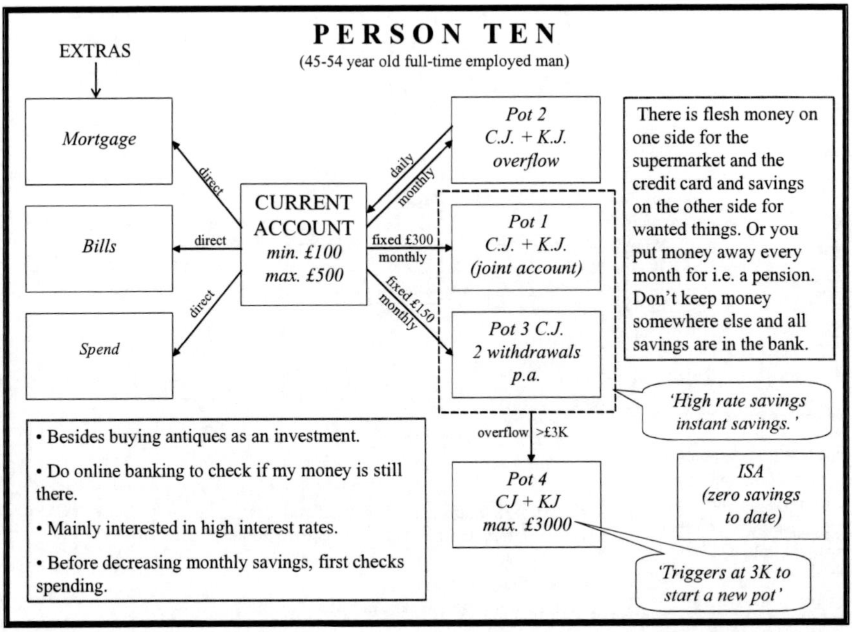
PERSON TEN
(45-54 year old full-time employed man)
EXTRAS
Mortgage
Bills
Spend
direct
direct
direct
CURRENT ACCOUNT
min. £100
max. £500
daily
monthly
fixed £300 monthly
fixed £150 monthly
Pot 2
C.J. + K.J.
overflow
Pot 1
C.J. + K.J.
(joint account)
Pot 3 C.J.
2 withdrawals
p.a.
overflow >£3K
Pot 4
CJ + KJ
max. £3000
There is flesh money on one side for the supermarket and the credit card and savings on the other side for wanted things. Or you put money away every month for i.e. a pension. Don't keep money somewhere else and all savings are in the bank.
'High rate savings instant savings.'
ISA
(zero savings to date)
'Triggers at 3K to start a new pot'
• Besides buying antiques as an investment.
• Do online banking to check if my money is still there.
• Mainly interested in high interest rates.
• Before decreasing monthly savings, first checks spending.

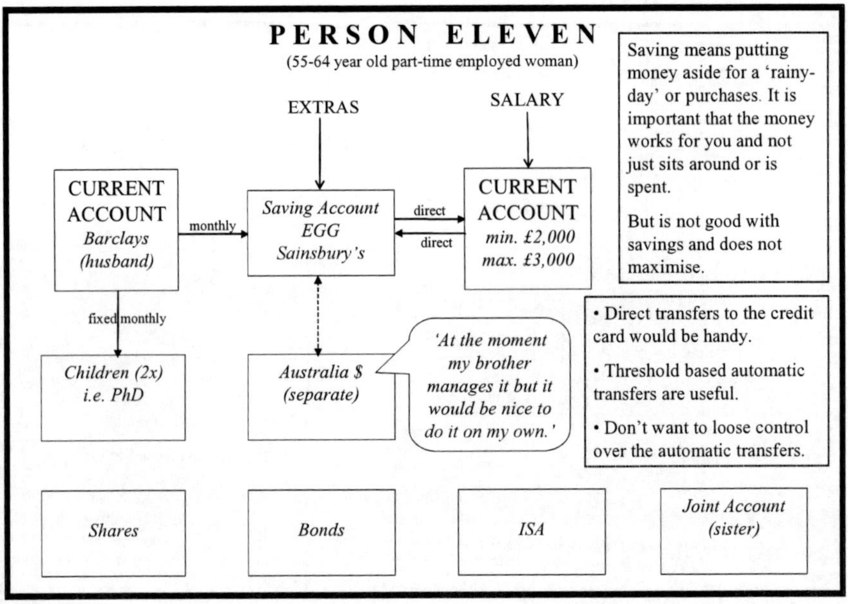
PERSON ELEVEN
(55-64 year old part-time employed woman)
EXTRAS
SALARY
CURRENT ACCOUNT
Barclays
(husband)
monthly
Saving Account
EGG
Sainsbury's
direct
direct
CURRENT ACCOUNT
min. £2,000
max. £3,000
fixed monthly
Children (2x)
i.e. PhD
Australia $
(separate)
'At the moment my brother manages it but it would be nice to do it on my own.'
Saving means putting money aside for a 'rainy-day' or purchases. It is important that the money works for you and not just sits around or is spent.
But is not good with savings and does not maximise.
• Direct transfers to the credit card would be handy.
• Threshold based automatic transfers are useful.
• Don't want to loose control over the automatic transfers.
Shares
Bonds
ISA
Joint Account
(sister)

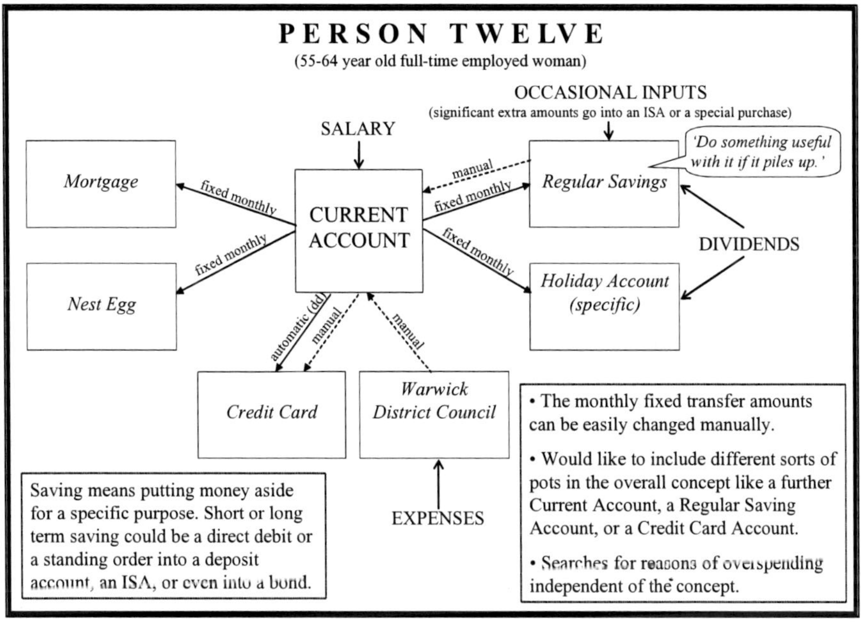
PERSON TWELVE
(55-64 year old full-time employed woman)
OCCASIONAL INPUTS
(significant extra amounts go into an ISA or a special purchase)
SALARY
Mortgage
fixed monthly
CURRENT ACCOUNT
manual
fixed monthly
Regular Savings
'Do something useful with it if it piles up.'
fixed monthly
Nest Egg
fixed monthly
DIVIDENDS
Holiday Account (specific)
automatic (dd)
manual
manual
Credit Card
Warwick District Council
EXPENSES
Saving means putting money aside for a specific purpose. Short or long term saving could be a direct debit or a standing order into a deposit account, an ISA, or even into a bond.
• The monthly fixed transfer amounts can be easily changed manually.
• Would like to include different sorts of pots in the overall concept like a further Current Account, a Regular Saving Account, or a Credit Card Account.
• Searches for reasons of overspending independent of the concept.

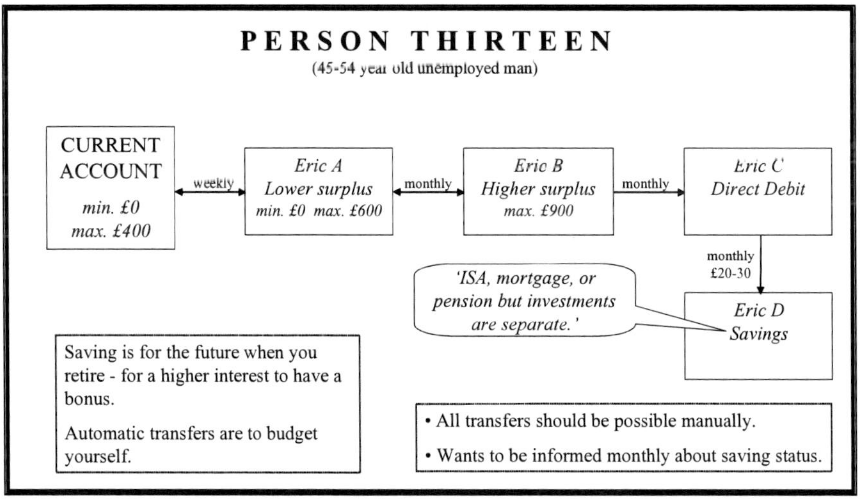
PERSON THIRTEEN
(45-54 year old unemployed man)
CURRENT ACCOUNT
min. £0
max. £400
weekly
Eric A
Lower surplus
min. £0 max. £600
monthly
Eric B
Higher surplus
max. £900
monthly
Eric C
Direct Debit
monthly
£20-30
'ISA, mortgage, or pension but investments are separate.'
Eric D
Savings
Saving is for the future when you retire - for a higher interest to have a bonus.
Automatic transfers are to budget yourself.
• All transfers should be possible manually.
• Wants to be informed monthly about saving status.

## Appendix B: The 10 Saving Factor Descriptions

| FACTOR 1<br>*SELF-CONTROL* | |
|---|---|
| *Eigenvalue* | *4.39* |
| To control my spending I would like to be able to lock money away so that I could not access it for a specific period. | 0.83 |
| I would like to have delayed access to some savings in order to decrease spending. | 0.82 |
| I would like to control my spending by limiting the ways in which I can get hold of my money. | 0.82 |
| I would like to structure my finances in such a way as to help me spend less. | 0.58 |
| I would be more reluctant to spend impulsively if I was being rewarded for maintaining a high saving balance. | 0.57 |
| I want to be sure I always have money at hand. | -0.13 |
| I would like to link investments (ISA's, Bonds, or Stocks, etc.) within my financial structure. | -0.13 |
| I feel uncomfortable if I do not have access to all my savings at any given time. | -0.13 |
| Maintaining hands-on control over my finances helps me to ensure it is sufficiently flexible to cope with unforeseen events. | -0.19 |
| I don't want to rely on one single company for all my finances. | -0.26 |
| **FACTOR 2**<br>***HANDS ON*** | |
| *Eigenvalue* | *3.06* |
| I need to be constantly aware of my complete financial situation. | 0.66 |
| It would be important that my financial structure is stable over time. | 0.64 |
| I would feel uncomfortable unless I understood every single part of my financial structure. | 0.60 |
| I want to be sure I always have money at hand. | 0.44 |
| Maintaining hands-on control over my finances helps me to ensure it is sufficiently flexible to cope with unforeseen events. | 0.42 |
| Being less aware of some of my money helps me to spend less. | -0.21 |
| I feel uncomfortable working out my financial situation on my own. | -0.33 |
| I would like to have automatic transfers to make me less aware of some of my money. | -0.35 |
| I don't enjoy taking care of my money. | -0.50 |
| I want to be less involved with my finances. | -0.58 |
| **FACTOR 3**<br>***ADVICE*** | |
| *Eigenvalue* | *2.83* |
| I would like to have independent external advice about my savings. | 0.82 |
| I would like to have regular financial advice about my financial structure. | 0.81 |
| I would like to have ongoing financial advice which helps me to save more. | 0.72 |
| I would like to be continually informed about my flows of money. | 0.39 |
| I like to have savings even if I am in debt. | 0.34 |
| I always want to keep a specific minimum amount of money in my current account. | -0.05 |
| I do not care how much I save as long I do not go overdrawn. | -0.09 |
| I want to keep the effort related to my finances low. | -0.10 |
| I would like to have automatic transfers to make me less aware of some of my | -0.11 |

| | |
|---|---|
| money. | |
| Being less aware of some of my money helps me to spend less. | -0.14 |
| **FACTOR 4** ***REGULAR SAVINGS*** | |
| *Eigenvalue* | *2.65* |
| I would set up standing orders to save regularly. | 0.74 |
| I want a minimum percentage of my income to be paid into my savings accounts. | 0.74 |
| There is a minimum amount I would want paid monthly into my savings accounts. | 0.71 |
| I would like to automate regular payments to ensure they are paid on time. | 0.37 |
| I would be more reluctant to spend impulsively if I was being rewarded for maintaining a high saving balance. | 0.34 |
| I don't enjoy taking care of my money. | -0.07 |
| A financial structure which was partially automated would be less secure. | -0.11 |
| I save until I reach the amount needed for something I wish to purchase. | -0.13 |
| I feel uncomfortable working out my financial situation on my own. | -0.18 |
| I need to be constantly aware of my complete financial situation. | -0.29 |

| | |
|---|---|
| **FACTOR 5** ***AUTOMATION*** | |
| *Eigenvalue* | *2.54* |
| I would like to automate regular transfers to save time. | 0.83 |
| I would like to automate regular transfers to savings accounts to overcome forgetfulness or laziness. | 0.65 |
| I would like to set up an automated financial structure and let it run. | 0.60 |
| I would like to automate regular payments to ensure they are paid on time. | 0.60 |
| I would like to have automatic transfers to make me less aware of some of my money. | 0.35 |
| I don't have a problem with being charged if I act against restrictions I have previously set. | -0.06 |
| I restrict myself by only spending a certain amount on different types of purchases | -0.10 |
| I would feel worried that I did not have complete understanding of my financial situation if it involved automated features. | -0.12 |
| I would feel uncomfortable unless I understood every single part of my financial structure. | -0.14 |
| A financial structure which was partially automated would be less secure. | -0.16 |
| **FACTOR 6** ***LOW EFFORT*** | |
| *Eigenvalue* | *2.08* |
| I want the bank to do the work for me. | 0.77 |
| I would like to keep my finances as simple as possible. | 0.73 |
| I want to keep the effort related to my finances low. | 0.54 |
| I feel uncomfortable if I do not have access to all my savings at any given time. | 0.37 |
| I want to be less involved with my finances. | 0.29 |
| Maintaining hands-on control over my finances helps me to ensure it is sufficiently flexible to cope with unforeseen events. | -0.08 |
| I would like to have automatic transfers to make me less aware of some of my money. | -0.10 |

| Item | Loading |
|---|---|
| I don't want to rely on one single company for all my finances. | -0.16 |
| I would set up standing orders to save regularly. | -0.16 |
| I would like to reach a specific saving level at a specified time. | -0.20 |
| **FACTOR 7** *INTEGRATION* | |
| *Eigenvalue* | *2.07* |
| I would like to link all my finances into one integrated framework. | 0.75 |
| I would like to keep all my finances together. | 0.70 |
| I would like to link investments (ISA's, Bonds, or Stocks, etc.) within my financial structure. | 0.58 |
| I would like to set up an automated financial structure and let it run. | 0.33 |
| I would like to have automatic transfers to make me less aware of some of my money. | 0.24 |
| I want to be less involved with my finances. | -0.12 |
| I don't want to rely on one single company for all my finances. | -0.13 |
| It would be important that my financial structure is stable over time. | -0.15 |
| I would like to keep my finances as simple as possible. | -0.17 |
| I prefer my savings and my current account to be separate. | -0.35 |
| **FACOTR 8** *SECURITY WORRIES* | |
| *Eigenvalue* | *2.04* |
| If I give the bank day to day control over my finances I would be worried that they might make errors that I never notice. | 0.77 |
| I would feel worried that I did not have complete understanding of my financial situation if it involves automated features. | 0.73 |
| A financial structure which was partially automated would be less secure. | 0.53 |
| I would like to be continually informed about my flows of money. | 0.29 |
| I restrict myself by only spending a certain amount on different types of purchases | 0.21 |
| I would like the savings I have available for leisure to be dependent on the overall savings I hold. | -0.10 |
| I want to keep the effort related to my finances low. | -0.10 |
| I would like to automate regular transfers to save time. | -0.10 |
| I know exactly what I am saving for. | -0.16 |
| I would like to set up an automated financial structure and let it run. | -0.18 |
| **FACTOR 9** *PLANNED BUDGET* | |
| *Eigenvalue* | *2.03* |
| I restrict myself by only spending a certain amount on different types of purchases | 0.74 |
| I know exactly what I am saving for. | 0.62 |
| I feel uncomfortable if I do not have access to all my savings at any given time. | 0.44 |
| I need to be constantly aware of my complete financial situation. | 0.44 |
| I would like to be continually informed about my flows of money. | 0.30 |
| I would like to automate regular transfers to savings accounts to overcome forgetfulness or laziness. | -0.16 |

| | |
|---|---|
| I would like to link investments (ISA's, Bonds, or Stocks, etc.) within my financial structure. | -0.17 |
| I don't enjoy taking care of my money. | -0.17 |
| It would be important that my financial structure is stable over time. | -0.22 |
| I would like to automate regular payments to ensure they are paid on time. | -0.22 |
| **FACTOR 10** ***DISTRIBUTED SAVINGS*** | |
| *Eigenvalue* | *1.98* |
| I would like to be able to distribute my regular savings between different accounts. | 0.81 |
| I would like to be able to divide my savings into different distinguishable saving categories. | 0.68 |
| I would like to link investments (ISA's, Bonds, or Stocks, etc.) within my financial structure. | 0.34 |
| I would like the savings I have available for leisure to be dependent on the overall savings I hold. | 0.32 |
| I would like to be able to specify maximum balances for specific savings accounts. | 0.29 |
| I would like to keep all my finances together. | -0.11 |
| I would like to structure my finances in such a way as to help me spend less. | -0.13 |
| I would like to have ongoing financial advice which helps me to save more. | -0.17 |
| A financial structure which was partially automated would be less secure. | -0.20 |
| I want to be sure I always have money at hand. | -0.21 |

## Appendix C: Individual Repgrid Results For The Concept 'Company'

The Ward clustering tree is shown as a measure of distance for the derived descriptors and companies.

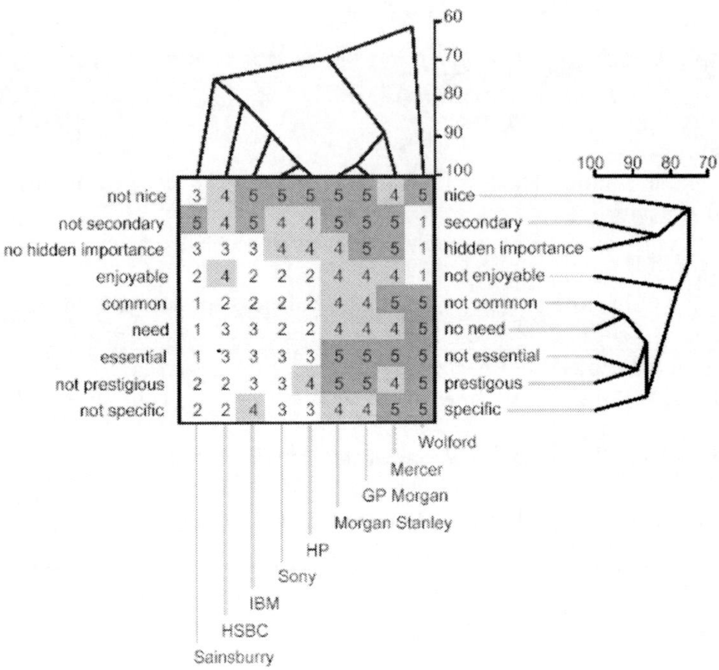

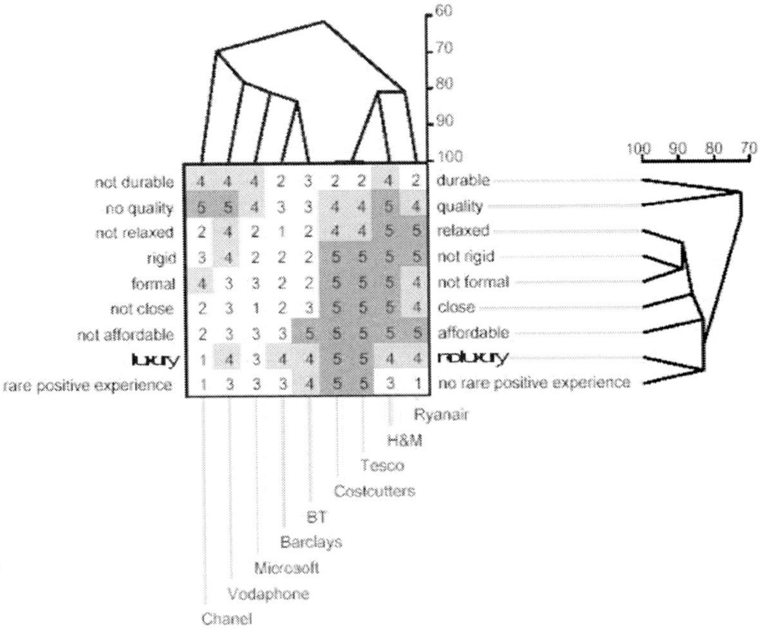
60
70
80
90
100
100 90 80 70
not durable 4 4 4 2 3 2 2 4 2 durable
no quality 5 5 4 3 3 4 4 5 4 quality
not relaxed 2 4 2 1 2 4 4 5 5 relaxed
rigid 3 4 2 2 2 5 5 5 5 not rigid
formal 4 3 3 2 2 5 5 5 4 not formal
not close 2 3 1 2 3 5 5 5 4 close
not affordable 2 3 3 3 5 5 5 5 5 affordable
luxury 1 4 3 4 4 5 5 4 4 noluxury
rare positive experience 1 3 3 3 4 5 5 3 1 no rare positive experience
Ryanair
H&M
Tesco
Costcutters
BT
Barclays
Microsoft
Vodaphone
Chanel

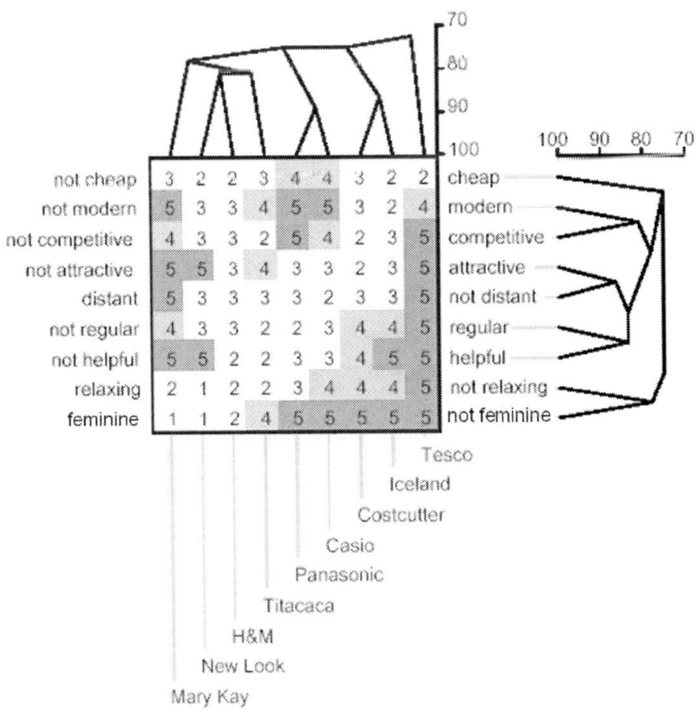
70
80
90
100
100 90 80 70
not cheap 3 2 2 3 4 4 3 2 2 cheap
not modern 5 3 3 4 5 5 3 2 4 modern
not competitive 4 3 3 2 5 4 2 3 5 competitive
not attractive 5 5 3 4 3 3 2 3 5 attractive
distant 5 3 3 3 3 2 3 3 5 not distant
not regular 4 3 3 2 2 3 4 4 5 regular
not helpful 5 5 2 2 3 3 4 5 5 helpful
relaxing 2 1 2 2 3 4 4 4 5 not relaxing
feminine 1 1 2 4 5 5 5 5 5 not feminine
Tesco
Iceland
Costcutter
Casio
Panasonic
Titacaca
H&M
New Look
Mary Kay

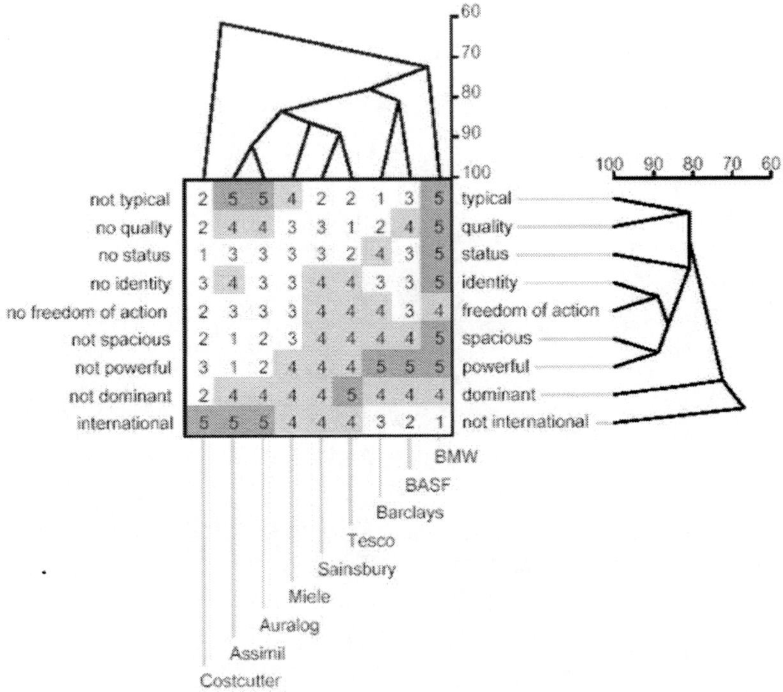
60
70
80
90
100
100 90 80 70 60
not typical 2 5 5 4 2 2 1 3 5 typical
no quality 2 4 4 3 3 1 2 4 5 quality
no status 1 3 3 3 3 2 4 3 5 status
no identity 3 4 3 3 4 4 3 3 5 identity
no freedom of action 2 3 3 3 4 4 4 3 4 freedom of action
not spacious 2 1 2 3 4 4 4 4 5 spacious
not powerful 3 1 2 4 4 4 5 5 5 powerful
not dominant 2 4 4 4 4 5 4 4 4 dominant
international 5 5 5 4 4 4 3 2 1 not international
BMW
BASF
Barclays
Tesco
Sainsbury
Miele
Auralog
Assimil
Costcutter

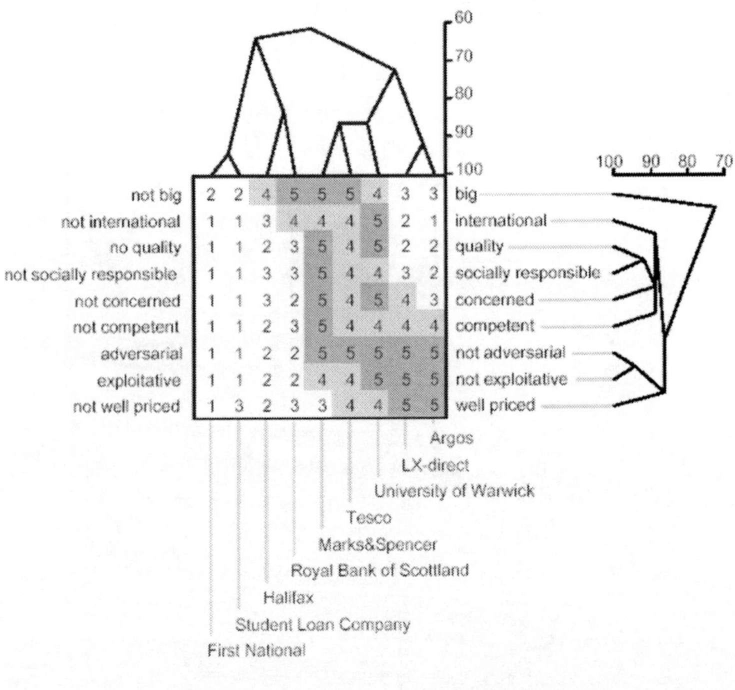
60
70
80
90
100
100 90 80 70
not big 2 2 4 5 5 5 4 3 3 big
not international 1 1 3 4 4 4 5 2 1 international
no quality 1 1 2 3 5 4 5 2 2 quality
not socially responsible 1 1 3 3 5 4 4 3 2 socially responsible
not concerned 1 1 3 2 5 4 5 4 3 concerned
not competent 1 1 2 3 5 4 4 4 4 competent
adversarial 1 1 2 2 5 5 5 5 5 not adversarial
exploitative 1 1 2 2 4 4 5 5 5 not exploitative
not well priced 1 3 2 3 3 4 4 5 5 well priced
Argos
LX-direct
University of Warwick
Tesco
Marks&Spencer
Royal Bank of Scottland
Halifax
Student Loan Company
First National

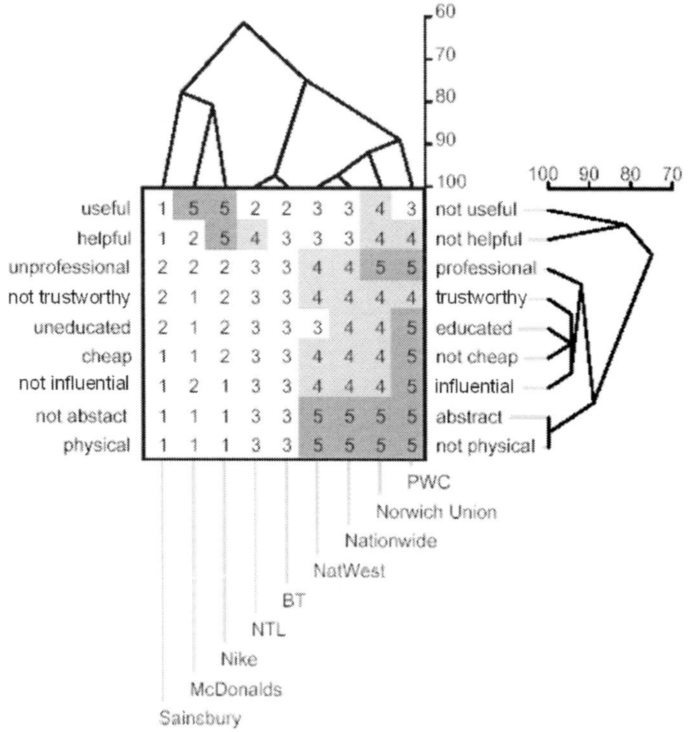
60
70
80
90
100
100 90 80 70
useful 1 5 5 2 2 3 3 4 3 not useful
helpful 1 2 5 4 3 3 3 4 4 not helpful
unprofessional 2 2 2 3 3 4 4 5 5 professional
not trustworthy 2 1 2 3 3 4 4 4 4 trustworthy
uneducated 2 1 2 3 3 3 4 4 5 educated
cheap 1 1 2 3 3 4 4 4 5 not cheap
not influential 1 2 1 3 3 4 4 4 5 influential
not abstact 1 1 1 3 3 5 5 5 5 abstract
physical 1 1 1 3 3 5 5 5 5 not physical
PWC
Norwich Union
Nationwide
NatWest
BT
NTL
Nike
McDonalds
Sainsbury

# INDEX

## A

academics, 22
accounting, 1, 9, 10, 11, 46, 56, 155, 177, 180, 182, 185
accuracy, 94, 95, 109, 121, 126, 127, 129, 135, 138, 163, 164, 165, 172
adaptation, 5, 7, 8, 93, 149, 167, 185
advertising, 89, 169
affective dimension, 10
affective meaning, 179
age, 25, 36, 50, 58, 72, 77, 82, 107, 119, 128
agents, 151, 153, 176
aggregates, 152
aggregation, 22, 27, 78
algorithm, 172
alternative, 3, 4, 39, 40, 89, 94, 95, 96, 101, 102, 103, 104, 105, 106, 113, 114, 115, 118, 122, 124, 132, 133, 134, 137, 139, 140, 141, 142, 147, 148, 152, 175
alternatives, 3, 4, 47, 49, 55, 101, 105, 107, 115, 118, 125, 142
analysis of variance, 110
anchoring, 4
ANOVA, 110, 121, 130
anthropology, 154
application, 26, 38, 40, 57, 61, 62, 89, 101, 102, 106, 113, 118, 124, 126, 127, 128, 129, 133, 137, 139, 165, 171, 180
arbitrage, 11
argument, 142
assessment, 183
assets, 10, 85, 174
assumptions, 19, 120, 151, 152
ATM, 24
attachment, 99, 102
attitudes, 20, 21, 69, 150, 172, 174, 185
attractiveness, 12, 71, 89, 174
automation, 64
automatization, 104, 175
autonomy, 46, 161
availability, 4, 56, 57, 162
aversion, 12, 183, 186
avoidance, 65
awareness, 62, 178

## B

banking, 57
banks, 73
behavioral aspects, 14
behavioral change, 160
behavioral effects, 15, 169
behavioral models, 152

behavioral theory, 159, 174
behavioral variation, 24, 29, 65, 88, 148, 150, 151
beliefs, 163
benchmark, 70
benchmarks, 176
benefits, 9, 48, 94, 138
Bernoulli, Daniel, 1
bias, 24, 90
bipolar, 72, 73, 74
blocks, 108, 109, 111, 113, 115, 116, 121, 123, 125, 126, 128, 129, 130, 134, 135, 142
bonus, 10, 45, 120
bonuses, 55, 59, 61
borrowing, 11
bottom-up, 49
boundedly rational, 2
brand perception, 71
buffer, 20, 52, 54
bundling, 184

## C

categorization, 8, 49, 70, 94, 98, 104, 105, 139, 142, 160, 166, 172, 173, 178, 179, 183
category d, 27
causal relationship, 13
causation, 13, 64, 166
channels, 21, 165, 186
classes, 27, 29, 31, 78, 88
classical, 11, 14
classification, 24, 173, 175, 176
clinical assessment, 163
cluster analysis, 27
clustering, xi, 28, 73, 78, 81, 200
clusters, xi, 27, 28, 29, 30, 31, 78, 80, 81
cognition, ix, 50, 93, 143, 165, 177, 180
cognitive development, 94
cognitive effort, 94, 101
cognitive function, 147, 154
cognitive models, 64
cognitive process, x, 13, 88, 94, 106
cognitive representations, 88
cognitive science, 14, 15, 148, 149, 180
cognitive system, 64
commerce, 87
commercial bank, 180
communication, 64
competence, 160
complexity, 56, 106, 116, 126, 135, 142, 153, 162, 179
components, 3, 46, 48, 65, 160
composition, 11
computational theory, 103, 138, 143, 144, 165
concentrates, 21
conceptualization, 47, 93, 100
concordance, 57
concrete, 40, 41, 179
conditioning, 169
confidentiality, 89
configuration, 50, 105, 115, 125
conflict, 11, 47, 63, 64, 182
conformity, 64
conjecture, 126
conjunction fallacy, 2, 3, 186
connectionist, 173, 178, 181, 182
consolidation, 184
constraints, 5, 11, 24, 57, 108, 148, 167, 170
construct validity, 183
construction, 50, 63
consumer choice, 185
consumer expenditure, 186
consumers, 176
consumption, 8, 9, 10, 11, 20, 21, 45, 46, 160, 161, 163, 168, 169, 170, 171, 175, 177, 181
consumption function, 168, 177
contingency, ix, 48, 55, 65, 161, 187
control, xi, 11, 16, 41, 45, 46, 47, 48, 49, 54, 55, 56, 57, 58, 59, 60, 61, 62, 64, 65, 151, 159, 161, 162, 170, 173, 175, 178, 180, 182, 196, 198
corporations, 22
correlation, xiii, 13, 27, 37, 38, 53, 85, 86, 120
correlations, 36, 62, 63, 85, 86

costs, xii, 9, 11, 23, 48, 55, 94, 96, 117, 120, 122, 127, 128, 129, 130, 135, 136, 137, 138, 139, 142
credibility, 184
credit, xi, 9, 11, 21, 23, 24, 25, 65, 170, 180, 181, 184
credit card, xi, 9, 11, 21, 24, 25, 65, 170, 180
creditworthiness, 107
criticism, 94, 119
cues, ix, 5, 55, 59, 65, 95, 96, 97, 101, 104, 105, 107, 109, 116, 119, 126, 128, 134, 135, 136
cultural differences, 162
culture, 165
current account, 51, 54, 197, 198
customers, 19, 22, 23, 24, 25, 26, 29, 31, 36, 38, 39, 40, 41, 52, 169, 170, 179

## D

danger, 49, 149
data analysis, ix, 15, 24
data processing, 23
data set, 30
database, 38, 50, 52, 85, 176
debt, 11, 58, 170, 180, 197
decision making, ix, x, 4, 7, 40, 70, 152, 163, 165, 166, 177, 178, 179, 181, 184, 187
decision task, 186
decisions, 1, 2, 4, 5, 6, 8, 65, 70, 90, 97, 98, 106, 108, 109, 120, 126, 141, 144, 148, 150, 153, 154, 161, 166, 170, 174, 177, 179, 184
decoupling, 184
defaults, 53
deficit, 47, 63, 65
deficits, 49
definition, 25, 49, 50, 51, 52, 56, 100
degrees of freedom, 114
demographic characteristics, 183
demographic data, 22
demographics, 23, 57, 58, 61
dependent variable, 14, 110, 121, 130
depreciation, 9, 169
designers, 171
detection, 8, 166
deviation, 48, 120
differentiation, 7, 21, 22, 26, 36, 38, 49, 62
direct action, 143
direct mail, 22, 39
directionality, 86
discipline, 153
discounting, 46, 173, 186
discrimination, 3, 101
distribution, xi, 6, 20, 25, 26, 38, 46, 165
diversification, 7, 161
diversity, 8, 9, 53, 65
dominance, 83
duration, 51
dynamic environment, 141

## E

earnings, 20
earth, 87
eating, 70
ecological, 2, 20, 50, 63
economic growth, 161
economic theory, 9, 11, 12, 40, 45, 90, 147, 152, 154, 175, 185
economics, ix, 1, 13, 152, 154, 171, 177, 183, 185, 187
education, 28, 32, 33, 34
elaboration, 48
elasticity, 20, 179
elasticity of demand, 20
emotional bias, 1
employees, 107, 120
employers, 73
employment, 89, 173
empowerment, 65
encouragement, 63
entrepreneurs, 29
environmental conditions, 5, 56
environmental factors, 57
estimating, 97, 106
ethical issues, 176
evolution, 65, 160

evolutionary process, 7
expenditures, 11
experimental condition, 108, 117
experimental design, 4, 97, 109, 129
exploitation, 6

## F

factor analysis, 29, 31, 59, 83
factor H, 87
factorial, 37, 82
failure, 7, 45, 47, 161
fairness, 83
family, 84, 85, 87
fee, 107
feedback, ix, 97, 98, 104, 106, 108, 109, 115, 116, 121, 126, 132, 136, 137, 138, 141, 157, 160, 165
feelings, 171
feminist, 3
field theory, 181
finance, ix, 1, 8, 148, 149, 153, 155, 182
financial institution, 19, 21, 24, 50
financial institutions, 19, 21
financial providers, 24
financial resources, 107, 120
financial sector, 26
financial support, 157
firms, 174
flexibility, 56, 62, 64, 65, 83, 95, 107, 120
food, 8, 70
forgetfulness, 197, 199
forgetting, 103, 111, 114, 123, 132, 140, 141
framing, 2, 3, 4, 12, 148
freedom, 46, 74, 87, 114
freedom of will, 46
Freud, 47, 168
funds, 7
future orientation, vii, 28, 29, 30, 32

## G

gambling, 1, 3, 163, 174
games, 139, 143, 162, 163, 164, 166, 184
gender, 37
generalizability, 21, 106, 114, 117, 118, 124, 127, 134, 136, 140, 174
generalization, 86
generalizations, 100, 140, 148
generation, 13, 72, 141, 165
genetics, 154, 185
goals, 45, 47, 50, 53, 56, 59, 89, 147, 165
government, 22
group characteristics, 58
grouping, 28, 48, 73, 81, 83
groups, xiii, 24, 25, 27, 60, 61, 73, 78, 83, 87
growth, 52, 56, 59, 85, 161
guessing, 184
guidance, 55, 59, 72

## H

hedonic, 9, 20
heterogeneity, 29, 152
heuristic, 5, 30, 95, 96, 126, 137, 139, 168, 177, 178
histogram, 120
homogeneity, 56, 73, 153
homogenous, 27
honesty, 70, 85, 87
household, 22, 40, 58, 165, 171, 174
household income, 58
households, 10, 11, 161
human, 1, 5, 8, 41, 49, 71, 93, 101, 159, 162, 163, 166, 184, 185, 187, 188
human behavior, 41, 163, 187
human cognition, 93, 159
humans, 8
hyperbolic, 46, 160, 170, 173
hypothesis, 9, 13, 20, 111, 160, 164, 165, 177, 182
hypothesis test, 13, 165

## I

identification, 38, 141, 178

identity, 75
illiquid asset, 151
illusion, 183
imagination, 103, 111, 114, 123, 132, 141
implementation, 39
impulsive, 20, 47, 161, 181
impulsiveness, 159
incentive, 64, 147
incentives, 12, 15, 49, 183
incidence, 163, 184
inclusion, 55, 58
income, 10, 20, 26, 36, 46, 54, 58, 59, 60, 163, 164, 197
independence, 3
indicators, 29, 89
individual differences, 14, 15, 19, 22, 29, 40, 42, 49, 58, 62, 65, 71, 150, 151, 167, 182
individual personality, 31, 72
induction, 168, 174
inferences, 93, 95, 96, 97, 99, 104, 105, 106, 110, 111, 115, 116, 118, 119, 125, 134, 136, 137, 138, 139, 141, 142, 143, 144, 162, 183
information processing, 138
Information Theory, 159
innovation, 70, 87
Innovation, ix, 83, 84, 85, 86, 87
insight, ix, 13, 187
iinstitutions, 24, 26
integration, ix, 46, 64, 90, 93, 176
intelligence, 162
intentions, 20, 169, 172, 185
interaction, 1, 5, 6, 7, 9, 64, 70, 110, 121, 131, 150
interactions, 6, 94
interdisciplinary, 153
interest rates, 11, 170
interview, 50, 51, 58, 72
interviews, 52
intrinsic, 6, 160
introspection, 13
investment, 1, 5, 8, 11, 12, 13, 16, 69, 147, 150, 151, 160, 165, 166, 170
investment incentive, 13
investors, 69

## J

judge, 87
judgment, 98, 144, 152, 162, 163, 164, 165, 169, 172, 173, 183
justice, 3

## K

Kahneman, Daniel, 2
Keynes, 45, 50, 56, 173
Keynesian, 177
knowledge transfer, 153

## L

labeling, 52
laboratory studies, 12
land, 41
law, 6, 185
LEA, 169
learning process, 6, 15, 95, 98, 103, 106, 109, 115, 117, 120, 126, 135, 136, 138, 139, 140, 147, 149
legislation, 41
leisure, 36, 198, 199
Libertarian, 184, 185
life cycle, 46, 160, 164, 177
life cycle hypothesis, 160, 177
life style, 23, 36, 39, 171, 180
lifecycle, 10, 20, 46, 61, 63, 174, 182
lifestyles, 21, 169
lifetime, 20
likelihood, 3, 36, 38, 39, 48, 104, 113, 114, 159, 165
Likert scale, 14, 58, 77, 82
limitation, 14
limitations, 2, 26, 48, 142, 154
linear, 12, 95, 102, 127, 141, 186
linear model, 95, 127, 141, 186
linkage, 15, 154
links, 89

liquid assets, 10, 11
liquidity, 11, 48, 55, 65, 170
loading, 30, 31, 87
loans, 39
locus, 63
losses, 12, 101, 127, 140
loyalty, 21, 180, 184

## M

maintenance, ix, 27, 32, 33, 34, 35, 36, 55
management, 15, 19, 36, 40, 41, 57, 107, 120, 172, 177
management practices, 177
manipulation, 23, 48, 59, 151
mapping, x, 6
market, 15, 21, 56, 64, 85, 147, 151, 153, 174, 180
market segment, 21, 174, 180
marketing, 15, 19, 21, 22, 23, 26, 36, 40, 41, 89, 165, 169, 176, 182
mathematical skills, 94
matrix, 107
meanings, 60
measurement, 58, 97, 110, 113, 116, 121, 130, 134, 135, 161, 164, 170, 174, 179
measures, x, xiii, 19, 30, 36, 63, 83, 85, 86, 89, 93, 164, 171
membership, 98
memorizing, 143
memory, xii, 2, 5, 10, 14, 94, 96, 104, 117, 118, 119, 122, 126, 137, 142, 143, 162, 165, 167, 171, 172, 175, 182
men, 107, 119, 128, 150
mental image, 159
mental imagery, 159
mental model, 148
mental processes, 13, 148, 149
mental representation, 47, 50
modeling, 93, 155, 163, 177
money, 24, 36, 45, 48, 52, 56, 173, 183, 196, 197, 198, 199, 200
motivation, 160, 182
motives, 45, 50, 52, 53, 56, 57, 58, 59, 63, 69, 89, 150, 168, 171
movement, 3
multiplication, 174
multivariate, 175
myopic, 47

## N

natural, ix, 15, 40, 57, 70, 71, 72, 88, 154, 167, 168
natural sciences, 154, 167
network, 104, 167, 169, 182
neural network, 104
neural systems, 176
neurobiology, 176
neuroeconomics, 161
nuclear, 3

## O

observable behavior, 57, 154
observations, 4, 8, 13, 25, 46, 153, 175
observed behavior, x, 3, 21, 22, 45, 63, 71
opportunity costs, 139
optimization, 6, 7, 30, 94, 113, 116, 125
optimization method, 30
orientation, 6, 14, 41, 47, 63, 65
outliers, 29, 78

## P

paradigm shift, 152
paradox, 1, 3
parameter, xiii, xiv, 99, 101, 102, 103, 113, 114, 116, 117, 124, 125, 126, 133, 134, 139
parameter estimates, 124
paternalism, 151, 184, 185
pay off, 11, 141
penalties, 48, 55, 60, 64, 151
penalty, 48
pension plans, 64
pensions, 164
perception, 13, 48, 70, 71, 86, 87, 88, 90, 171, 176

perceptions, 161
performance indicator, 89
permanent income hypothesis, 20, 164
personality, x, 14, 22, 31, 36, 41, 45, 58, 60, 62, 69, 70, 71, 75, 76, 86, 89, 147, 150, 155, 159, 164, 168
personality dimensions, 71, 86
personality factors, 22, 60, 86, 89
personality measures, x
personality research, 63, 71
PET, 179
phenotypic, 149
philosophy, 3
physical environment, 187
plausibility, 101
pleasure principle, 47
polymorphism, 149
poor, 53
population, 8, 25, 149
portfolio, 69, 182
portfolios, 69
power, 19, 70, 77, 78, 81, 85, 87, 175
predictability, 148
prediction, 12, 100, 101, 102, 106, 108, 109, 111, 113, 115, 117, 118, 120, 122, 123, 125, 129, 132, 136, 139, 142, 153, 154
predictors, 39, 86, 93
preference, 3, 99, 102, 111, 113, 114, 117, 123, 124, 125, 126, 129, 132, 133, 135, 137, 138, 174, 186
preparedness, 49
pressure, 96, 141, 163, 181
prestige, 70, 78, 81, 87
prices, 3
primary data, 23
private, 26, 29
probability, 2, 3, 12, 39, 93, 95, 97, 99, 100, 101, 103, 105, 111, 113, 115, 116, 117, 118, 122, 124, 125, 126, 132, 133, 134, 135, 140, 167, 172, 183, 186
probability judgment, 12, 93, 186
probability theory, 2
probe, 104, 105, 115
problem solving, 64, 177
product design, 62
production, 139, 162
profit, 85
profitability, 22
profits, 21, 172
program, 2, 3
property, 128
prospect theory, 4, 12, 186
protection, 41
protocol, 160, 179
prototype, 160, 176
psychological adaptations, 149
psychology, 1, 5, 6, 13, 98, 144, 149, 154, 165, 169, 173, 182, 187
psychometric approach, 21
psychophysics, 1
public, 41, 64, 70, 87, 89, 161, 176
public policy, 64, 161, 176

## Q

qualifications, 107, 120
questionnaire, 58, 62
questionnaires, 14

## R

random, 99, 107, 108, 128, 137
range, 4, 11, 45, 69, 71, 82, 83, 90
rating scale, 14
ratings, ix, 14, 16, 73, 77, 137
rationality, 2, 151, 167, 168, 174
reading, 166
reality, 47, 63
reasoning, 10, 144, 167, 183, 186
recognition, 94, 166, 171, 178
reconcile, 9
reconstruction, 88
recruiting, 154
redistribution, 64
regional, 89, 151
regression, 39, 164
regular, 10, 23, 25, 75, 196, 197, 199
regulation, 47, 161

reinforcement, 6, 99, 100, 102, 103, 105, 136, 139, 140, 141, 143, 162, 166, 167, 182
reinforcement learning, 6, 102, 105, 143, 166, 167
relationship, 9, 19, 89, 167, 172, 177, 178
relationship management, 172
relationships, 13
rent, 29
repetitions, 109
representativeness, 4, 58
research design, 62
resource allocation, 94
resources, 22, 41, 107, 120, 181
retail, 23, 175
retention, 21, 167
retirement, 49, 52, 64, 150, 161, 166, 167, 173, 179, 180, 183
rewards, 6, 48, 64, 176, 183
risk, 7, 11, 12, 14, 40, 150, 161, 162, 164, 166, 168, 170, 172, 180, 184, 187
risk aversion, 12
risk behaviors, 187
risk orientation, vii
risk perception, 187
robustness, 38

## S

salary, 10
sales, 85
sample, xi, 11, 22, 24, 25, 26, 38, 39, 58, 73, 75, 106
sampling, 25, 184
saving rate, 63
savings, 10, 19, 49, 52, 53, 54, 56, 57, 64, 174, 175, 177, 180, 185, 196, 197, 198, 199
savings account, 197, 199
scientific understanding, 153
scores, 23, 29, 38, 40, 60
search, 96, 97, 113, 116, 119, 128, 130, 135, 136, 137, 138, 139, 142, 164, 170, 179
seasonal pattern, 25
security, 10, 52, 56, 57, 59, 69
segmentation, 19, 21, 38, 40, 163, 175, 180, 187
segregation, 46
selecting, 30, 95, 99, 101, 117, 138, 139, 141, 180
self-awareness, 62
self-control, ix, 1, 11, 16, 46, 47, 48, 49, 50, 51, 54, 55, 56, 57, 58, 59, 60, 61, 62, 63, 64, 65, 147, 151, 161, 170, 171, 173, 179, 180, 181, 182, 185, 186, 187
self-efficacy, 160
self-regulation, 47
semantic, 16, 70, 71, 75, 76, 87, 147, 166, 170, 171, 172, 178, 179, 185
sensation, 14, 63, 188
sensation seeking, 14, 63, 188
sensitivity, 102, 117
sentence processing, 166
separation, 9, 23, 47, 55
series, 173, 179, 186
services, x, 21, 23, 26, 36, 39, 41, 63, 167
shaping, 89
shares, 104
short run, 11
SIC, 23
sign, 9, 114, 116, 134
similarity, 4, 28, 73, 100, 105, 115, 178
simulation, 160
skill acquisition, 139, 185
skills, 94
social cognition, 104
social context, 94
social control, 64
social exchange, 165
social justice, 3
social psychology, 159
social relations, 168
social responsibility, 21
social sciences, 187
social security, 10, 29
socially responsible, 75
socioeconomic, 183
specificity, 148
spectrum, 65, 75
speculation, 165

stability, 4, 14, 29, 40, 81, 89, 165
standard model, 40, 152
stimulus, 99, 104
stock, 20, 153, 160, 164
storage, 15, 21, 167
strategy use, 49
strength, 9, 86, 87
stress, 12, 24, 50, 65, 98, 149, 163
structuring, 48, 50, 51, 87, 166
students, 72, 77, 107, 119, 128
subjective, 30, 51, 93, 105, 120
superiority, 102, 143
supervisors, 157
supplements, 138
supply, 8, 177
suppression, 55
sure thing principle, 3
surplus, 55
survey design, 172
survival, 7
sustainability, 21
switching, 26, 104
symbolic, 174
symptoms, 97
system analysis, 176

## T

taxonomy, 168
telephone, 173
temporal, 9, 20, 40, 46, 47, 48, 64, 169
temporal distribution, 20
thinking, 41, 45
time constraints, 108
time pressure, 96, 141, 181
tracking, 15, 89
trade-off, 6, 94, 135, 138
trading, 150
tradition, 1, 5, 8, 98
traits, 21
transactions, 16, 23, 24, 25, 27, 37, 41, 183
transfer, 153, 154
transformation, 174
translation, 87, 171
travel, 36
trial, 6, 99, 100, 108, 109, 111, 113, 115, 116, 121, 123, 126, 128, 129, 130, 132, 137, 141
trust, 8, 56, 61, 82, 87
trustworthiness, 83

## U

uncertainty, 4, 12, 46, 93, 148, 166, 168, 169, 172, 175, 186
uniform, 70
universality, 4, 15, 86, 148, 185
updating, 103

## V

validation, 163
validity, 50, 95, 119, 120, 121, 126, 134, 162, 183
values, xiii, xiv, 3, 27, 38, 61, 76, 77, 78, 85, 89, 95, 102, 103, 105, 107, 113, 114, 115, 116, 119, 125, 126, 133, 134, 137, 172
variability, 2, 14, 20, 63, 73, 77, 89, 142, 147, 165
variables, 13, 14, 23, 29, 30, 36, 56, 57, 61, 89, 154, 171
variance, 30, 60, 77, 110
variation, 4, 26, 51, 52, 57, 59, 77, 148, 149, 150, 151, 152, 154, 161, 187
varimax rotation, 60
venture capital, 13, 175, 187
verbal fluency, 51
visible, 107
visualization, 45
volatility, xi, 25

## W

wealth, 7, 9, 10, 46, 52, 161, 177
wealth distribution, 46
women, 107, 119, 128, 150, 172
word recognition, 94, 166
working memory, 14, 162